Who
We
Are

BLACKS

Who We Are

BLACKS

BY THE NEW STRATEGIST EDITORS

New Strategist Publications, Inc.
Ithaca, New York

New Strategist Publications, Inc.
P.O. Box 242, Ithaca, New York 14851
800/848-0842; 607/273-0913
www.newstrategist.com

ISBN 978-1-933588-81-0
ISBN 1-933588-81-0

Printed in the United States of America

Table of Contents

List of Tables

Chapter 3. Housing

Chapter 4. Income

Chapter 5. Labor Force

Chapter 9. Time Use

Chapter 10. Wealth

List of Illustrations

Introduction

The 2000 census counted not only more people than had been projected, but more diversity than had been expected. Now, with the 21st century well underway, the composition of the U.S. population is continuing its rapid change. Hispanics have become the largest minority. Asians are the most affluent segment of the population. Blacks are making significant gains in education and earning power. Only by understanding each of these increasingly important segments of the population can policymakers and business people hope to tailor their programs and products to the wants and needs of more than 300 million Americans.

The first edition of *Who We Are: Blacks* provides a comprehensive look at the characteristics of this fast growing segment of the U.S. population as the 21st century unfolds. In addition to detailed estimates of the numbers of blacks nationally and by state and metropolitan area, *Who We Are: Blacks* includes the latest socioeconomic data on the black population. It has detailed spending data for black households and the latest data on black household wealth. Results from the American Time Use Survey are also presented here, profiling black time use and comparing it to the averages.

Understanding the demographics and lifestyles of racial and ethnic groups is of vital importance to researchers and policy makers. *Who We Are: Blacks* provides the key to understanding both the similarities and the differences between blacks and other Americans. Regardless of race or ethnic origin, there is no doubt Americans are more alike than different, and *Who We Are: Blacks* documents our many similarities. But there are also important differences among racial and ethnic groups that, if not taken into account, can derail public policy efforts and business strategies. The living arrangements of blacks differ from those of the average American, for example, and those differences affect not only lifestyles but also consumer behavior. The substantial educational, employment, and economic gains made by blacks, documented in these pages, are contrary to popular perception, but they are of utmost importance to policy makers and business leaders.

Race and Hispanic origin classifications

The 2000 census transformed racial and ethnic classification in the United States. The census allowed Americans, for the first time in modern history, to identify themselves as belonging to more than one racial group. This makes the analysis of racial and ethnic diversity more complex—and more rewarding—than ever before.

Most of the government's ongoing surveys now use the new racial classification scheme. Consequently, researchers have a wealth of racial and ethnic data available to them.

The federal government's new racial classification system has resulted in different racial and ethnic combinations. Three terms are used to distinguish groups from one another. The "race alone" population consists of people who identify themselves as being of only one race. The "race in combination" population consists of people who identify themselves as being of more than one race, such as black and white. The "race, alone or in combination" population includes both those who identify themselves as being of one race and those who identify themselves as being of more than one race. For example, the "black, alone or in combination" population includes those who say they are black alone and those who say they are black and white and those who say they are black, white, and Asian, and so on.

While the new classification system is a goldmine for researchers, the numbers no longer add up. This may frustrate some, but it provides a more accurate picture of each racial group than the previous methodology did, which required the multiracial to align with only one race. Under the new scheme, however, tables showing the "race alone" population exclude the multiracial. Tables showing the "race in combination" population count some people more than once. To make matters even more complex, Hispanics are considered an ethnic group rather than a race and they can be black, white, or Asian. Keep these factors in mind as you peruse the numbers.

Whenever possible, the tables in *Who We Are: Blacks* show the "race alone or in combination" populations. We prefer this classification because it includes everyone who identifying with a particular racial group and does not exclude the multiracial. In some instances, the "race alone or in combination" population figures are not available. In these cases, the "race alone" population is shown. The racial classification used is noted at the bottom of each table, if available. Note that some data sources do not define their racial classifications.

How to use this book

Who We Are: Blacks is designed for easy use. It is divided into 10 chapters arranged alphabetically: Education, Health, Housing, Income, Labor Force, Living Arrangements, Population, Spending, Time Use, and Wealth. Descriptive text and charts accompany most of the tables, highlighting the important trends.

Most of the tables in *Who We Are: Blacks* are based on data collected by the federal government, in particular the Census Bureau, the Bureau of Labor Statistics, the National Center for Education Statistics, and the National Center for Health Statistics. The federal government continues to be the best source of up-to-date, reliable information on the changing characteristics of Americans.

Several government surveys are of particular importance to *Who We Are: Blacks*. One is the Census Bureau's Current Population Survey. The CPS is a nationally representative survey of the civilian noninstitutional population aged 15 or older. The Census Bureau takes it monthly, collecting information from 50,000 households on employment and unemployment. Each year, the March survey includes a demographic supplement that is the source of most national data on the characteristics of Americans, such as their educational attainment, living arrangements, and incomes. CPS data appear in many tables of this book.

The American Community Survey is another important source of data for *Who We Are: Blacks*. The ACS, an ongoing nationwide survey of 250,000 households per month, provides detailed demographic data at the community level. Designed to replace the census long-form questionnaire, the ACS includes more than 60 questions that formerly appeared on the long form, such as inquiries regarding the language spoken at home, or householders' income and education. ACS data are available for the nation, regions, states, counties, metropolitan areas, and smaller geographic units.

The Consumer Expenditure Survey is the data source for the Spending chapter. Sponsored by the Bureau of Labor Statistics, the CEX is an ongoing study of the day-to-day spending of American households. The data collected by the survey are used to update prices for the Consumer Price Index. The CEX includes an interview survey and a diary survey administered to two separate, nationally representative samples. The average spending figures shown in the Spending chapters of this book are the integrated data from both the diary and interview components of the survey. For the interview survey, about 7,500 consumer units are interviewed on a rotating panel basis each quarter for five consecutive quarters. For the diary survey, another 7,500 consumer units keep weekly diaries of spending for two consecutive weeks.

The Bureau of Labor Statistics' American Time Use Survey is the source of data for the Time Use chapter. Through telephone interviews with a nationally representative sample of noninstitutionalized Americans aged 15 or older, the ATUS collects information in minute detail about what survey respondents did during the previous 24 hours—or diary day. Time use data allow social scientists to better understand our economy and lifestyle and how policy decisions affect our lives.

The data in the Wealth chapter comes from the Survey of Consumer Finances, a triennial survey taken by the Federal Reserve Board. The SCF collects data on the assets, debt, and net worth of American households. The latest data available are from the 2004 survey, for which the Federal Reserve Board interviewed a representative sample of 4,522 households. The SCF provides wealth data for only two racial and ethnic groups: "non-Hispanic whites" and "non-whites and Hispanics."

Value added

While the government collected the data presented in *Who We Are: Blacks*, the tables published here are not reprints from government reports—as is the case in many reference books. Instead, New Strategist's editors spent hundreds of hours scouring web sites, compiling numbers into meaningful statistics, and creating tables with calculations revealing the trends. Government web sites are useful for obtaining generalized summary data or for tapping into complex databases that often require statistical programs for analysis. New Strategist has done the work for you, delving into the data and providing analysis and comparisons, placing the important information about blacks at your fingertips. Researchers who want even more can use the source listed at the bottom of each table to explore the original data. The book contains a comprehensive table list to help readers locate the information they need. For a more detailed search, use the index at the back of the book. Also in the back of the book is the glossary, which defines most of the terms commonly used in the tables and text.

Who We Are: Blacks gives you the opportunity to discover and become familiar with the growing black population and its many unique characteristics. Armed with such knowledge, you will be closer to understanding what the future holds for our vast and complex nation.

Executive Summary

What You Need to Know about Blacks

The United States is rapidly becoming more diverse. To keep track of the changing racial and ethnic makeup of the nation requires more than hearsay and hunches. It requires an understanding of the size and characteristics of the country's growing minority populations. Whether you are a marketer, retailer, manufacturer, politician, policy maker, or social service provider, the nation's Asians, blacks, and Hispanics are a growing share of your customers and constituents.

Unfortunately, many Americans know little about the racial and ethnic make-up of the population. The public often wildly overestimates the size of minority groups while at the same time underestimating or even ignoring their powerful influence. In these fast-changing times, getting it wrong may be the difference between profit and loss, winning and losing, successful programs and failures. To keep you informed, the summary charts below highlight the most important facts you need to know about the nation's black or African American population. More details are available in the chapters that follow. Use these charts as a starting point for generating product ideas, developing marketing insights, and creating innovative policies.

1. Blacks are the second-largest minority in the United States

Shortly after the 2000 census, the number of Hispanics surpassed the number of blacks. Today, there are 40 million blacks and 44 million Hispanics in the United States. Because the Asian, black, and Hispanic populations are growing faster than the non-Hispanic white population, the non-Hispanic white share of the population is shrinking. The nation's minorities now account for one in three Americans. (For more information, see the Population chapter.)

Thirteen percent of Americans are black

(percent distribution of population by race and Hispanic origin, 2006)

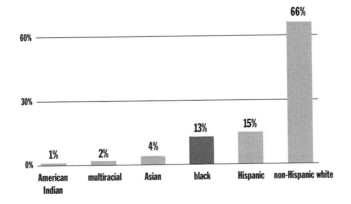

2. More than half of blacks live in the South

The 54 percent majority of blacks live in the South, where they account for a large share of the populations of several states. Few blacks live in the West. In California, the nation's most populous state, only 7 percent of the population is black. (For more information, see the Population chapter.)

Few blacks live in the West

(percent distributiuon of the black population, by region, 2006)

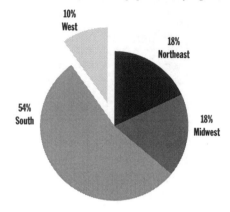

3. Blacks are a large share of some state populations

Blacks account for more than one in four residents of six states, all in the South. In some metropolitan areas, blacks are an even larger share of residents. They account for more than 40 percent of the population of 10 metros, including Jackson, Mississippi; Memphis, Tennessee; and Montgomery, Alabama. (For more information, see the Population chapter.)

Thirty percent of Georgia's population is black

(black share of population in the states in which blacks account for at least 25 percent of residents, 2006)

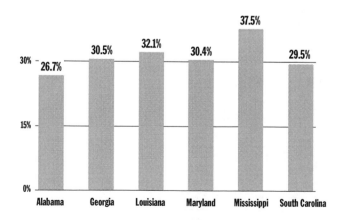

4. Black incomes are below average

Black household incomes are below average because married couples—the most affluent household type—head relatively few black households. Female-headed families—one of the poorest household types—are almost as numerous as married couples among black households, pulling down black household income statistics. (For more information, see the Income chapter.)

Black households have less to spend

(median income of total and black households, 2005)

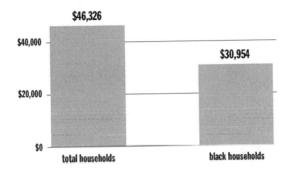

But black couples have relatively high incomes

(median income of black households by household type, 2005)

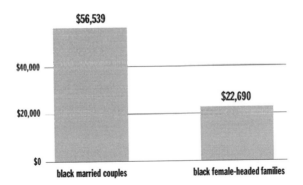

5. Married couples head few black households

Married couples head the 51 percent majority of the nation's households. Among black households, however, married couples head a smaller 30 percent. Female-headed families represent a much larger share of black households (29 percent) than households nationally (12 percent). These differences in black household composition explain why black household incomes are below average. (For more information, see the Living Arrangements chapter.)

Only 30 percent of black households are headed by married couples

(percent of total and black households headed by married couples and female-headed families, 2006)

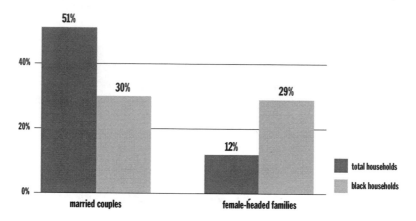

6. Most black children are born out-of-wedlock

Black women gave birth to 616,000 babies in 2005, and 69 percent of those children were born out-of-wedlock. This high rate of out-of-wedlock childbearing creates female-headed families, boosting the black poverty rate and lowering black household incomes. (For more information, see the Health chapter.)

Nearly 70 percent of black babies are born to single mothers

(percent of total and black babies born out-of-wedlock, 2005)

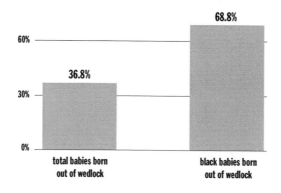

7. Black incomes are rising

The median household income of blacks grew by 14 percent between 1990 and 2005, after adjusting for inflation—twice as fast as the median income of all households during those years. The median income of black men also has been rising faster than average. Behind the rising incomes of blacks is their growing educational attainment. (For more information, see the Income chapter.)

Black household incomes are growing faster than average

(percent change in median income of total and black households, 1990 to 2005; in 2005 dollars)

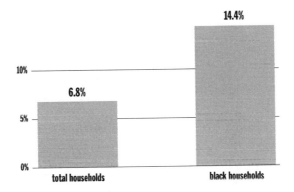

The incomes of black men are also growing faster than average

(percent change in median income of total and black men, 1990 to 2005; in 2005 dollars)

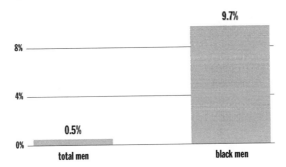

8. Fewer blacks are poor

The poverty rate of blacks is nearly double the rate among all Americans, but it is much lower than it used to be as blacks make gains in education and employment. The black poverty rate fell from 31.9 percent in 1990 to 24.7 percent in 2005. Among black married couples, only 8.2 percent are poor. (For more information, see the Income chapter.)

One in four blacks lives in poverty

(percent of blacks with incomes below poverty level, 1990 and 2005)

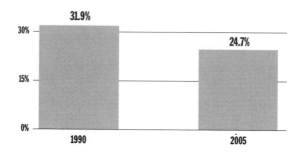

9. Blacks spend less than the average household

The average annual spending of black households is 29 percent below average, largely because so many are female-headed families. On a number of individual items, however, blacks spend more than the average household. They spend 20 percent more than average on residential telephone service. They control more than one-quarter of the market for children's shoes. (For more information, see the Spending chapter.)

Black households spend about $33,000 a year

(average annual spending of total and black households, 2005)

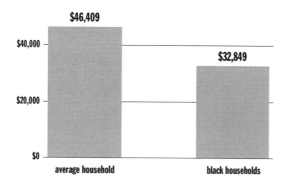

10. Blacks spend more time in religious activities

Nothing distinguishes black time use from average time use as much as their involvement in religious activities. On an average day, blacks spend twice as much time as the average person participating in religious activities. Other activities at which blacks spend more time than the average person include going to school, watching television, and making telephone calls. (For more information, see the Time Use chapter.)

One in eight blacks participates in religious activities on an average day

(percent of total people and blacks aged 15 or older who participate in religious activities as a primary activity on an average day, 2005)

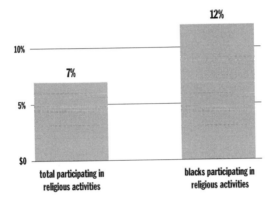

1

Education

■ More than 80 percent of blacks aged 25 or older are high school graduates, a share not far below the 85 percent of all Americans with a high school diploma.

■ By state, the percentage of blacks with a college degree is highest, at 29 percent, in Maryland and lowest, at 12 percent, in Indiana.

■ Of the nation's 76 million students, more than 12 million—or 16 percent—are black. In some states, blacks are the majority or near majority of public school students.

■ Among the nation's 17 million college students, 14 percent are black. Fifty-six percent of black college students are enrolled in four-year colleges, 30 percent in two-year schools, and 14 percent in graduate school.

■ Of the 1.4 million bachelor's degrees awarded in 2004–05, blacks earned 9 percent. In that school year, blacks earned a larger 12 percent of associate's degrees, 9 percent of master's degrees, 6 percent of doctoral degrees, and 7 percent of first-professional degrees.

■ Nearly half of the nation's 23 million blacks aged 16 or older participated in adult education programs during the 2004–05 academic year.

Black Educational Attainment Has Grown Rapidly

Blacks are almost as likely as the average American to be high school graduates.

More than 80 percent of blacks aged 25 or older are high school graduates, a share not far below the 85 percent of all Americans with a high school diploma. Blacks still lag in college experience. Only 19 percent of blacks have a college degree compared with 28 percent for the population as a whole.

The educational attainment of blacks varies greatly by age. Among blacks under age 55, at least 85 percent have graduated from high school. Among those aged 65 or older, the proportion is just 55 percent. Among blacks under age 45, at least one in five has a college degree compared with only about one in ten blacks aged 65 or older. The greater opportunity available to younger generations of blacks is clearly evident in these statistics.

■ The proportion of blacks with a college education will continue to climb, but only if college remains affordable for the middle class.

Many more blacks are high school graduates

(percent of blacks aged 25 or older with a high school diploma, 1980 and 2006)

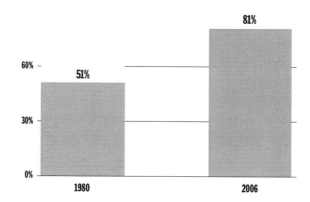

Table 1.1 Total and Black Educational Attainment, 1980 to 2006

(percent of total people and blacks aged 25 or older completing high school or college, 1980 to 2006; percentage point change, 1980–2006)

	high school graduates		college graduates	
	total	black	total	black
2006	85.5%	80.7%	28.0%	18.5%
2005	85.2	81.1	27.7	17.6
2004	85.2	80.6	27.7	17.6
2003	84.6	80.0	27.2	17.3
2002	84.1	78.7	26.7	17.0
2001	84.1	78.8	26.2	15.7
2000	84.1	78.5	25.6	16.5
1999	83.4	77.0	25.2	15.4
1998	82.8	76.0	24.4	14.7
1997	82.1	74.9	23.9	13.3
1996	81.7	74.3	23.6	13.6
1995	81.7	73.8	23.0	13.2
1994	80.9	72.9	22.2	12.9
1993	80.2	70.4	21.9	12.2
1992	79.4	67.7	21.4	11.9
1991	78.4	66.7	21.4	11.5
1990	77.6	66.2	21.3	11.3
1989	76.9	64.6	21.1	11.8
1988	76.2	63.5	20.3	11.2
1987	75.6	63.4	19.9	10.7
1986	74.7	62.3	19.4	10.9
1985	73.9	59.8	19.4	11.1
1984	73.3	58.5	19.1	10.4
1983	72.1	56.8	18.8	9.5
1982	71.0	54.9	17.7	8.8
1981	69.7	52.9	17.1	8.2
1980	68.6	51.2	17.0	7.9
Percentage point change				
2000 to 2006	1.4	2.2	2.5	2.2
1980 to 2006	16.9	29.5	11.0	10.6

Note: From 2003 through 2006, blacks are those who identify themselves as being of the race alone.
Source: Bureau of the Census, Current Population Surveys, Internet site http://www.census.gov/population/www/socdemo/ educ-attn.html; calculations by New Strategist

Table 1.2 Educational Attainment of Blacks by Age, 2006

(number and percent distribution of blacks aged 25 or older by educational attainment and age, 2006; numbers in thousands)

	total	25 to 34	35 to 44	45 to 54	55 to 64	65 or older
Total blacks	**22,137**	**5,366**	**5,505**	**5,081**	**3,132**	**3,053**
Not a high school graduate	4,245	726	676	763	715	1,361
High school graduate only	7,805	1,903	2,048	1,879	1,073	902
Some college, no degree	4,237	1,260	1,109	1,001	529	339
Associate's degree	1,714	386	461	482	266	122
Bachelor's degree	2,827	811	856	638	328	193
Master's degree	1,032	217	278	252	177	108
Professional degree	167	38	50	38	26	17
Doctoral degree	110	24	27	29	18	12
High school grad. or more	17,892	4,639	4,829	4,319	2,417	1,693
Some college or more	10,087	2,736	2,781	2,440	1,344	791
Bachelor's degree or more	4,136	1,090	1,211	957	549	330
PERCENT DISTRIBUTION						
Total blacks	**100.0%**	**100.0%**	**100.0%**	**100.0%**	**100.0%**	**100.0%**
Not a high school graduate	19.2	13.5	12.3	15.0	22.8	44.6
High school graduate only	35.3	35.5	37.2	37.0	34.3	29.5
Some college, no degree	19.1	23.5	20.1	19.7	16.9	11.1
Associate's degree	7.7	7.2	8.4	9.5	8.5	4.0
Bachelor's degree	12.8	15.1	15.5	12.6	10.5	6.3
Master's degree	4.7	4.0	5.0	5.0	5.7	3.5
Professional degree	0.8	0.7	0.9	0.7	0.8	0.6
Doctoral degree	0.5	0.4	0.5	0.6	0.6	0.4
High school grad. or more	80.8	86.5	87.7	85.0	77.2	55.5
Some college or more	45.6	51.0	50.5	48.0	42.9	25.9
Bachelor's degree or more	18.7	20.3	22.0	18.8	17.5	10.8

Note: Blacks are those who identify themselves as being of the race alone or as being of the race in combination with one or more other races.
Source: Bureau of the Census, 2006 Current Population Survey Annual Social and Economic Supplement, Educational Attainment in the United States: 2006, Detailed Tables, Internet site http://www.census.gov/population/www/socdemo/education/cps2006.html; calculations by New Strategist

Table 1.3 Educational Attainment of Black Men by Age, 2006

(number and percent distribution of black men aged 25 or older by educational attainment and age, 2006; numbers in thousands)

	total	25 to 34	35 to 44	45 to 54	55 to 64	65 or older
Total black men	**9,808**	**2,448**	**2,474**	**2,324**	**1,376**	**1,185**
Not a high school graduate	1,932	346	349	363	315	555
High school graduate only	3,701	986	977	912	487	340
Some college, no degree	1,808	533	504	433	211	129
Associate's degree	664	154	164	209	98	36
Bachelor's degree	1,179	348	353	250	159	70
Master's degree	392	59	93	115	85	39
Professional degree	68	10	17	21	11	7
Doctoral degree	65	12	17	20	10	8
High school grad. or more	7,877	2,102	2,125	1,960	1,061	629
Some college or more	4,176	1,116	1,148	1,048	574	289
Bachelor's degree or more	1,704	429	480	406	265	124

PERCENT DISTRIBUTION

	total	25 to 34	35 to 44	45 to 54	55 to 64	65 or older
Total black men	**100.0%**	**100.0%**	**100.0%**	**100.0%**	**100.0%**	**100.0%**
Not a high school graduate	19.7	14.1	14.1	15.6	22.9	46.8
High school graduate only	37.7	40.3	39.5	39.2	35.4	28.7
Some college, no degree	18.4	21.8	20.4	18.6	15.3	10.9
Associate's degree	6.8	6.3	6.6	9.0	7.1	3.0
Bachelor's degree	12.0	14.2	14.3	10.8	11.6	5.9
Master's degree	4.0	2.4	3.8	4.9	6.2	3.3
Professional degree	0.7	0.4	0.7	0.9	0.8	0.6
Doctoral degree	0.7	0.5	0.7	0.9	0.7	0.7
High school grad. or more	80.3	85.9	85.9	84.3	77.1	53.1
Some college or more	42.6	45.6	46.4	45.1	41.7	24.4
Bachelor's degree or more	17.4	17.5	19.4	17.5	19.3	10.5

Note: Blacks are those who identify themselves as being of the race alone or as being of the race in combination with one or more other races.
Source: Bureau of the Census, 2006 Current Population Survey Annual Social and Economic Supplement, Educational Attainment in the United States: 2006, Detailed Tables, Internet site http://www.census.gov/population/www/socdemo/education/cps2006.html; calculations by New Strategist

Table 1.4 Educational Attainment of Black Women by Age, 2006

(number and percent distribution of black women aged 25 or older by educational attainment and age, 2006; numbers in thousands)

	total	25 to 34	35 to 44	45 to 54	55 to 64	65 or older
Total black women	**12,329**	**2,917**	**3,031**	**2,757**	**1,756**	**1,868**
Not a high school graduate	2,313	381	328	399	400	805
High school graduate only	4,104	917	1,071	967	587	562
Some college, no degree	2,429	727	605	569	318	210
Associate's degree	1,051	231	296	270	166	86
Bachelor's degree	1,648	464	503	388	170	123
Master's degree	640	157	185	137	92	69
Professional degree	99	26	32	17	14	10
Doctoral degree	46	12	10	9	9	4
High school grad. or more	10,017	2,534	2,702	2,357	1,356	1,064
Some college or more	5,913	1,617	1,631	1,390	769	502
Bachelor's degree or more	2,433	659	730	551	285	206

PERCENT DISTRIBUTION

	total	25 to 34	35 to 44	45 to 54	55 to 64	65 or older
Total black women	**100.0%**	**100.0%**	**100.0%**	**100.0%**	**100.0%**	**100.0%**
Not a high school graduate	18.8	13.1	10.8	14.5	22.8	43.1
High school graduate only	33.3	31.4	35.3	35.1	33.4	30.1
Some college, no degree	19.7	24.9	20.0	20.6	18.1	11.2
Associate's degree	8.5	7.9	9.8	9.8	9.5	4.6
Bachelor's degree	13.4	15.9	16.6	14.1	9.7	6.6
Master's degree	5.2	5.4	6.1	5.0	5.2	3.7
Professional degree	0.8	0.9	1.1	0.6	0.8	0.5
Doctoral degree	0.4	0.4	0.3	0.3	0.5	0.2
High school grad. or more	81.2	86.9	89.1	85.5	77.2	57.0
Some college or more	48.0	55.4	53.8	50.4	43.8	26.9
Bachelor's degree or more	19.7	22.6	24.1	20.0	16.2	11.0

Note: Blacks are those who identify themselves as being of the race alone or as being of the race in combination with one or more other races.
Source: Bureau of the Census, 2006 Current Population Survey Annual Social and Economic Supplement, Educational Attainment in the United States: 2006, Detailed Tables, Internet site http://www.census.gov/population/www/socdemo/education/cps2006.html; calculations by New Strategist

Blacks in the West Are the Best Educated

Blacks in the South lag behind those in the rest of the country.

Black educational attainment varies by region, and blacks living in the West are the most highly educated. Eighty-seven percent of blacks aged 25 or older in the West have a high school diploma compared with a low of 79 percent in the South. Twenty-five percent of blacks in the West have a college degree compared with only 17 to 18 percent of blacks in the Midwest and South.

By state, the percentage of blacks with a college degree is lowest, at just 12 percent, in Indiana and Kentucky. The figure is highest, at 28 to 29 percent, in Colorado, Maryland, and Washington.

■ The educational attainment of blacks is rising, but wide variations by region and state remain.

Black educational attainment varies by region

(percent of blacks aged 25 or older with a bachelor's degree, by region, 2006)

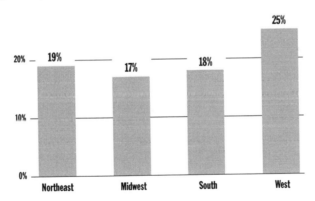

Table 1.5 Educational Attainment of Blacks by Age and Region, 2006

(percent of blacks aged 25 or older by selected educational attainment, age, and region, 2006)

	Northeast	Midwest	South	West
HIGH SCHOOL GRAD. OR MORE				
Total blacks	**80.3%**	**84.3%**	**78.8%**	**87.1%**
Aged 25 to 34	86.4	88.0	85.2	90.3
Aged 35 to 44	83.4	89.1	88.2	90.5
Aged 45 to 54	86.5	89.5	82.4	88.7
Aged 55 to 64	75.4	82.0	74.3	88.0
Aged 65 or older	60.2	62.9	48.7	70.8
SOME COLLEGE OR MORE				
Total blacks	**43.1**	**49.6**	**43.0**	**57.7**
Aged 25 to 34	52.7	52.1	48.3	59.8
Aged 35 to 44	48.4	54.5	48.7	58.1
Aged 45 to 54	43.9	54.2	45.0	62.0
Aged 55 to 64	35.3	49.6	39.9	62.1
Aged 65 or older	25.0	28.8	22.6	41.3
BACHELOR'S DEGREE OR MORE				
Total blacks	**19.2**	**16.7**	**18.1**	**24.6**
Aged 25 to 34	21.3	16.1	20.8	23.8
Aged 35 to 44	22.3	21.2	21.4	25.4
Aged 45 to 54	20.9	17.7	17.0	27.8
Aged 55 to 64	17.2	18.4	16.0	25.6
Aged 65 or older	10.1	7.0	10.9	19.1

Note: Blacks are those who identify themselves as being of the race alone or as being of the race in combination with one or more other races.
Source: Bureau of the Census, 2006 Current Population Survey Annual Social and Economic Supplement, Educational Attainment in the United States: 2006, Detailed Tables, Internet site http://www.census.gov/population/www/socdemo/education/cps2006.html; calculations by New Strategist

Table 1.6 Educational Attainment of Blacks by State, 2006

(percent of blacks aged 25 or older who are high school or college graduates, for the 25 most populous states, 2006)

	high school graduate or more	college graduate
Total blacks	**80.8%**	**18.7%**
Alabama	77.9	14.3
Arizona	88.7	20.4
California	86.6	25.3
Colorado	87.7	28.2
Florida	75.2	18.9
Georgia	83.0	19.1
Illinois	82.8	19.3
Indiana	83.4	11.9
Kentucky	90.8	12.3
Maryland	87.1	28.9
Massachusetts	89.0	20.1
Michigan	87.4	16.8
Minnesota	83.8	20.3
Missouri	85.9	12.5
New Jersey	80.5	18.2
New York	78.9	21.2
North Carolina	78.2	15.3
Ohio	84.8	17.0
Pennsylvania	82.2	14.8
South Carolina	77.9	15.1
Tennessee	78.5	14.8
Texas	82.6	19.8
Virginia	79.6	21.9
Washington	89.7	28.2
Wisconsin	81.0	13.8

Note: Blacks are those who identify themselves as being of the race alone or as being of the race in combination with one or more other races.
Source: Bureau of the Census, 2006 Current Population Survey Annual Social and Economic Supplement, Educational Attainment in the United States: 2006, Detailed Tables, Internet site http://www.census.gov/population/www/socdemo/education/cps2006 .html; calculations by New Strategist

Blacks Represent a Large Share of the Nation's Students

Black women are much more likely than black men to be in school.

Of the nation's 76 million students, more than 12 million—or 16 percent—are black. More than 90 percent of blacks are in school through the 16-to-17 age group. At ages 18 to 19, nearly two-thirds of blacks are still in school. The proportion drops below the 50 percent mark among blacks aged 20 or older.

Among students aged 20 or older, black women are much more likely than black men to be in school. In the 20-to-21 age group, fully 41 percent of black women are in school compared with 35 percent of black men. In the 22-to-24 age group the proportions are 31 and 24 percent, respectively.

In some states, blacks are the majority or a near majority of public elementary and secondary students. They account for 51 percent of students in Mississippi, 48 percent in Louisiana, and 41 percent in South Carolina.

■ If college was made more affordable, a larger proportion of blacks in their twenties would be in school.

Among black students aged 20 or older, women greatly outnumber men

(number of black students aged 20 or older, by sex, 2005)

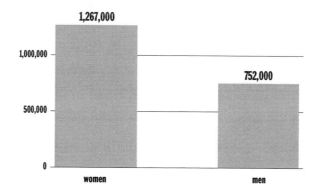

Table 1.7 Total and Black School Enrollment by Age, 2005

(total number of people aged 3 or older enrolled in school, number of blacks enrolled, and black share of total, by age, October 2005; numbers in thousands)

		black	
	total	number	share of total
Total aged 3 or older	**75,780**	**12,118**	**16.0%**
Aged 3 to 4	4,383	700	16.0
Aged 5 to 6	7,486	1,251	16.7
Aged 7 to 9	11,628	1,875	16.1
Aged 10 to 13	16,308	2,781	17.1
Aged 14 to 15	8,375	1,398	16.7
Aged 16 to 17	8,472	1,346	15.9
Aged 18 to 19	5,109	747	14.6
Aged 20 to 21	4,069	460	11.3
Aged 22 to 24	3,254	489	15.0
Aged 25 to 29	2,340	313	13.4
Aged 30 to 34	1,344	250	18.6
Aged 35 to 44	1,762	291	16.5
Aged 45 to 54	913	169	18.5
Aged 55 or older	336	47	14.0

Note: Blacks are those who identify themselves as being of the race alone or as being of the race in combination with one or more other races.
Source: Bureau of the Census, School Enrollment—Social and Economic Characteristics of Students: October 2005, Detailed Tables, Internet site http://www.census.gov/population/www/socdemo/school/cps2005.html; calculations by New Strategist

Table 1.8 School Enrollment of Blacks by Age and Sex, 2005

(number and percent of blacks aged 3 or older enrolled in school, by age and sex, October 2005; numbers in thousands)

	total		female		male	
	number	percent	number	percent	number	percent
Total blacks enrolled	**12,118**	**33.5%**	**6,325**	**32.4%**	**5,793**	**34.6%**
Aged 3 to 4	700	51.3	341	50.0	358	52.5
Aged 5 to 6	1,251	96.1	621	97.1	630	95.1
Aged 7 to 9	1,875	98.5	954	99.4	920	97.5
Aged 10 to 13	2,781	98.6	1,362	99.3	1,419	97.9
Aged 14 to 15	1,398	95.9	736	97.8	662	93.8
Aged 16 to 17	1,346	92.9	683	92.0	663	93.8
Aged 18 to 19	747	62.5	359	59.1	388	66.2
Aged 20 to 21	460	38.1	249	41.3	211	34.9
Aged 22 to 24	489	27.8	298	31.1	190	23.9
Aged 25 to 29	313	11.7	199	13.8	114	9.3
Aged 30 to 34	250	9.9	181	12.8	69	6.1
Aged 35 to 44	291	5.3	214	7.1	77	3.1
Aged 45 to 54	169	3.4	99	3.6	70	3.1
Aged 55 or older	47	0.8	27	0.8	21	0.8

Note: Blacks are those who identify themselves as being of the race alone or as being of the race in combination with one or more other races.
Source: Bureau of the Census, School Enrollment—Social and Economic Characteristics of Students: October 2005, Detailed Tables, Internet site http://www.census.gov/population/www/socdemo/school/cps2005.html; calculations by New Strategist

Table 1.9 Black Enrollment in Public Elementary and Secondary Schools by State, 1994 and 2004

(percentage of students enrolled in public elementary and secondary schools who are black, by state, 1994 and 2004; percentage point change, 1994–2004)

	2004	1994	percentage point change
Total enrolled	**17.3%**	**16.7%**	**0.6**
Alabama	36.1	35.8	0.3
Alaska	4.6	4.8	−0.2
Arizona	5.0	4.3	0.7
Arkansas	23.0	23.9	−0.9
California	8.1	8.7	−0.6
Colorado	5.9	5.4	0.5
Connecticut	13.8	13.3	0.5
Delaware	32.3	29.1	3.2
District of Columbia	84.5	88.0	−3.5
Florida	24.1	25.0	−0.9
Georgia	38.9	37.5	1.4
Hawaii	2.4	2.7	−0.3
Idaho	1.0	–	–
Illinois	20.7	21.0	−0.3
Indiana	12.4	11.2	1.2
Iowa	4.8	3.2	1.6
Kansas	8.7	8.4	0.3
Kentucky	10.5	9.7	0.8
Louisiana	47.7	45.7	2.0
Maine	1.9	0.7	1.2
Maryland	38.1	34.7	3.4
Massachusetts	8.9	8.0	0.9
Michigan	19.9	17.5	2.4
Minnesota	8.2	4.5	3.7
Mississippi	50.8	50.9	−0.1
Missouri	17.9	15.8	2.1
Montana	0.8	0.5	0.3
Nebraska	7.4	5.8	1.6
Nevada	–	9.3	
New Hampshire	1.6	0.8	0.8
New Jersey	17.7	18.6	−0.9
New Mexico	2.5	2.4	0.1
New York	19.9	20.2	−0.3
North Carolina	31.6	30.5	1.1
North Dakota	1.2	0.8	0.4
Ohio	17.1	15.1	2.0
Oklahoma	10.8	10.4	0.4
Oregon	3.3	2.5	0.8
Pennsylvania	16.0	13.9	2.1
Rhode Island	8.6	7.0	1.6
South Carolina	40.8	41.7	−0.9
South Dakota	1.6	0.8	0.8
Tennessee	25.1	23.0	2.1
Texas	14.2	14.3	−0.1
Utah	1.2	0.7	0.5
Vermont	1.4	0.7	0.7
Virginia	27.1	26.2	0.9
Washington	5.7	4.6	1.1
West Virginia	4.8	3.9	0.9
Wisconsin	10.5	9.3	1.2
Wyoming	1.4	1.0	0.4

Note: "–" means data are not available.
Source: National Center for Education Statistics, Digest of Education Statistics 2006, Internet site http://nces.ed.gov/programs/digest/; calculations by New Strategist

The Black College Enrollment Rate Is Slipping

Family income greatly affects black college enrollment.

Most black students who graduate from high school enroll in college within 12 months of getting their diploma. But trends in the black enrollment rate are troubling. Since 2000, the black rate has failed to keep pace with the average rate, and it fell between 2004 and 2005. The rapid increase in college costs may be preventing blacks from enrolling in college.

Family income greatly influences whether young adults are enrolled in a four-year college. Overall, 26 percent of black dependents aged 18 to 24 are students at a four-year school. The proportion is just 20 percent among those with family incomes below $25,000 and rises to 48 percent among those with incomes of $75,000 or more.

Among the nation's 17 million college students, 14 percent are black. Fifty-six percent of black college students are enrolled in four-year colleges, 30 percent in two-year schools, and 14 percent in graduate school.

■ Financial aid is critical to boosting the percentage of blacks with a college degree.

Black enrollment rises sharply with family income

(percent of black dependent family members aged 18 to 24 who attend a four-year college, by family income, 2005)

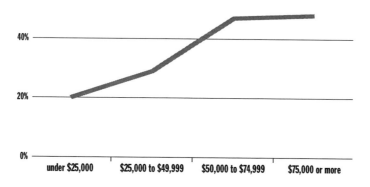

under $25,000	$25,000 to $49,999	$50,000 to $74,999	$75,000 or more

Table 1.10 Total and Black College Enrollment Rate, 1990 to 2005

(percent of total people and blacks aged 16 to 24 having graduated from high school in the previous 12 months who were enrolled in college as of October, 1990 to 2005; percentage point change in enrollment rate for selected years)

	total people	blacks
2005	68.6%	55.7%
2004	66.7	62.5
2003	63.9	57.5
2002	65.2	59.4
2001	61.8	55.0
2000	63.3	54.9
1999	62.9	58.9
1998	65.6	61.9
1997	67.0	58.5
1996	65.0	56.0
1995	61.9	51.2
1994	61.9	50.8
1993	62.6	55.6
1992	61.9	48.2
1991	62.6	46.4
1990	60.1	46.8
Percentage point change		
2000 to 2005	5.3	0.8
1990 to 2005	8.5	8.9

Source: National Center for Education Statistics, Digest of Education Statistics 2006, Internet site http://nces.ed.gov/programs/digest/; calculations by New Strategist

Table 1.11 Total and Black College Enrollment, 1976 to 2005

(number of total people and blacks aged 15 or older enrolled in institutions of higher education, and black share of total, 1976 to 2005; numbers in thousands)

	total enrolled	black number	black share of total
2005	17,488	2,215	12.7%
2004	17,272	2,165	12.5
2003	16,901	2,069	12.2
2002	16,612	1,979	11.9
2001	15,928	1,850	11.6
2000	15,312	1,730	11.3
1999	14,791	1,641	11.1
1998	14,507	1,583	10.9
1997	14,502	1,551	10.7
1996	14,368	1,506	10.5
1995	14,262	1,474	10.3
1990	13,819	1,247	9.0
1980	12,087	1,107	9.2
1976	10,986	1,033	9.4

Note: Enrollment figures are based on a survey of institutions of higher education. They differ from enrollment figures in other tables, which are based on household surveys.
Source: National Center for Education Statistics, Digest of Education Statistics 2006, Internet site http://nces.ed.gov/programs/ digest/; calculations by New Strategist

Table 1.12 College Enrollment Status of Blacks Aged 18 to 24, 2005

(total number of black dependent family members aged 18 to 24, and number and percent enrolled in a four-year college by family income, 2005; numbers in thousands)

	total	enrolled in four-year college number	enrolled in four-year college percent
Total black dependent family members aged 18 to 24	**2,540**	**678**	**26.7%**
Less than $25,000	882	177	20.1
$25,000 to $49,999	901	263	29.2
$50,000 to $74,999	132	62	47.0
$75,000 and over	60	29	48.3

Note: Blacks are those who identify themselves as being of the race alone or as being of the race in combination with one or more other races. Numbers will not add to total because not reported is not shown.
Source: Bureau of the Census, School Enrollment—Social and Economic Characteristics of Students: October 2005, Detailed Tables, Internet site http://www.census.gov/population/www/socdemo/school/cps2005.html; calculations by New Strategist

Table 1.13 Total and Black College Enrollment by Age, 2005

(total number of people aged 15 or older enrolled in college, number of blacks enrolled, and black share of total, by age, October 2005; numbers in thousands)

		black	
	total	number	share of total
Total enrolled in college	**17,472**	**2,386**	**13.7%**
Under age 20	3,909	513	13.1
Aged 20 to 21	3,945	428	10.8
Aged 22 to 24	3,162	461	14.6
Aged 25 to 29	2,291	299	13.1
Aged 30 to 34	1,309	230	17.6
Aged 35 to 39	948	143	15.1
Aged 40 to 44	709	110	15.5
Aged 45 to 49	515	103	20.0
Aged 50 to 54	368	56	15.2
Aged 55 or older	318	43	13.5

Note: Blacks are those who identify themselves as being of the race alone or as being of the race in combination with one or more other races.
Source: Bureau of the Census, School Enrollment—Social and Economic Characteristics of Students: October 2005, Detailed Tables, Internet site http://www.census.gov/population/www/socdemo/school/cps2005.html; calculations by New Strategist

Table 1.14 College Enrollment of Blacks by Age and Type of School, 2005

(number and percent distribution of blacks aged 15 or older enrolled in college by age and type of school, October 2005; numbers in thousands)

	total	two-year college	four-year college	graduate school
Total blacks enrolled	**2,386**	**725**	**1,335**	**326**
Under age 20	513	178	335	0
Aged 20 to 21	428	113	296	19
Aged 22 to 24	461	108	309	44
Aged 25 to 29	299	115	124	60
Aged 30 to 34	230	73	101	56
Aged 35 or older	455	139	171	145
PERCENT DISTRIBUTION BY TYPE OF SCHOOL				
Total blacks enrolled	**100.0%**	**30.4%**	**56.0%**	**13.7%**
Under age 20	100.0	34.7	65.3	0.0
Aged 20 to 21	100.0	26.4	69.2	4.4
Aged 22 to 24	100.0	23.4	67.0	9.5
Aged 25 to 29	100.0	38.5	41.5	20.1
Aged 30 to 34	100.0	31.7	43.9	24.3
Aged 35 or older	100.0	30.5	37.6	31.9
PERCENT DISTRIBUTION BY AGE				
Total blacks enrolled	**100.0%**	**100.0%**	**100.0%**	**100.0%**
Under age 20	21.5	24.6	25.1	0.0
Aged 20 to 21	17.9	15.6	22.2	5.8
Aged 22 to 24	19.3	14.9	23.1	13.5
Aged 25 to 29	12.5	15.9	9.3	18.4
Aged 30 to 34	9.6	10.1	7.6	17.2
Aged 35 or older	19.1	19.2	12.8	44.5

Note: Blacks are those who identify themselves as being of the race alone or as being of the race in combination with one or more other races.
Source: Bureau of the Census, School Enrollment—Social and Economic Characteristics of Students: October 2005, Detailed Tables, Internet site http://www.census.gov/population/www/socdemo/school/cps2005.html; calculations by New Strategist

Blacks Earn Nine Percent of Bachelor's Degrees

They earn a larger 12 percent of associate's degrees.

Of the 1.3 million bachelor's degrees awarded in 2004–05, blacks earned 9 percent. This figure is less than the black share of the total population and may slip in the future if black college enrollment rates continue to fall. Blacks earned a larger 12 percent of associate's degrees awarded in 2004–05. At the master's level, blacks earned 9 percent of degrees, including 18 percent of degrees in public administration. Only 6 percent of doctoral degrees are awarded to blacks.

Blacks earned a relatively small 7 percent of first-professional degrees awarded in 2004–05, but in theology they accounted for a much larger 15 percent of degrees. Of those receiving degrees in medicine and law in 2004–05, blacks accounted for 7 percent.

■ Blacks are making inroads into higher education, but the rising cost of college is limiting their gains.

Blacks earn one in eight associate's degrees

(percent of degrees earned by blacks, by level of degree, 2004–05)

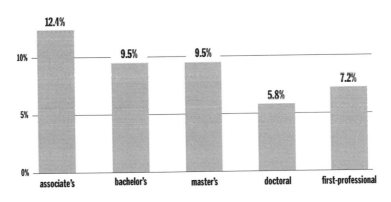

Table 1.15 Associate's Degrees Earned by Total People and Blacks by Field of Study, 2004–05

(total number of associate's degrees conferred and number and percent earned by blacks, by field of study, 2004–05)

	total	earned by blacks	
		number	share of total
Total associate's degrees	**696,660**	**86,402**	**12.4%**
Agriculture and natural resources	6,404	38	0.6
Architecture and related programs	583	37	6.3
Area, ethnic, and cultural studies	115	25	21.7
Biological and biomedical sciences	1,709	132	7.7
Business	112,378	17,842	15.9
Communications, journalism, and related programs	2,545	263	10.3
Communications technologies	3,516	411	11.7
Computer and information sciences	36,173	5,554	15.4
Construction trades	3,512	243	6.9
Education	13,329	2,250	16.9
Engineering	2,441	300	12.3
Engineering technologies	33,548	3,691	11.0
English language and literature, letters	995	91	9.1
Family and consumer sciences	9,707	2,036	21.0
Foreign languages, literature, and linguistics	1,234	80	6.5
Health professions and related sciences	122,520	15,578	12.7
Legal professions and studies	9,885	1,673	16.9
Liberal arts and sciences, general studies, and humanities	240,131	25,669	10.7
Library science	108	9	8.3
Mathematics and statistics	807	37	4.6
Mechanics and repair technologies	13,619	966	7.1
Military technologies	355	87	24.5
Multi- and interdisciplinary studies	13,888	1,561	11.2
Parks, recreation, leisure, and fitness	966	116	12.0
Philosophy and religion	422	17	4.0
Physical sciences and science technologies	2,814	217	7.7
Precision production	2,039	88	4.3
Psychology	1,942	181	9.3
Public administration and social service professions	4,027	1,070	26.6
Security and protective services	23,749	3,221	13.6
Social sciences and history	6,533	735	11.3
Theology and religious vocations	581	107	18.4
Transportation and materials moving	1,435	91	6.3
Visual and performing arts	22,650	1,986	8.8

Source: National Center for Education Statistics, Digest of Education Statistics 2006, Internet site http://nces.ed.gov/programs/digest/; calculations by New Strategist

Table 1.16 Bachelor's Degrees Earned by Total People and Blacks by Field of Study, 2004–05

(total number of bachelor's degrees conferred and number and percent earned by blacks, by field of study, 2004–05)

		earned by blacks	
	total	number	share of total
Total bachelor's degrees	**1,439,264**	**136,122**	**9.5%**
Agriculture and natural resources	23,002	654	2.8
Architecture and related services	9,237	426	4.6
Area, ethnic, cultural, and gender studies	7,569	1,051	13.9
Biological and biomedical sciences	64,611	5,146	8.0
Business	311,574	34,464	11.1
Communications, journalism, and related programs	72,715	7,048	9.7
Communications technologies	2,523	262	10.4
Computer and information sciences	54,111	6,438	11.9
Construction trades	117	8	6.8
Education	105,451	6,434	6.1
Engineering	64,906	3,386	5.2
Engineering technologies	14,482	1,537	10.6
English language, literature, and letters	54,379	4,200	7.7
Family and consumer sciences	20,074	2,057	10.2
Foreign languages, literature, and linguistics	18,386	753	4.1
Health professions and related clinical sciences	80,685	8,989	11.1
Legal professions and studies	3,161	618	19.6
Liberal arts and sciences, general studies, and humanities	43,751	5,657	12.9
Library science	76	3	3.9
Mathematics and statistics	14,351	885	6.2
Mechanics and repair technologies	238	15	6.3
Military technologies	40	1	2.5
Multi- and interdisciplinary studies	30,243	2,674	8.8
Parks, recreation, leisure, and fitness	22,888	2,042	8.9
Philosophy and religious studies	11,584	604	5.2
Physical sciences and science technologies	18,905	1,105	5.8
Precision production	64	0	0.0
Psychology	85,614	9,703	11.3
Public administration and social service professions	21,769	4,946	22.7
Security and protective services	30,723	5,545	18.0
Social sciences and history	156,892	14,323	9.1
Theology and religious vocations	9,284	538	5.8
Transportation and materials moving	4,904	291	5.9
Visual and performing arts	80,955	4,319	5.3

Source: National Center for Education Statistics, Digest of Education Statistics 2006, Internet site http://nces.ed.gov/programs/digest/; calculations by New Strategist

Table 1.17 Master's Degrees Earned by Total People and Blacks by Field of Study, 2004–05

(total number of master's degrees conferred and number and percent earned by blacks, by field of study, 2004–05)

	total	earned by blacks number	earned by blacks share of total
Total master's degrees	**574,618**	**54,482**	**9.5%**
Agriculture and natural resources	4,746	112	2.4
Architecture and related services	5,674	268	4.7
Area, ethnic, cultural, and gender studies	1,755	168	9.6
Biological and biomedical sciences	8,199	426	5.2
Business	142,617	16,025	11.2
Communications, journalism, and related programs	6,762	678	10.0
Communications technologies	433	48	11.1
Computer and information sciences	18,416	1,024	5.6
Education	167,490	16,977	10.1
Engineering	32,633	885	2.7
Engineering technologies	2,500	203	8.1
English language, literature, and letters	8,468	366	4.3
Family and consumer sciences	1,827	196	10.7
Foreign languages, literature, and linguistics	3,407	81	2.4
Health professions and related clinical sciences	46,703	4,386	9.4
Legal professions and studies	4,170	201	4.8
Liberal arts and sciences, general studies, and humanities	3,680	306	8.3
Library science	6,213	288	4.6
Mathematics and statistics	4,477	143	3.2
Multi- and interdisciplinary studies	4,252	322	7.6
Parks, recreation, leisure, and fitness	3,740	318	8.5
Philosophy and religious studies	1,647	80	0.0
Physical sciences and science technologies	5,678	127	2.2
Precision production	6	0	0.0
Psychology	18,830	2,493	13.2
Public administration and social service professions	29,552	5,374	18.2
Security and protective services	3,991	663	16.6
Social sciences and history	16,952	1,206	7.1
Theology and religious vocations	5,815	489	8.4
Transportation and materials moving	802	48	6.0
Visual and performing arts	13,183	581	4.4

Source: National Center for Education Statistics, Digest of Education Statistics 2006, Internet site http://nces.ed.gov/programs/digest/; calculations by New Strategist

Table 1.18 Doctoral Degrees Earned by Total People and Blacks by Field of Study, 2004–05

(total number of doctoral degrees conferred and number and percent earned by blacks, by field of study, 2004–05)

	total	earned by blacks number	earned by blacks share of total
Total doctoral degrees	**52,631**	**3,056**	**5.8%**
Agriculture and natural resources	1,173	23	2.0
Architecture and related services	179	5	2.8
Area, ethnic, cultural, and gender studies	189	24	12.7
Biological and biomedical sciences	5,578	155	2.8
Business	1,498	123	8.2
Communications, journalism, and related programs	465	25	5.4
Communications technologies	3	0	0.0
Computer and information sciences	1,119	22	2.0
Education	7,681	1,206	15.7
Engineering	6,547	111	1.7
Engineering technologies	54	0	0.0
English language, literature, and letters	1,212	80	6.6
Family and consumer sciences	331	37	11.2
Foreign languages, literature, and linguistics	1,027	11	1.1
Health professions and related clinical sciences	5,868	257	4.4
Legal professions and studies	98	1	1.0
Liberal arts and sciences, general studies, and humanities	109	2	1.8
Library science	42	0	0.0
Mathematics and statistics	1,176	20	1.7
Multi- and interdisciplinary studies	983	64	6.5
Parks, recreation, leisure, and fitness	207	8	3.9
Philosophy and religious studies	586	25	4.3
Physical sciences and science technologies	4,114	60	1.5
Psychology	5,106	323	6.3
Public administration and social service professions	673	92	13.7
Security and protective services	94	6	6.4
Social sciences and history	3,819	195	5.1
Theology and religious vocations	1,422	153	10.8
Visual and performing arts	1,278	28	2.2

Source: National Center for Education Statistics, Digest of Education Statistics 2006, Internet site http://nces.ed.gov/programs/digest/; calculations by New Strategist

Table 1.19 First-Professional Degrees Earned by Total People and Blacks by Field of Study, 2004–05

(total number of first-professional degrees conferred and number and percent earned by blacks, by field of study, 2004–05)

	total	earned by blacks	
		number	share of total
Total first-professional degrees	**87,289**	**6,313**	**7.2%**
Dentistry (D.D.S. or D.M.D.)	4,454	192	4.3
Medicine (M.D.)	15,461	1,083	7.0
Optometry (O.D.)	1,252	36	2.9
Osteopathic medicine (D.O.)	2,762	88	3.2
Pharmacy (Pharm.D.)	8,885	791	8.9
Podiatry (Pod.D., D.P., or D.P.M.)	343	34	9.9
Veterinary medicine (D.V.M.)	2,354	43	1.8
Chiropractic (D.C. or D.C.M.)	2,560	135	5.3
Naturopathic medicine	262	13	5.0
Law (LL.B. or J.D.)	43,423	3,052	7.0
Theology (M.Div., M.H.L., B.D., or Ord.)	5,533	846	15.3

Source: National Center for Education Statistics, Digest of Education Statistics 2006, Internet site http://nces.ed.gov/programs/digest/; calculations by New Strategist

Blacks Are Most Likely to Participate in Adult Education

The largest share of blacks takes work-related courses.

Blacks are more likely than Asians or Hispanics to participate in adult education. Nearly half—46 percent—of the nation's 23 million blacks aged 16 or older participated in adult education programs during the 2004–05 academic year. Twenty-seven percent of blacks took a work-related course, and almost as many (24 percent) took a personal interest course.

Black participation in other types of adult education programs is minimal. Just 2 percent of blacks took GED classes in 2004–05, and an equal share participated in apprenticeship programs. A larger 4 percent of blacks are in a part-time college degree program.

■ Blacks are more likely than Asians to be in an apprenticeship program.

Black participation is above that of Asians or Hispanics

(percent of people aged 16 or older who take adult education classes, by race and Hispanic origin, 2004–05)

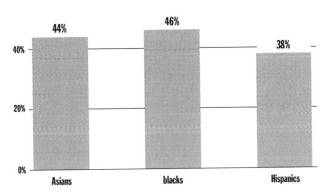

Table 1.20 Participation in Adult Education, 2004–05

(number and percent of people aged 16 or older participating in adult education, by type of educational activity, race, and Hispanic origin, 2004–05; numbers in thousands)

	black	Asian	Hispanic
Total aged 16 or older, number	**23,467**	**7,080**	**26,101**
Total aged 16 or older, percent	**100.0%**	**100.0%**	**100.0%**
Participated in any formal adult education activity	46.0	44.0	38.0
English-as-a-second-language classes	0.0	2.0	6.0
Basic skills, GED classes	2.0	0.0	3.0
Part-time college degree programs	4.0	6.0	4.0
Part-time vocational degree or diploma programs	1.0	0.0	1.0
Apprenticeships	2.0	0.0	2.0
Work-related courses	27.0	24.0	17.0
Personal interest courses	24.0	23.0	15.0

Source: National Center for Education Statistics, Adult Education Participation in 2004-05; National Household Education Surveys Program, Internet site http://nces.ed.gov/pubs2006/adulted/tables.asp; calculations by New Strategist

2

Health

■ Only 45 percent of blacks aged 18 or older say their health is excellent or very good, which is well below the 55 percent of all adults who rate their health highly.

■ Only 35 percent of blacks are current regular drinkers compared with a much larger 48 percent of all adults.

■ Sixty-five percent of black adults are overweight. Thirty-two percent are obese.

■ Of the 4.1 million births in the United States in 2005, blacks accounted for a substantial 15 percent. Sixty-nine percent of black births are to unmarried women.

■ The 80 percent majority of blacks had health insurance coverage in 2006. The percentage of blacks with no health insurance reaches a high of 35 percent in the 18-to-24 age group.

■ Blacks aged 18 or older suffer from a variety of health conditions at a higher than average rate, including high blood pressure, asthma, diabetes, and kidney disease.

■ At birth, blacks can expect to live 73.3 years, which is well below the 77.8 years of life expectancy for the average American.

Blacks Are Less Likely to Say Their Health Is Excellent or Very Good

The percentage of blacks who rate their health as excellent or very good has declined.

Only 45 percent of blacks aged 18 or older say their health is excellent or very good, according to the federal government's Behavioral Risk Factor Surveillance System. This share is well below the 55 percent of all adults who rate their health highly. Blacks are much more likely than the average person to say their health is only fair or poor.

Between 2000 and 2006, the percentage of blacks who rated their health as excellent fell by 2 percentage points. During those same years, the proportion rating their health as only good or fair climbed nearly 2 percentage points. Five percent of blacks reported poor health in 2006, about the same as in 2000.

■ A lack of health insurance and problems accessing health care services may be affecting the health status of blacks.

Blacks are less likely than the average Americans to rate their health highly

(percent of total people and blacks aged 18 or older who rate their health as excellent or very good, 2006)

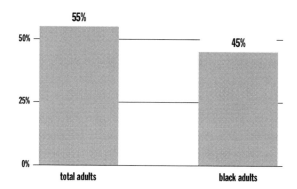

Table 2.1 Health Status of Total and Black Adults, 2006

(percent distribution of total people and blacks aged 18 or older by self-reported health status, and index of black to total, 2006)

	total	black	index black to total
Total people	**100.0%**	**100.0%**	–
Excellent	20.7	16.4	79
Very good	34.4	28.2	82
Good	30.2	35.0	116
Fair	10.9	15.4	141
Poor	3.7	5.0	135

Note: "–" means not applicable.
Source: Centers for Disease Control and Prevention, Behavioral Risk Factor Surveillance System, Prevalence Data, Internet site http://apps.nccd.cdc.gov/brfss/index.asp; calculations by New Strategist

Table 2.2 Black Health Status, 2000 and 2006

(percent distribution of blacks aged 18 or older by self-reported health status, 2000 and 2006, percentage point change, 2000–06)

	2006	2000	percentage point change
Total blacks	**100.0%**	**100.0%**	–
Excellent	16.4	18.3	–1.9
Very good	28.2	28.9	–0.7
Good	35.0	33.3	1.7
Fair	15.4	13.8	1.6
Poor	5.0	5.1	–0.1

Note: "–" means not applicable.
Source: Centers for Disease Control and Prevention, Behavioral Risk Factor Surveillance System, Prevalence Data, Internet site http://apps.nccd.cdc.gov/brfss/index.asp; calculations by New Strategist

Among Blacks, One in Five Smokes Cigarettes

Blacks are much less likely than the average American to drink alcohol.

Blacks smoke cigarettes at an average rate. Twenty-one percent of blacks aged 18 or older are current smokers, the same percentage as among all adults in the United States. Sixty-four percent of blacks aged 18 or older have never smoked, a larger share than the 57 percent of all Americans who never started smoking.

Only 35 percent of blacks are current regular drinkers, meaning they have had more than 12 alcoholic drinks in the past year. This compares with a much larger 48 percent of all adults who are current regular drinkers. More than one-third of blacks (36 percent) are lifetime abstainers versus a smaller 24 percent of all Americans.

■ Only 14 percent of blacks are former smokers compared with 21 percent of all adults.

Blacks are equally likely to smoke, but less likely to drink, than the average American

(percent of total people and blacks aged 18 or older by smoking and drinking status, 2005)

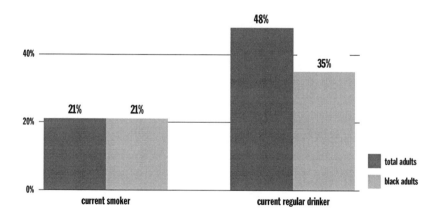

Table 2.3 Smoking Status of Total and Black Adults, 2005

(number and percent distribution of total people and blacks aged 18 or older by smoking status, 2005)

	total		blacks	
	number	percent distribution	number	percent distribution
Total people	**217,774**	**100.0%**	**24,817**	**100.0%**
All current smokers	45,131	20.7	5,243	21.1
Every-day smoker	36,454	16.7	3,936	15.9
Some-day smoker	8,678	4.0	1,307	5.3
Former smoker	46,522	21.4	3,400	13.7
Nonsmoker	124,257	57.1	15,863	63.9

Note: Current smokers have smoked at least 100 cigarettes in lifetime and still smoke; every-day smokers are current smokers who smoke every day; some-day smokers are current smokers who smoke on some days; former smokers have smoked at least 100 cigarettes in lifetime but currently do not smoke; nonsmokers have smoked fewer than 100 cigarettes in lifetime. Numbers by smoking status may not add to total because unknown is not shown. Blacks are those who identify themselves as being of the race alone.
Source: National Center for Health Statistics, Summary Health Statistics for U.S. Adults: National Health Interview Survey, 2005, Series 10, No. 232, 2006, Internet site http://www.cdc.gov/nchs/nhis.htm; calculations by New Strategist

Table 2.4 Drinking Status of Total and Black Adults, 2005

(number and percent distribution of total people and blacks aged 18 or older by drinking status, 2005)

	total		blacks	
	number	percent distribution	number	percent distribution
Total people	**217,774**	**100.0%**	**24,817**	**100.0%**
Current regular drinker	103,672	47.6	8,566	34.5
Current infrequent drinker	25,502	11.7	2,699	10.9
Former drinker	30,357	13.9	3,605	14.5
Lifetime abstainer	51,420	23.6	8,995	36.2

Note: A lifetime abstainer had fewer than 12 drinks in lifetime; a former drinker had more than 12 drinks in lifetime, but no drinks in past year; current drinker had more than 12 drinks in lifetime, and had drinks in past year; infrequent drinker had fewer than 12 drinks in one year; a regular drinker had more than 12 drinks in one year. Numbers by drinking status may not add to total because unknown is not shown. Blacks are those who identify themselves as being of the race alone.
Source: National Center for Health Statistics, Summary Health Statistics for U.S. Adults: National Health Interview Survey, 2005, Series 10, No. 232, 2006, Internet site http://www.cdc.gov/nchs/nhis.htm; calculations by New Strategist

Most Blacks Are Overweight

Nearly one in three is obese.

Black men aged 20 or older weigh 190 pounds, on average, according to a government study that put a representative sample of Americans on a scale to measure their weight. Black women aged 20 or older weigh 183 pounds, on average. Among black adults, weight does not vary much by age.

Blacks are significantly more likely to be overweight than is the general population. Sixty-five percent of blacks are overweight, having a body mass index of 25 or more. Among all adults, a slightly smaller 58 percent are overweight. Thirty-one percent of blacks are obese, having a body mass index of 30 or more. Among all adults, 24 percent are obese.

■ Only 30 percent of blacks aged 18 or older have a healthy weight compared with 36 percent of all adults.

Few blacks have a healthy weight

(percent distribution of blacks aged 18 or older by weight status, 2005)

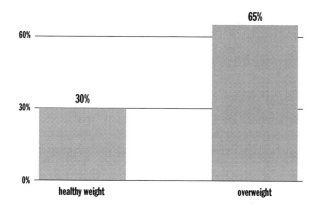

Table 2.5 Weight of Blacks by Age and Sex, 1999–2002

(average weight in pounds of non-Hispanic blacks aged 20 or older by age and sex, 1999–2002)

	men	women
Total blacks	**190.0 lbs.**	**182.8 lbs.**
Aged 20 to 39	189.7	179.6
Aged 40 to 59	191.4	189.3
Aged 60 or older	187.3	177.2

Note: Data are based on measured weight of a sample of the civilian noninstitutionalized population.
Source: National Center for Health Statistics, Anthropometric Reference Data for Children and Adults: U.S. Population, 1999–2002, Advance Data, No. 361, 2005, Internet site http://www.cdc.gov/nchs/about/major/nhanes/advancedatas.htm

Table 2.6 Weight Status of Total and Black Adults, 2005

(percent distribution of total people and blacks aged 18 or older by body weight status, and index of black to total, 2005)

	total	blacks	index black to total
Total people	**100.0%**	**100.0%**	–
Underweight	1.9	1.0	54
Healthy weight	36.1	29.9	83
Overweight, total	57.7	64.8	112
Overweight, not obese	33.8	33.5	99
Obese	23.9	31.3	131

Note: Underweight is a body mass index (BMI) below 18.5; healthy weight is a BMI of 18.5 to 24.9; overweight is a BMI of 25.0 or higher; obese is a BMI of 30.0 or more. BMI is calculated by dividing weight in kilograms by height in meters squared. Data are based on self-reported heights and weights of a representative sample of the civilian noninstitutional population. Numbers may not add to total because weight unknown is not shown. Blacks are those who identify themselves as being of the race alone. "–" means not applicable.
Source: National Center for Health Statistics, Summary Health Statistics for U.S. Adults: National Health Interview Survey, 2005, Series 10, No. 232, 2006, Internet site http://www.cdc.gov/nchs/nhis.htm; calculations by New Strategist

Most Black Children Are Born to Single Mothers

More than two out of three black births are to unmarried women.

Of the 4.1 million births in the United States in 2005, blacks accounted for a substantial 15 percent. Blacks account for one in four births to women aged 15 to 19 and for an even larger 42 percent of births to women under age 15.

In 2004, the 69 percent majority of black births were to unmarried women. The percentage of births to single mothers falls with age, from more than 95 percent of births to black women under age 20 to less than half of births to black women aged 30 or older.

Although blacks account for 15 percent of births nationwide, in some states the black share is much higher. The black share of births is at least 30 percent in Alabama, Georgia, Louisiana, Maryland, Mississippi, and South Carolina.

■ Because single mothers are such a large proportion of black families, the black poverty rate is well above average.

The percentage of babies born to single mothers falls with age

(percentage of black babies born to unmarried mothers, by age of mother, 2004)

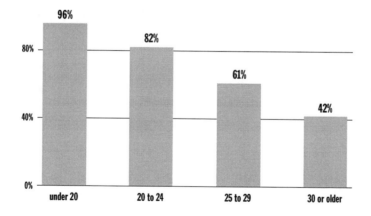

Table 2.7 Births to Total and Black Women by Age, 2005

(total number of births, number and percent distribution of births to blacks, and black share of total, by age, 2005)

		black		
	total	number	percent distribution	share of total
Total births	**4,140,419**	**632,625**	**100.0%**	**15.3%**
Under age 15	6,717	2,835	0.4	42.2
Aged 15 to 19	414,406	103,733	16.4	25.0
Aged 20 to 24	1,040,399	203,579	32.2	19.6
Aged 25 to 29	1,132,293	155,989	24.7	13.8
Aged 30 to 34	952,013	100,953	16.0	10.6
Aged 35 to 39	483,401	51,600	8.2	10.7
Aged 40 to 44	104,644	13,191	2.1	12.6
Aged 45 to 54	6,546	745	0.1	11.4

Source: National Center for Health Statistics, Births: Preliminary Data for 2005, Health E-Stats, Internet site http://www.cdc .gov/nchs/products/pubs/pubd/hestats/prelimbirths05/prelimbirths05.htm; calculations by New Strategist

Table 2.8 Births to Black Women by Age and Marital Status, 2004

(total number of births to blacks, number of births to unmarried blacks, and unmarried share of total, by age, 2004)

		unmarried	
	total	number	share of total
Births to blacks	**616,074**	**423,950**	**68.8%**
Under age 15	2,827	2,811	99.4
Aged 15 to 19	102,793	98,828	96.1
Aged 20 to 24	200,398	164,645	82.2
Aged 25 to 29	147,858	89,601	60.6
Aged 30 to 34	99,083	43,259	43.7
Aged 35 to 39	50,043	19,647	39.3
Aged 40 or older	13,072	5,159	39.5

Source: National Center for Health Statistics, Births: Final Data for 2004, National Vital Statistics Reports, Vol. 55, No. 1, 2006, Internet site http://www.cdc.gov/nchs/products/pubs/pubd/nvsr/nvsr.htm; calculations by New Strategist

Table 2.9 Births to Total and Black Women by Birth Order, 2005

(total number of births, number and percent distribution of births to blacks, and black share of total, by birth order, 2005)

	total	black number	black percent distribution	black share of total
Total births	**4,140,419**	**632,625**	**100.0%**	**15.3%**
First child	1,638,962	241,867	38.2	14.8
Second child	1,327,927	181,666	28.7	13.7
Third child	699,891	110,144	17.4	15.7
Fourth or later child	456,497	94,693	15.0	20.7

Note: Numbers will not add to total because "not stated" is not shown.
Source: National Center for Health Statistics, Births: Preliminary Data for 2005, Health E-Stats, Internet site http://www.cdc .gov/nchs/products/pubs/pubd/hestats/prelimbirths05/prelimbirths05.htm; calculations by New Strategist

Table 2.10 Births to Total and Black Women by State, 2005

(total number of births, number and percent distribution of births to blacks, and black share of total, by state, 2005)

	total	black births		
		number	percent distribtution	share of total
Total births	**4,140,419**	**632,625**	**100.0%**	**15.3%**
Alabama	60,447	18,137	2.9	30.0
Alaska	10,463	424	0.1	4.1
Arizona	96,231	3,648	0.6	3.8
Arkansas	39,196	7,470	1.2	19.1
California	549,626	32,410	5.1	5.9
Colorado	68,963	3,123	0.5	4.5
Connecticut	41,717	5,279	0.8	12.7
Delaware	11,648	2,911	0.5	25.0
District of Columbia	7,893	5,268	0.8	66.7
Florida	226,280	56,520	8.9	25.0
Georgia	142,256	45,818	7.2	32.2
Hawaii	17,925	487	0.1	2.7
Idaho	23,062	146	0.0	0.6
Illinois	179,061	30,733	4.9	17.2
Indiana	87,282	9,885	1.6	11.3
Iowa	39,312	1,507	0.2	3.8
Kansas	39,893	3,125	0.5	7.8
Kentucky	56,385	5,085	0.8	9.0
Louisiana	61,005	24,109	3.8	39.5
Maine	14,113	265	0.0	1.9
Maryland	74,986	26,491	4.2	35.3
Massachusetts	76,920	8,805	1.4	11.4
Michigan	127,799	22,480	3.6	17.6
Minnesota	70,969	6,897	1.1	9.7
Mississippi	42,398	18,660	2.9	44.0
Missouri	78,619	11,686	1.8	14.9
Montana	11,602	62	0.0	0.5
Nebraska	26,148	1,719	0.3	6.6
Nevada	37,258	3,206	0.5	8.6
New Hampshire	14,426	233	0.0	1.6
New Jersey	113,700	19,967	3.2	17.6
New Mexico	28,834	538	0.1	1.9
New York	246,354	54,358	8.6	22.1
North Carolina	123,118	28,441	4.5	23.1
North Dakota	8,393	130	0.0	1.5
Ohio	148,916	24,233	3.8	16.3
Oklahoma	51,746	4,817	0.8	9.3
Oregon	45,937	1,010	0.2	2.2
Pennsylvania	145,584	22,886	3.6	15.7
Rhode Island	12,680	1,286	0.2	10.1
South Carolina	57,728	20,376	3.2	35.3
South Dakota	11,457	143	0.0	1.2
Tennessee	81,743	18,484	2.9	22.6
Texas	385,963	44,088	7.0	11.4
Utah	51,554	484	0.1	0.9
Vermont	6,475	78	0.0	1.2
Virginia	104,592	22,916	3.6	21.9
Washington	82,705	4,228	0.7	5.1
West Virginia	20,838	708	0.1	3.4
Wisconsin	70,978	6,796	1.1	9.6
Wyoming	7,239	63	0.0	0.9

Source: National Center for Health Statistics, Births: Preliminary Data for 2005, Health E-Stats, Internet site http://www.cdc .gov/nchs/products/pubs/pubd/hestats/prelimbirths05/prelimbirths05.htm; calculations by New Strategist

Most Blacks Have Private Health Insurance

One in five has no health insurance.

The 80 percent majority of blacks had health insurance coverage in 2006, including 86 percent of black children. Although most blacks have private health insurance, only 27 percent have employment-based coverage through their own employer. Almost as many, 23 percent, were covered by Medicaid (the government's health insurance program for the poor), and 11 percent were on Medicare (the government's health insurance program for people aged 65 or older). Twenty percent of blacks are without health insurance.

The largest share of black children is covered by private insurance (49 percent), while a smaller 41 percent are on Medicaid. The proportion of blacks with employment-based coverage through their own job tops 50 percent only in the 45-to-54 age group. The percentage of blacks with no health insurance reaches a high of 35 percent in the 18-to-24 age group.

■ Many of the nation's uninsured seek care at emergency rooms, driving up health care costs.

Blacks are more likely to be covered by private than by government insurance

(percent distribution of blacks by health insurance coverage, 2006)

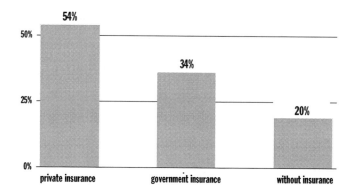

Table 2.11 Health Insurance Coverage of Total People and Blacks by Age, 2006

(number of total people and blacks with and without health insurance coverage and black share of total, 2006; numbers in thousands)

	with health insurance			without health insurance		
	total	black	black share of total	total	black	black share of total
Total people	**249,829**	**31,162**	**12.5%**	**46,995**	**7,921**	**16.9%**
Under age 18	65,440	10,737	16.4	8,661	1,708	19.7
Aged 18 to 24	20,081	2,761	13.7	8,323	1,473	17.7
Aged 25 to 34	29,154	3,666	12.6	10,713	1,751	16.3
Aged 35 to 44	34,744	4,200	12.1	8,018	1,221	15.2
Aged 45 to 54	36,819	4,105	11.1	6,642	1,065	16.0
Aged 55 to 64	28,096	2,645	9.4	4,095	624	15.2
Aged 65 or older	35,494	3,047	8.6	541	80	14.8

Source: Bureau of the Census, 2007 Current Population Survey, Annual Social and Economic Supplement, detailed tables, Internet site http://pubdb3.census.gov/macro/032007/health/toc.htm; calculations by New Strategist

Table 2.12 Health Insurance Coverage of Blacks by Age, 2006

(number and percent distribution of blacks by age and health insurance coverage status, 2006; numbers in thousands)

		with health insurance coverage during year			not covered at any time during the year
	total	total	private	government	
Total blacks	**39,083**	**31,162**	**20,966**	**13,121**	**7,921**
Under age 18	12,445	10,737	6,129	5,522	1,708
Aged 18 to 24	4,234	2,761	1,998	898	1,473
Aged 25 to 34	5,417	3,666	2,863	984	1,751
Aged 35 to 44	5,421	4,200	3,464	909	1,221
Aged 45 to 54	5,170	4,105	3,380	953	1,065
Aged 55 to 64	3,268	2,645	1,905	955	624
Aged 65 or older	3,128	3,047	1,228	2,899	80
PERCENT DISTRIBUTION BY COVERAGE STATUS					
Total blacks	**100.0%**	**79.7%**	**53.6%**	**33.6%**	**20.3%**
Under age 18	100.0	86.3	49.2	44.4	13.7
Aged 18 to 24	100.0	65.2	47.2	21.2	34.8
Aged 25 to 34	100.0	67.7	52.9	18.2	32.3
Aged 35 to 44	100.0	77.5	63.9	16.8	22.5
Aged 45 to 54	100.0	79.4	65.4	18.4	20.6
Aged 55 to 64	100.0	80.9	58.3	29.2	19.1
Aged 65 or older	100.0	97.4	39.3	92.7	2.6

Note: Blacks are those who identify themselves as being of the race alone or as being of the race in combination with one or more other races. Numbers may not add to total because some people have more than one type of health insurance.
Source: Bureau of the Census, 2007 Current Population Survey, Annual Social and Economic Supplement, detailed tables, Internet site http://pubdb3.census.gov/macro/032007/health/toc.htm; calculations by New Strategist

Table 2.13 Blacks with Private Health Insurance Coverage by Age, 2006

(number and percent distribution of blacks by age and private health insurance coverage status, 2006; numbers in thousands)

| | | with private health insurance | | | |
| | | total | employment based | | |
	total	total	total	own	direct purchase
Total blacks	**39,083**	**20,966**	**19,257**	**10,441**	**1,835**
Under age 18	12,445	6,129	5,698	33	428
Aged 18 to 24	4,234	1,998	1,650	675	186
Aged 25 to 34	5,417	2,863	2,711	2,267	202
Aged 35 to 44	5,421	3,464	3,301	2,644	217
Aged 45 to 54	5,170	3,380	3,243	2,597	230
Aged 55 to 64	3,268	1,905	1,770	1,477	189
Aged 65 or older	3,128	1,228	885	747	383
PERCENT DISTRIBUTION BY COVERAGE STATUS					
Total blacks	**100.0%**	**53.6%**	**49.3%**	**26.7%**	**4.7%**
Under age 18	100.0	49.2	45.8	0.3	3.4
Aged 18 to 24	100.0	47.2	39.0	15.9	4.4
Aged 25 to 34	100.0	52.9	50.0	41.8	3.7
Aged 35 to 44	100.0	63.9	60.9	48.8	4.0
Aged 45 to 54	100.0	65.4	62.7	50.2	4.4
Aged 55 to 64	100.0	58.3	54.2	45.2	5.8
Aged 65 or older	100.0	39.3	28.3	23.9	12.2

Note: Blacks are those who identify themselves as being of the race alone or as being of the race in combination with one or more other races. Numbers will not add to total because some people have more than one type of health insurance.
Source: Bureau of the Census, 2007 Current Population Survey, Annual Social and Economic Supplement, detailed tables, Internet site http://pubdb3.census.gov/macro/032007/health/toc.htm; calculations by New Strategist

Table 2.14 Blacks with Government Health Insurance Coverage by Age, 2006

(number and percent distribution of blacks by age and government health insurance coverage status, 2006; numbers in thousands)

| | total | with government health insurance | | | |
		total	Medicaid	Medicare	military
Total blacks	**39,083**	**13,121**	**9,086**	**4,127**	**1,289**
Under age 18	12,445	5,522	5,152	115	359
Aged 18 to 24	4,234	898	760	47	119
Aged 25 to 34	5,417	984	830	97	121
Aged 35 to 44	5,421	909	648	153	179
Aged 45 to 54	5,170	953	604	320	178
Aged 55 to 64	3,268	955	474	523	182
Aged 65 or older	3,128	2,899	618	2,871	150
PERCENT DISTRIBUTION BY COVERAGE STATUS					
Total blacks	**100.0%**	**33.6%**	**23.2%**	**10.6%**	**3.3%**
Under age 18	100.0	44.4	41.4	0.9	2.9
Aged 18 to 24	100.0	21.2	17.9	1.1	2.8
Aged 25 to 34	100.0	18.2	15.3	1.8	2.2
Aged 35 to 44	100.0	16.8	12.0	2.8	3.3
Aged 45 to 54	100.0	18.4	11.7	6.2	3.4
Aged 55 to 64	100.0	29.2	14.5	16.0	5.6
Aged 65 or older	100.0	92.7	19.8	91.8	4.8

Note: Blacks are those who identify themselves as being of the race alone or as being of the race in combination with one or more other races. Number may not add to total because some people have more than one type of health insurance.
Source: Bureau of the Census, 2007 Current Population Survey, Annual Social and Economic Supplement, detailed tables, Internet site http://pubdb3.census.gov/macro/032007/health/toc.htm; calculations by New Strategist

Ten Percent of Blacks Have Diabetes

Blacks account for a disproportionate share of Americans experiencing a number of chronic conditions.

Blacks aged 18 or older suffer from a variety of health conditions at a higher than average rate. Twenty-nine percent of black adults have high blood pressure, 25 percent have chronic lower back pain, and 19 percent have arthritis. Blacks account for 11 percent of the population, but are an even larger share of those with hypertension, stroke, asthma, prostate cancer, diabetes, and kidney disease.

Black children are also more likely than average to experience a variety of health conditions. Seventeen percent have been diagnosed with asthma, and blacks account for more than one in five children with asthma in the United States. Black children account for 18 percent of those with a learning disability, although only 7 percent of black children have been diagnosed with the problem. Fourteen percent of black children have allergies, and 13 percent have taken prescription medicine regularly for at least three months.

Sixteen percent of blacks aged 18 or older have difficulties in physical functioning. A substantial 9 percent find it difficult or impossible to walk a quarter mile, and 10 percent have trouble standing for two hours. Blacks make up the largest share of cumulative AIDS cases, at 42 percent. Non-Hispanic whites account for a smaller 40 percent of the nation's total AIDS cases.

■ The poorer health of the black population is due in part to their lower socioeconomic status and lesser access to health care services.

Among AIDS cases, blacks outnumber non-Hispanic whites

(percent distribution of cumulative AIDS cases by race and Hispanic origin, through 2005)

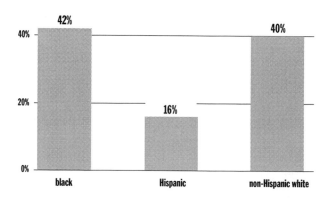

Table 2.15 Health Conditions among Total and Black Adults, 2005

(number of total people and blacks aged 18 or older with selected health conditions, percent of blacks with condition, and black share of total with condition, 2005; numbers in thousands)

	total	blacks number	percent with condition	share of total
Total people	217,774	24,817	100.0%	11.4%
Selected circulatory diseases				
Heart disease, all types	25,583	2,258	9.1	8.8
Coronary	14,088	1,311	5.3	9.3
Hypertension	48,759	7,097	28.6	14.6
Stroke	5,166	706	2.8	13.7
Selected respiratory conditions				
Emphysema	3,791	180	0.7	4.7
Asthma				
Ever had	23,334	2,899	11.7	12.4
Still have	15,697	2,048	8.3	13.0
Hay fever	18,651	1,502	6.1	8.1
Sinusitis	29,517	3,292	13.3	11.2
Chronic bronchitis	8,912	1,063	4.3	11.9
Cancer				
Any cancer	15,995	816	3.3	5.1
Breast cancer (all adults)	2,623	169	0.7	6.4
Cervical cancer (women only)	1,215	67	0.3	5.5
Prostate cancer (men only)	1,830	244	1.0	13.3
Other selected diseases and conditions				
Diabetes	16,186	2,513	10.1	15.5
Ulcers	15,104	1,327	5.3	8.8
Kidney disease	3,791	570	2.3	15.0
Liver disease	2,965	314	1.3	10.6
Arthritis	46,941	4,718	19.0	10.1
Chronic joint symptoms	58,863	5,593	22.5	9.5
Migraines or severe headaches	32,826	3,621	14.6	11.0
Pain in neck	32,294	2,954	11.9	9.1
Pain in lower back	61,965	6,303	25.4	10.2
Pain in face or jaw	9,639	964	3.9	10.0
Selected sensory problems				
Hearing	36,454	2,155	8.7	5.9
Vision	20,255	2,538	10.2	12.5
Absence of all natural teeth	16,310	2,014	8.1	12.3

Note: The conditions shown are those that have ever been diagnosed by a doctor, except as noted. Hay fever, sinusitis, and chronic bronchitis have been diagnosed in the past 12 months. Kidney and liver disease have been diagnosed in the past 12 months and exclude kidney stones, bladder infections, and incontinence. Chronic joint symptoms are shown if respondent had pain, aching, or stiffness in or around a joint (excluding back and neck) and the condition began more than three months ago. Migraines, pain in neck, lower back, face, or jaw are shown only if pain lasted a whole day or more.
Source: National Center for Health Statistics, Summary Health Statistics for U.S. Adults: National Health Interview Survey, 2005, Series 10, No. 232, 2007, Internet site http://www.cdc.gov/nchs/nhis.htm

Table 2.16 Health Conditions among Total and Black Children, 2005

(number of total people and blacks under age 18 with selected health conditions, percent of blacks with condition, and black share of total, 2005; numbers in thousands)

	total	black number	black percent with condition	black share of total
Total children	**73,376**	**11,152**	**100.0%**	**15.2%**
Asthma				
Ever had	9,287	1,949	17.5	21.0
Still have	6,531	1,467	13.2	22.5
Experienced in last 12 months				
Hay fever	7,708	962	8.6	12.5
Respiratory allergies	8,534	1,047	9.4	12.3
Other allergies	9,170	1,519	13.6	16.6
Ever told had*				
Learning disability	4,244	774	6.9	18.2
Attention deficit hyperactivity disorder	3,998	634	5.7	15.9
Prescription medication taken regularly for at least 3 months	9,724	1,405	12.6	14.4

* Ever told by a school representative or health professional. Data exclude children under age 3.
Note: Other allergies include food or digestive allergies, eczema, and other skin allergies.
Source: National Center for Health Statistics, Summary Health Statistics for U.S. Children: National Health Interview Survey, 2005, Series 10, No. 231, 2006, Internet site http://www.cdc.gov/nchs/nhis.htm

Table 2.17 Physician Office Visits by Total People and Blacks by Age, 2004

(number of total physician office visits, number and percent distribution of visits by blacks, black share of total, and average number of visits by blacks per person per year, by age, 2004)

	total (000s)	visits by blacks number (000s)	visits by blacks percent distribution	visits by blacks share of total	visits by blacks per person per year
Total visits	**910,857**	**98,001**	**100.0%**	**10.8%**	**2.7**
Under age 15	147,910	16,626	17.0	11.2	1.8
Aged 15 to 24	70,593	7,799	8.0	11.0	1.3
Aged 25 to 44	194,261	24,767	25.3	12.7	1.3
Aged 45 to 64	264,103	28,903	29.5	10.9	3.8
Aged 65 to 74	113,426	11,763	12.0	10.4	7.0
Aged 75 or older	120,565	8,143	8.3	6.8	6.7

Source: National Center for Health Statistics, National Ambulatory Medical Care Survey: 2004 Summary, Advance Data No. 374, 2006, Internet site http://www.cdc.gov/nchs/about/major/ahcd/adata.htm; calculations by New Strategist

Table 2.18 Difficulties in Physical Functioning among Total and Black Adults, 2005

(number of total people and blacks aged 18 or older, number with difficulties in physical functioning, percent of blacks with difficulty, and black share of total, by type of difficulty, 2005; numbers in thousands)

	total	black number	percent with difficulty	share of total
TOTAL PEOPLE	217,774	24,817	100.0%	11.4%
Total with any physical difficulty	32,405	4,067	16.4	12.6
Walk quarter of a mile	15,418	2,188	8.8	14.2
Climb up 10 steps without resting	11,669	1,808	7.3	15.5
Stand for two hours	19,047	2,500	10.1	13.1
Sit for two hours	7,011	891	3.6	12.7
Stoop, bend, or kneel	19,077	2,354	9.5	12.3
Reach over head	5,418	742	3.0	13.7
Grasp or handle small objects	4,008	566	2.3	14.1
Lift or carry 10 pounds	9,635	1,538	6.2	16.0
Push or pull large objects	14,674	2,053	8.3	14.0

Note: Respondents were classified as having difficulties if they responded "very difficult" or "can't do at all."
Source: National Center for Health Statistics, Summary Health Statistics for U.S. Adults: National Health Interview Survey, 2005, Series 10, No. 232, 2007, Internet site http://www.cdc.gov/nchs/nhis.htm; calculations by New Strategist

Table 2.19 Cumulative AIDS Cases by Race and Hispanic Origin, through 2005

(cumulative number and percent distribution of AIDS cases by race and Hispanic origin, through December 2005)

	number	percent distribution
Total cases	956,666	100.0%
American Indian	3,251	0.3
Asian	7,739	0.8
Black, non-Hispanic	399,637	41.8
Hispanic	156,026	16.3
White, non-Hispanic	386,552	40.4

Source: Centers for Disease Control and Prevention, Cases of HIV Infection and AIDS in the United States and Dependent Areas, 2005, HIV/AIDS Surveillance Report, Vol. 17, 2006, Internet site http://www.cdc.gov/hiv/topics/surveillance/resources/reports/2005report/default.htm

Heart Disease Is the Leading Cause of Death among Blacks

Cancer ranks second as a cause of death.

Heart disease is the leading cause of death among blacks, accounting for 26 percent of all deaths among blacks in 2004. Cancer is the only other disease that accounts for at least 20 percent of deaths among blacks.

Cerebrovascular disease (stroke) accounts for 6 percent of deaths among blacks, while diabetes is in fourth place at 4 percent. Homicide is the sixth leading cause of death among blacks, and HIV infection is ninth.

At birth, blacks can expect to live 73.3 years. This figure is well below the 77.8 years of life expectancy for the average American. At age 65, blacks can expect to live 17.3 more years, or 1.4 years below average.

■ Although black life expectancy has been rising, it is still well below the life expectancy of the average American.

Black life expectancy is nearly five years below average

(years of life remaining at birth for total people and blacks, 2004)

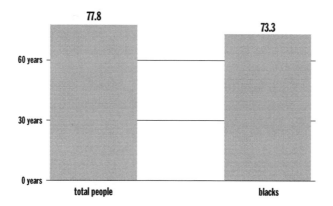

Table 2.20 Leading Causes of Death among Blacks, 2004

(number and percent distribution of deaths to blacks accounted for by the 10 leading causes of death among blacks, 2004)

	number	percent distribution
Total deaths among blacks	**287,315**	**100.0%**
1. Diseases of the heart (1)	74,225	25.8
2. Malignant neoplasms (cancer) (2)	62,499	21.8
3. Cerebrovascular diseases (3)	18,118	6.3
4. Diabetes mellitus (6)	12,834	4.5
5. Accidents (5)	12,670	4.4
6. Homicide (15)	8,135	2.8
7. Nephritis, nephrotic syndrome, nephrosis (9)	7,834	2.7
8. Chronic lower respiratory disease (4)	7,400	2.6
9. Human immunodeficiency virus infection	7,271	2.5
10. Septicemia (10)	6,010	2.1
All other causes	70,319	24.5

Note: Number in parentheses shows rank for all Americans if the cause of death is among top 15.
Source: National Center for Health Statistics, Health United States, 2006, Internet site http://www.cdc.gov/nchs/hus.htm; calculations by New Strategist

Table 2.21 Life Expectancy of Total People and Blacks at Birth and Age 65, 2004

(expected number of years of life remaining for total people and blacks at birth and age 65 and difference between total and black, by sex, 2004)

	total	females	males
Total life expectancy at birth	**77.8**	**80.4**	**75.2**
Black life expectancy at birth	73.3	76.5	69.8
Difference	4.5	3.9	5.4
Total life expectancy at age 65	**18.7**	**20.0**	**17.1**
Black life expectancy at age 65	17.3	18.7	15.3
Difference	1.4	1.3	1.8

Source: National Center for Health Statistics, Health, United States, 2006, Internet site http://www.cdc.gov/nchs/hus.htm; calculations by New Strategist

3

Housing

■ Forty-eight percent of the nation's black households owned their home in 2006, up from 42 percent in 1994. The homeownership rate peaks at 68 percent among black householders aged 65 or older.

■ Among black married couples, 71 percent own their home.

■ Among black householders in the South, the 53 percent majority are homeowners.

■ More than 80 percent of black homeowners have three or more bedrooms in their home. Half have two or more bathrooms.

■ Only 12 percent of black homeowners report crime to be a problem in their neighborhood. Three out of four are satisfied with the local public elementary school.

■ The median value of the homes owned by blacks stood at $113,855 in 2005, well below the $165,344 median value of all owned homes.

■ With a mobility rate of 16 percent, blacks are significantly more likely to move in a given year than is the average American.

Nearly Half of Black Households Are Homeowners

The black homeownership rate is well below average.

Forty-eight percent of the nation's black households owned their home in 2006. This share is well below the 69 percent homeownership rate for all households. Homeownership among blacks is increasing, the rate rising from 42 percent in 1994.

The black homeownership rate rises with age, first surpassing 50 percent in the 45-to-54 age group. It rises as high as 68 percent among black householders aged 65 or older. Blacks account for 9 percent of the nation's homeowners and for a larger 21 percent of the nation's renters.

■ Because so many black households are female-headed families—one of the poorest household types—black homeownership is well below average.

Black homeownership has increased

(percentage of black households owning their home, 1994 and 2006)

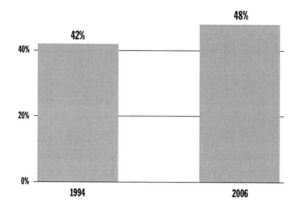

Table 3.1 Total and Black Homeownership Rate, 1994 to 2006

(homeownership rate of total and black households and index of black to total, 1994 to 2006; percentage point change in homeownership rate, 1994–2006)

	homeownership rate		index,
	total	black	black to total
2006	68.8%	47.9%	70
2005	68.9	48.2	70
2004	69.0	49.1	71
2003	68.3	48.1	70
2002	67.9	47.3	70
2001	67.8	47.7	70
2000	67.4	47.2	70
1999	66.8	46.3	69
1998	66.3	45.6	69
1997	65.7	44.8	68
1996	65.4	44.1	67
1995	64.7	42.7	66
1994	64.0	42.3	66
Percentage point change			
2000 to 2006	1.4	0.7	–
1994 to 2006	4.8	5.6	–

Note: Blacks include only those who identify themselves as being of the race alone. The index is calculated by dividing the black homeownership rate by the total rate and multiplying by 100. "–" means not applicable.
Source: Bureau of the Census, Housing Vacancies and Homeownership, Annual Statistics: 2006, Internet site http://www.census .gov/hhes/www/housing/hvs/annual06/ann06t20.html; calculations by New Strategist

Table 3.2 Total and Black Homeownership Rate by Age of Householder, 2005

(percent of total and black households owning a home, by age of householder, 2005)

	homeownership rate		index,
	total	black	black to total
Total households	**68.8%**	**48.1%**	**70**
Under age 25	23.9	11.0	46
Aged 25 to 29	40.2	17.2	43
Aged 30 to 34	56.7	34.2	60
Aged 35 to 44	68.7	47.8	70
Aged 45 to 54	76.7	58.0	76
Aged 55 to 64	81.1	61.2	76
Aged 65 to 74	82.9	68.4	82
Aged 75 or older	77.7	67.5	87

Note: Blacks include only those who identify themselves as being of the race alone. The index is calculated by dividing the black homeownership rate by the total rate and multiplying by 100.
Source: Bureau of the Census, American Housing Survey for the United States: 2005, Internet site http://www.census.gov/hhes/ www/housing/ahs/ahs05/ahs05.html; calculations by New Strategist

Table 3.3 Black Homeownership Status by Age of Householder, 2005

(number and percent distribution of black households by age of householder and homeownership status, 2005; numbers in thousands)

	total	owner	renter
Total black households	**13,447**	**6,471**	**6,975**
Under age 25	961	106	855
Aged 25 to 29	1,232	212	1,019
Aged 30 to 34	1,458	498	960
Aged 35 to 44	2,944	1,407	1,537
Aged 45 to 54	2,842	1,649	1,193
Aged 55 to 64	1,888	1,156	732
Aged 65 to 74	1,255	858	397
Aged 75 or older	867	585	282
PERCENT DISTRIBUTION BY HOMEOWNERSHIP STATUS			
Total black households	**100.0%**	**48.1%**	**51.9%**
Under age 25	100.0	11.0	89.0
Aged 25 to 29	100.0	17.2	82.7
Aged 30 to 34	100.0	34.2	65.8
Aged 35 to 44	100.0	47.8	52.2
Aged 45 to 54	100.0	58.0	42.0
Aged 55 to 64	100.0	61.2	38.8
Aged 65 to 74	100.0	68.4	31.6
Aged 75 or older	100.0	67.5	32.5

Note: Blacks include only those who identify themselves as being of the race alone.
Source: Bureau of the Census, American Housing Survey for the United States: 2005, Internet site http://www.census.gov/hhes/ www/housing/ahs/ahs05/ahs05.html; calculations by New Strategist

Table 3.4 Total and Black Homeowners by Age of Householder, 2005

(number of total homeowners, number and percent distribution of black homeowners, and black share of total, by age, 2005; numbers in thousands)

		black		
	total	number	percent distribution	share of total
Total homeowners	**74,931**	**6,471**	**100.0%**	**8.6%**
Under age 25	1,436	106	1.6	7.4
Aged 25 to 29	3,402	212	3.3	6.2
Aged 30 to 34	5,777	498	7.7	8.6
Aged 35 to 44	15,419	1,407	21.7	9.1
Aged 45 to 54	17,305	1,649	25.5	9.5
Aged 55 to 64	13,773	1,156	17.9	8.4
Aged 65 to 74	9,185	858	13.3	9.3
Aged 75 or older	8,633	585	9.0	6.8

Note: Blacks include only those who identify themselves as being of the race alone.
Source: Bureau of the Census, American Housing Survey for the United States: 2005, Internet site http://www.census.gov/hhes/ www/housing/ahs/ahs05/ahs05.html; calculations by New Strategist

Table 3.5 Total and Black Renters by Age of Householder, 2005

(number of total renters, number and percent distribution of black renters, and black share of total, by age, 2005; numbers in thousands)

	total	black number	black percent distribution	black share of total
Total renters	**33,940**	**6,975**	**100.0%**	**20.6%**
Under age 25	4,577	855	12.3	18.7
Aged 25 to 29	5,056	1,019	14.6	20.2
Aged 30 to 34	4,408	960	13.8	21.8
Aged 35 to 44	7,036	1,537	22.0	21.8
Aged 45 to 54	5,270	1,193	17.1	22.6
Aged 55 to 64	3,215	732	10.5	22.8
Aged 65 to 74	1,897	397	5.7	20.9
Aged 75 or older	2,482	282	4.0	11.4

Note: Blacks include only those who identify themselves as being of the race alone.
Source: Bureau of the Census, American Housing Survey for the United States: 2005, Internet site http://www.census.gov/hhes/www/housing/ahs/ahs05/ahs05.html; calculations by New Strategist

Most Black Married Couples Own Their Home

Renters dominate other types of black households.

Seventy-one percent of black married couples own their home. This share is less than the 84 percent homeownership rate for all married couples, but well above the 47 percent homeownership rate for all black households in 2006. Other black household types are more likely to rent than to own their home.

Because so many black households are female-headed families, they account for a disproportionate share of the nation's female-headed family homeowners. Among the 7 million female-headed families nationwide that own a home, blacks account for a substantial 21 percent. Among the 7 million female-headed families nationally that rent their home, blacks account for an even larger 38 percent.

■ Because few black households are headed by married couples, the black homeownership rate will remain low for years to come.

Black female-headed families are more likely to rent than own

(percentage of black households that own their home, by household type, 2006)

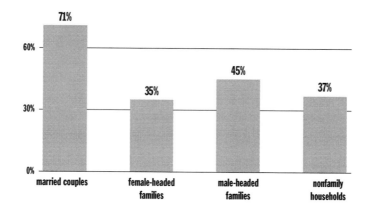

Table 3.6 Total and Black Homeownership Rate by Household Type, 2006

(percent of total and black households owning a home, by type of household, 2005)

| | homeownership rate | | index, |
	total	black	black to total
Total households	**68.5%**	**47.1%**	**69**
Family households	75.7	52.4	69
Married couples	83.6	71.2	85
Female hh, no spouse present	49.2	34.8	71
Male hh, no spouse present	58.5	45.0	77
Nonfamily households	53.4	37.5	70
Female householder	57.5	40.5	70
Male householder	48.3	33.3	69

Note: Blacks include those who identify themselves as being of the race alone or as being of the race in combination with one or more other races. The index is calculated by dividing the black homeownership rate by the total rate and multiplying by 100.
Source: Bureau of the Census, America's Families and Living Arrangements: 2006, Detailed Tables, Internet site http://www .census.gov/population/www/socdemo/hh-fam/cps2006.html; calculations by New Strategist

Table 3.7 Black Homeownership Status by Household Type, 2006

(number and percent distribution of black households by household type and homeownership status, 2006; numbers in thousands)

	total	owners	renters
Total black households	**14,399**	**6,778**	**7,622**
Family households	9,295	4,866	4,429
Married couples	4,249	3,027	1,222
Female hh, no spouse present	4,215	1,465	2,750
Male hh, no spouse present	831	374	458
Nonfamily households	5,104	1,912	3,192
Female householder	2,932	1,188	1,744
Male householder	2,172	724	1,448
PERCENT DISTRIBUTION BY HOMEOWNERSHIP STATUS			
Total black households	**100.0%**	**47.1%**	**52.9%**
Family households	100.0	52.4	47.6
Married couples	100.0	71.2	28.8
Female hh, no spouse present	100.0	34.8	65.2
Male hh, no spouse present	100.0	45.0	55.1
Nonfamily households	100.0	37.5	62.5
Female householder	100.0	40.5	59.5
Male householder	100.0	33.3	66.7

Note: Blacks include those who identify themselves as being of the race alone or as being of the race in combination with one or more other races.
Source: Bureau of the Census, America's Families and Living Arrangements: 2006, Detailed Tables, Internet site http://www .census.gov/population/www/socdemo/hh-fam/cps2006.html; calculations by New Strategist

Table 3.8 Total and Black Homeowners by Type of Household, 2006

(number of total homeowners, number and percent distribution of black homeowners, and black share of total, by type of household, 2006; numbers in thousands)

		black owners		
	total	number	percent distribution	share of total
Total homeowners	**78,330**	**6,778**	**100.0%**	**8.7%**
Family households	58,599	4,866	71.8	8.3
Married couples	48,663	3,027	44.7	6.2
Female hh, no spouse present	6,934	1,465	21.6	21.1
Male hh, no spouse present	3,001	374	5.5	12.5
Nonfamily households	19,731	1,912	28.2	9.7
Female householder	11,642	1,188	17.5	10.2
Male householder	8,089	724	10.7	9.0

Note: Blacks include those who identify themselves as being of the race alone or as being of the race in combination with one or more other races.
Source: Bureau of the Census, America's Families and Living Arrangements: 2006, Detailed Tables, Internet site http://www .census.gov/population/www/socdemo/hh-fam/cps2006.html; calculations by New Strategist

Table 3.9 Total and Black Renters by Type of Household, 2006

(number of total renters, number and percent distribution of black renters, and black share of total, by type of household, 2006; numbers in thousands)

		black renters		
	total	number	percent distribution	share of total
Total renters	**36,055**	**7,622**	**100.0%**	**21.1%**
Family households	18,803	4,429	58.1	23.6
Married couples	9,516	1,222	16.0	12.8
Female hh, no spouse present	7,158	2,750	36.1	38.4
Male hh, no spouse present	2,129	458	6.0	21.5
Nonfamily households	17,252	3,192	41.9	18.5
Female householder	8,588	1,744	22.9	20.3
Male householder	8,664	1,448	19.0	16.7

Note: Blacks include those who identify themselves as being of the race alone or as being of the race in combination with one or more other races.
Source: Bureau of the Census, America's Families and Living Arrangements: 2006, Detailed Tables, Internet site http://www .census.gov/population/www/socdemo/hh-fam/cps2006.html; calculations by New Strategist

Most Black Homeowners Live in the South

The black homeownership rate is highest in the South.

Among the 7 million black households in the South, the 53 percent majority owns their home. The South is the only region in which the majority of black households are homeowners. Sixty percent of all black homeowners live in the region. The black homeownership rate is lowest in the Northeast, at just 38 percent.

Blacks account for only 9 percent of the nation's homeowners, but in the South the proportion is a larger 14 percent. Blacks account for nearly 30 percent of renters in the South. The black share of renters is also substantial in the Northeast (22 percent) and Midwest (19 percent). Because few blacks live in the West, they account for a small share of homeowners or renters in the region.

■ Steep housing prices in the Northeast and West limit the homeownership of blacks.

Black homeownership is low in the Northeast and West

(percent of black households owning their home by region, 2005)

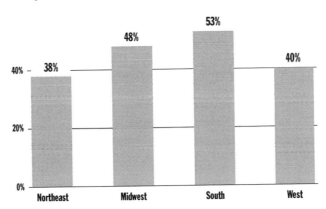

Table 3.10 Total and Black Homeownership Rate by Region, 2005

(percent of total and black households owning a home, by region, 2005)

	homeownership rate		index, black to total
	total	black	
Total black households	**68.8%**	**48.1%**	**70**
Northeast	65.0	37.9	58
Midwest	73.6	48.1	65
South	70.5	52.9	75
West	64.3	39.9	62

Note: Blacks include only those who identify themselves as being of the race alone. The index is calculated by dividing the black homeownership rate by the total rate and multiplying by 100.
Source: Bureau of the Census, American Housing Survey for the United States: 2005, Internet site http://www.census.gov/hhes/ www/housing/ahs/ahs05/ahs05.html; calculations by New Strategist

Table 3.11 Black Homeownership Status by Region, 2005

(number and percent distribution of black households by homeownership status and region, 2005; numbers in thousands)

	total	owners	renters
Total black households	**13,447**	**6,471**	**6,975**
Northeast	2,473	938	1,535
Midwest	2,447	1,178	1,269
South	7,342	3,883	3,460
West	1,184	473	711
PERCENT DISTRIBUTION BY HOMEOWNERSHIP STATUS			
Total black households	**100.0%**	**48.1%**	**51.9%**
Northeast	100.0	37.9	62.1
Midwest	100.0	48.1	51.9
South	100.0	52.9	47.1
West	100.0	39.9	60.1

Note: Blacks include only those who identify themselves as being of the race alone.
Source: Bureau of the Census, American Housing Survey for the United States: 2005, Internet site http://www.census.gov/hhes/ www/housing/ahs/ahs05/ahs05.html; calculations by New Strategist

Table 3.12 Total and Black Homeowners by Region, 2005

(number of total homeowners, number and percent distribution of black homeowners, and black share of total, by region, 2005; numbers in thousands)

	total	black owners		
		number	percent distribution	share of total
Total homeowners	**74,931**	**6,471**	**100.0%**	**8.6%**
Northeast	13,217	938	14.5	7.1
Midwest	18,360	1,178	18.2	6.4
South	28,003	3,883	60.0	13.9
West	15,350	473	7.3	3.1

Note: Blacks include only those who identify themselves as being of the race alone.
Source: Bureau of the Census, American Housing Survey for the United States: 2005, Internet site http://www.census.gov/hhes/www/housing/ahs/ahs05/ahs05.html; calculations by New Strategist

Table 3.13 Total and Black Renters by Region, 2005

(number of total renters, number and percent distribution of black renters, and black share of total, by region, 2005; numbers in thousands)

	total	black renters		
		number	percent distribution	share of total
Total renters	**33,940**	**6,975**	**100.0%**	**20.6%**
Northeast	7,120	1,535	22.0	21.6
Midwest	6,595	1,269	18.2	19.2
South	11,719	3,460	49.6	29.5
West	8,507	711	10.2	8.4

Note: Blacks include only those who identify themselves as being of the race alone.
Source: Bureau of the Census, American Housing Survey for the United States: 2005, Internet site http://www.census.gov/hhes/www/housing/ahs/ahs05/ahs05.html; calculations by New Strategist

Black Homeowners Are Achieving the American Dream

Most black homeowners have three or more bedrooms in their home.

Black homeowners are much better off than black renters, and the differences can be seen in the housing statistics. More than three out of four black homeowners live in a single-family detached unit. Among renters, only 21 percent live in a single-family home, while 70 percent live in an apartment.

More than 80 percent of black homeowners have three or more bedrooms in their home. Among black renters, a smaller 30 percent have that many bedrooms. Half of black homeowners have two or more bathrooms compared with only 16 percent of renters. Not surprisingly, black homeowners are more likely than renters to have porches, garages, and fireplaces. Thirty-one percent of black renters do not have a vehicle available for their use.

■ More than one in five black homeowners has a room in their home used for business.

Most black homeowners live in a single-family detached house

(percentage of black households living in a single-family detached house, by homeownership status, 2005)

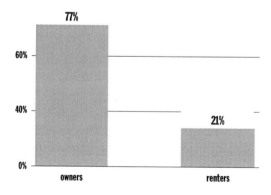

Table 3.14 Characteristics of Housing Units Occupied by Blacks, 2005

(number and percent distribution of housing units occupied by blacks by selected housing characteristics and homeownership status, 2005; numbers in thousands)

	total black households	owners number	owners percent distribution	renters number	renters percent distribution
UNITS IN STRUCTURE					
Total black households	**13,447**	**6,471**	**100.0%**	**6,975**	**100.0%**
1, detached	6,453	4,999	77.3	1,454	20.8
1, attached	1,153	661	10.2	492	7.1
2 to 4	1,688	177	2.7	1,511	21.7
5 to 9	1,127	20	0.3	1,106	15.9
10 to 19	1,022	66	1.0	955	13.7
20 to 49	644	23	0.4	621	8.9
50 or more	751	63	1.0	689	9.9
Mobile home or trailer	609	462	7.1	148	2.1
Median square footage of unit*	1,618	1,712	–	1,314	–
NUMBER OF BEDROOMS					
Total black households	**13,447**	**6,471**	**100.0**	**6,975**	**100.0**
None	144	0	0.0	144	2.1
One	2,000	130	2.0	1,871	26.8
Two	3,923	1,049	16.2	2,874	41.2
Three	5,392	3,649	56.4	1,743	25.0
Four or more	1,987	1,644	25.4	343	4.9
NUMBER OF COMPLETE BATHROOMS					
Total black households	**13,447**	**6,471**	**100.0**	**6,975**	**100.0**
None	121	41	0.6	80	1.1
One	6,755	1,841	28.5	4,914	70.5
One-and-one-half	2,224	1,367	21.1	857	12.3
Two or more	4,347	3,223	49.8	1,124	16.1
ROOM USED FOR BUSINESS					
Total black households	**13,447**	**6,471**	**100.0**	**6,975**	**100.0**
With room(s) used for business	2,302	1,393	21.5	910	13.0
SELECTED AMENITIES					
Porch, deck, balcony, or patio	10,284	5,633	87.0	4651	66.7
Telephone available	12,936	6,265	96.8	6,671	95.6
Usable fireplace	2,682	2,123	32.8	559	8.0
Separate dining room	6,030	3,833	59.2	2,197	31.5
With two or more living or recreation rooms	2,455	2,128	32.9	327	4.7
Garage or carport	5,149	3,785	58.5	1,364	19.6
No cars, trucks, or vans available	2,712	526	8.1	2,186	31.3

* Single-family detached and mobile/manufactured homes only.
Note: Blacks include only those who identify themselves as being of the race alone. – means not applicable.
Source: Bureau of the Census, American Housing Survey for the United States: 2005, Internet site http://www.census.gov/hhes/ www/housing/ahs/ahs05/ahs05.html; calculations by New Strategist

Most Black Homeowners Live in Neighborhoods with Single-Family Homes

Nearly half of black renters live near commercial or institutional complexes, however.

Black homeowners are likely to live in neighborhoods filled with single-family houses. Fully 86 percent of black homeowners reported single-family homes within 300 feet of their house in 2005. A smaller 65 percent of black renters reported single-family homes nearby. Nearly half of black renters reported commercial or institutional buildings within 300 feet compared with only 24 percent of black homeowners.

Few black householders complain of problems in their neighborhood. Crime and street noise are the most common problems, and 12 percent of black homeowners and 17 percent of black renters report crime to be a problem in their neighborhood. Seventy-six percent of black homeowners are satisfied with the local public elementary school, as are 68 of renters. Most black householders are also satisfied with public transportation, neighborhood shopping, and police protection.

■ For black households, street noise is almost as big a problem in their neighborhood as crime.

Most black households are satisfied with the local public elementary school

(percentage of black households satisfied with the local elementary school, by homeownership status, 2005)

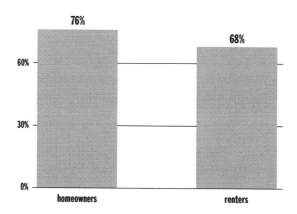

Table 3.15 Neighborhood Characteristics of Black Households, 2005

(number and percent distribution of black households by selected neighborhood characteristics and homeownership status, 2005; numbers in thousands)

	total black households	owners		renters	
		number	percent of total	number	percent of total
DESCRIPTION OF AREA WITHIN 300 FEET OF HOME					
Total black households	**13,447**	**6,471**	**100.0%**	**6,975**	**100.0%**
Single-family detached homes	10,132	5,576	86.2	4,556	65.3
Single-family attached homes	2,632	960	14.8	1,673	24.0
One to three story multiunit	3,898	886	13.7	3,012	43.2
Four to six story multiunit	983	163	2.5	820	11.8
Seven or more story multiunit	504	82	1.3	422	6.1
Manufactured/mobile homes	1,282	900	13.9	382	5.5
Commercial or institutional buildings	5,011	1,568	24.2	3,443	49.4
Industrial establishments or factories	745	228	3.5	517	7.4
Open space, park, woods, farm, or ranch	3,844	1,875	29.0	1,969	28.2
Four-or-more lane highway, railroad, or airport	2,340	773	11.9	1,567	22.5
With waterfront property	111	46	0.7	65	0.9
NEIGHBORHOOD PROBLEMS					
Total black households	**13,447**	**6,471**	**100.0**	**6,975**	**100.0**
Bothersome street noise problem	1,767	719	11.1	1,048	15.0
Bothersome neighborhood crime problem	1,927	748	11.6	1,179	16.9
Bothersome odor problem	676	202	3.1	474	6.8
Noise problem	415	155	2.4	260	3.7
Litter or housing deterioration	405	168	2.6	237	3.4
Poor city or county services	230	102	1.6	128	1.8
Undesirable commercial, institutional, industrial sites	93	33	0.5	60	0.9
People problem	664	283	4.4	381	5.5
Other problems	1,223	610	9.4	613	8.8
PUBLIC SCHOOLS					
Total black households with children under 14	**4,644**	**2,091**	**100.0**	**2,553**	**100.0**
Satisfactory public elementary school	3,311	1,580	75.6	1,731	67.8
PUBLIC SERVICES					
Total black households	**13,447**	**6,471**	**100.0**	**6,975**	**100.0**
With public transportation	9,344	3,888	60.1	5,455	78.2
Satisfactory neighborhood shopping	10,818	4,935	76.3	5,882	84.3
Satisfactory police protection	11,466	5,543	85.7	5,923	84.9

Note: Blacks include only those who identify themselves as being of the race alone.
Source: Bureau of the Census, American Housing Survey for the United States: 2005, Internet site http://www.census.gov/hhes/ www/housing/ahs/ahs05/ahs05.html; calculations by New Strategist

Most Blacks Rate Their House Highly

The homes owned by blacks are below average in value, however.

The median value of the homes owned by blacks stood at $113,855 in 2005, well below the $165,344 median value of all owned homes. Black home values are below average because most black homeowners live in the South, where housing prices are lower. Only 5 percent of black homeowners have a house valued at $300,000 or more compared with a much larger 25 percent of homeowners nationally.

Despite the lower value of the homes owned by blacks, most black homeowners rate their house and neighborhood highly. On a scale of 1 (worst) to 10 (best), nearly three out of four black homeowners give their house an 8 or higher. Two out of three give their neighborhood a rating of 8 or higher. Black renters are not as enthusiastic, with only 53 percent rating their house an 8 or higher and slightly less than 50 percent giving their neighborhood a high rating.

■ The relatively low value of the homes owned by blacks limits the net worth of black households.

The median value of black homes is below average

(median home value for all homeowners and black homeowners, 2005)

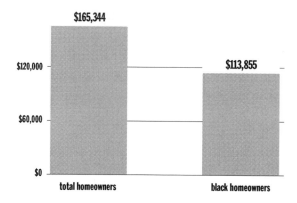

Table 3.16 Housing Value for Total and Black Homeowners, 2005

(number and percent distribution of total and black homeowners by value of home, black share of total, and median value of home, 2005; number of homeowners in thousands)

	total		black		
	number	percent distribution	number	percent distribution	share of total
Total homeowners	**74,931**	**100.0%**	**6,471**	**100.0%**	**8.6%**
Under $10,000	1,762	2.4	152	2.3	8.6
$10,000 to $19,999	1,231	1.6	133	2.1	10.8
$20,000 to $29,999	1,266	1.7	174	2.7	13.7
$30,000 to $39,999	1,429	1.9	167	2.6	11.7
$40,000 to $49,999	1,721	2.3	195	3.0	11.3
$50,000 to $59,999	1,954	2.6	400	6.2	20.5
$60,000 to $69,999	2,883	3.8	358	5.5	12.4
$70,000 to $79,999	3,357	4.5	492	7.6	14.7
$80,000 to $99,999	6,370	8.5	828	12.8	13.0
$100,000 to $119,999	5,123	6.8	486	7.5	9.5
$120,000 to $149,999	7,377	9.8	727	11.2	9.9
$150,000 to $199,999	9,751	13.0	756	11.7	7.8
$200,000 to $249,999	6,658	8.9	454	7.0	6.8
$250,000 to $299,999	4,949	6.6	260	4.0	5.3
$300,000 or more	19,100	25.5	889	13.7	4.7
Median home value	$165,344	–	$113,855	–	–

Note: Blacks include only those who identify themselves as being of the race alone. "–" means not applicable.
Source: Bureau of the Census, American Housing Survey for the United States: 2005, Internet site http://www.census.gov/hhes/www/housing/ahs/ahs05/ahs05.html; calculations by New Strategist

Table 3.17 Opinion of Housing Unit and Neighborhood among Blacks, 2005

(number and percent distribution of black households by opinion of housing unit and neighborhood, by homeownership status, 2005; numbers in thousands)

	total black households	owners number	owners percent distribution	renters number	renters percent distribution
OPINION OF HOUSING UNIT					
Total black households	**13,447**	**6,471**	**100.0%**	**6,975**	**100.0%**
1 (worst)	135	22	0.3	114	1.6
2	66	5	0.1	60	0.9
3	147	31	0.5	116	1.7
4	183	32	0.5	151	2.2
5	1,012	266	4.1	746	10.7
6	853	264	4.1	589	8.4
7	1,906	739	11.4	1,166	16.7
8	3,418	1,688	26.1	1,729	24.8
9	1,660	953	14.7	707	10.1
10 (best)	3,425	2,140	33.1	1,285	18.4
Not reported	644	331	5.1	313	4.5
OPINION OF NEIGHBORHOOD					
Total black households	**13,447**	**6,471**	**100.0**	**6,975**	**100.0**
1 (worst)	250	52	0.8	198	2.8
2	165	60	0.9	105	1.5
3	254	55	0.8	199	2.9
4	303	106	1.6	197	2.8
5	1,263	391	6.0	871	12.5
6	882	362	5.6	520	7.5
7	1,929	855	13.2	1,074	15.4
8	3,187	1,673	25.9	1,514	21.7
9	1,622	920	14.2	702	10.1
10 (best)	2,889	1,643	25.4	1,246	17.9
Not reported	703	354	5.5	348	5.0

Note: Blacks include only those who identify themselves as being of the race alone.
Source: Bureau of the Census, American Housing Survey for the United States: 2005, Internet site http://www.census.gov/hhes/ www/housing/ahs/ahs05/ahs05.html; calculations by New Strategist

Black Mobility Is above Average

Most black movers stay within the same county.

Six million blacks moved between March 2004 and March 2005, according to the Census Bureau. With a mobility rate of 16 percent, blacks are significantly more likely to move in a given year than is the average American. Among black movers, 63 percent moved within the same county, and only 20 percent moved to a different state.

As is true for all movers in the United States, most moves by blacks are spurred by housing-related needs. Among black movers, the need to establish an independent household and the need for a larger house or apartment were the top reasons for moving. Only 5 percent cited a new job or job transfer. When choosing their new home, the largest share of black movers said financial reasons were behind their choice, followed by room layout and the size of the home.

■ Black mobility is above average because most blacks are renters, and renters are more likely to move than homeowners.

More than 16 percent of blacks moved between 2004 and 2005

(percent of total people and blacks aged 1 or older moving between March 2004 and March 2005)

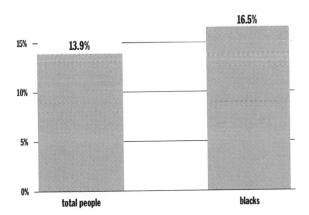

Table 3.18 Total and Black Movers by Age, 2004—05

(number of total people and blacks aged 1 or older moving and black share of total, percent of total people and blacks aged 1 or older moving, and index of black mobility rate to total, by age, March 2004 to March 2005; numbers in thousands)

	movers		black share
	total	black	of total
NUMBER MOVING			
Total movers	**39,889**	**6,193**	**15.5%**
Aged 1 to 4	3,481	720	20.7
Aged 5 to 9	3,140	674	21.5
Aged 10 to 14	2,623	601	22.9
Aged 15 to 17	1,377	281	20.4
Aged 18 to 19	1,311	207	15.8
Aged 20 to 24	6,176	789	12.8
Aged 25 to 29	5,503	747	13.6
Aged 30 to 34	3,947	590	14.9
Aged 35 to 39	2,979	410	13.8
Aged 40 to 44	2,575	374	14.5
Aged 45 to 49	2,087	293	14.0
Aged 50 to 54	1,417	192	13.5
Aged 55 to 59	1,065	130	12.2
Aged 60 to 61	309	38	12.3
Aged 62 to 64	409	36	8.8
Aged 65 or older	1,485	111	7.5

	movers		index,
	total	black	black to total
PERCENT MOVING			
Total movers	**13.9%**	**16.5%**	**119**
Aged 1 to 4	21.4	26.5	123
Aged 5 to 9	16.1	20.7	129
Aged 10 to 14	12.5	16.8	134
Aged 15 to 17	10.5	13.1	125
Aged 18 to 19	17.2	17.6	102
Aged 20 to 24	30.3	26.4	87
Aged 25 to 29	28.2	27.6	98
Aged 30 to 34	19.9	22.7	114
Aged 35 to 39	14.4	15.5	108
Aged 40 to 44	11.3	13.2	116
Aged 45 to 49	9.4	10.9	116
Aged 50 to 54	7.2	8.6	119
Aged 55 to 59	6.4	7.6	119
Aged 60 to 61	5.7	6.8	119
Aged 62 to 64	5.6	5.2	93
Aged 65 or older	4.2	3.7	88

Note: Blacks include those who identify themselves as being of the race alone or as being of the race in combination with one or more other races. The index is calculated by dividing the black mobility rate by the total rate and multiplying by 100.
Source: Bureau of the Census, Geographic Mobility: 2004 to 2005, Detailed Tables, Internet site http://www.census.gov/ population/www/socdemo/migrate/cps2005.html; calculations by New Strategist

Table 3.19 Geographical Mobility of Blacks by Age, 2004–05

(total number of blacks aged 1 or older, number who moved between March 2004 and March 2005, and percent distribution of movers, by age and type of move; numbers in thousands)

	total	movers total	same county	different county, same state	different state	abroad
Total blacks	**37,540**	**6,193**	**3,923**	**898**	**1,217**	**155**
Aged 1 to 4	2,721	720	507	82	119	12
Aged 5 to 9	3,257	674	419	80	162	13
Aged 10 to 14	3,575	601	351	94	139	17
Aged 15 to 17	2,140	281	197	16	60	8
Aged 18 to 19	1,177	207	142	21	34	10
Aged 20 to 24	2,983	789	479	153	138	19
Aged 25 to 29	2,702	747	492	104	125	26
Aged 30 to 34	2,599	590	381	124	71	14
Aged 35 to 39	2,640	410	236	63	101	10
Aged 40 to 44	2,832	374	215	66	81	12
Aged 45 to 49	2,695	293	184	38	65	6
Aged 50 to 54	2,244	192	114	32	43	3
Aged 55 to 59	1,716	130	87	10	32	1
Aged 60 to 61	561	38	19	5	14	0
Aged 62 to 64	693	36	21	1	13	1
Aged 65 or older	3,006	111	82	7	20	2

PERCENT DISTRIBUTION BY MOBILITY STATUS

		total	same county	different county, same state	different state	abroad
Total blacks	–	**100.0%**	**63.3%**	**14.5%**	**19.7%**	**2.5%**
Aged 1 to 4	–	100.0	70.4	11.4	16.5	1.7
Aged 5 to 9	–	100.0	62.2	11.9	24.0	1.9
Aged 10 to 14	–	100.0	58.4	15.6	23.1	2.8
Aged 15 to 17	–	100.0	70.1	5.7	21.4	2.8
Aged 18 to 19	–	100.0	68.6	10.1	16.4	4.8
Aged 20 to 24	–	100.0	60.7	19.4	17.5	2.4
Aged 25 to 29	–	100.0	65.9	13.9	16.7	3.5
Aged 30 to 34	–	100.0	64.6	21.0	12.0	2.4
Aged 35 to 39	–	100.0	57.6	15.4	24.6	2.4
Aged 40 to 44	–	100.0	57.5	17.6	21.7	3.2
Aged 45 to 49	–	100.0	62.8	13.0	22.2	2.0
Aged 50 to 54	–	100.0	59.4	16.7	22.4	1.6
Aged 55 to 59	–	100.0	66.9	7.7	24.6	0.8
Aged 60 to 61	–	100.0	50.0	13.2	36.8	0.0
Aged 62 to 64	–	100.0	58.3	2.8	36.1	2.8
Aged 65 or older	–	100.0	73.9	6.3	18.0	1.8

Note: Blacks include those who identify themselves as being of the race alone or as being of the race in combination with one or more other races. "–" means not applicable.
Source: Bureau of the Census, Geographic Mobility: 2004 to 2005, Detailed Tables, Internet site http://www.census.gov/ population/www/socdemo/migrate/cps2005.html; calculations by New Strategist

Table 3.20 Reasons for Moving among Black Movers, 2005

(number and percent distribution of black households with respondents who moved in the past 12 months by main reason for move and for choosing new neighborhood and house, 2005; numbers in thousands)

	total black movers	
	number	percent distribution
MAIN REASON FOR LEAVING PREVIOUS HOUSING UNIT		
Total black movers	**2,880**	**100.0%**
All reported reasons equal	33	1.1
Private displacement	21	0.7
Government displacement	13	0.5
Disaster loss (fire, flood, etc.)	24	0.8
New job or job transfer	155	5.4
To be closer to work/school/other	203	7.0
Other financial/employment reason	122	4.2
To establish own household	426	14.8
Needed larger house or apartment	319	11.1
Married, widowed, divorced, separated	140	4.9
Other family/personal reason	221	7.7
Wanted better home	263	9.1
Change from owner to renter/renter to owner	104	3.6
Wanted lower rent or maintenance	139	4.8
Other housing related reasons	154	5.3
Evicted from residence	15	0.5
Other	401	13.9
Not reported	127	4.4
MAIN REASON FOR CHOOSING PRESENT NEIGHBORHOOD		
Total black movers	**2,880**	**100.0**
All reported reasons equal	37	1.3
Convenient to job	512	17.8
Convenient to friends or relatives	469	16.3
Convenient to leisure activities	11	0.4
Convenient to public transportation	61	2.1
Good schools	165	5.7
Other public services	45	1.6
Looks/design of neighborhood	378	13.1
House was most important consideration	366	12.7
Other	759	26.4
Not reported	76	2.6

(continued)

	total black movers	
	number	percent distribution
MAIN REASON FOR CHOOSING PRESENT HOME		
Total black movers	**2,880**	**100.0%**
All reported reasons equal	52	1.8
Financial reasons	873	30.3
Room layout/design	479	16.6
Kitchen	20	0.7
Size	441	15.3
Exterior appearance	104	3.6
Yard/trees/view	67	2.3
Quality of construction	51	1.8
Only one available	206	7.2
Other	511	17.7
Not reported	76	2.6

Note: Blacks include only those who identify themselves as being of the race alone.
Source: Bureau of the Census, American Housing Survey for the United States: 2005, Internet site http://www.census.gov/hhes/ www/housing/ahs/ahs05/ahs05.html; calculations by New Strategist

4

Income

■ Between 1990 and 2005, the median income of black households grew 14 percent, after adjusting for inflation—more than the 7 percent gain for all households during those years.

■ Among black households, married couples had a median income of $56,539 in 2005. Black householders with a college degree had a median income of $61,471.

■ The median income of black men stood at $22,609 in 2005, up 21 percent since 1990, after adjusting for inflation.

■ Among black men with a professional degree who work full-time, 55 percent earn $100,000 or more.

■ The black share of the poverty population fell from 29 to 26 percent between 1990 and 2005. One-third of black children are poor.

Black Incomes Have Been Growing

Since 1990, black household income grew more than twice as fast as the average.

Among racial and ethnic groups, black household incomes are the lowest. Their $30,954 median household income in 2005 was well below the all-household median of $46,326—and lower than that of any other racial or ethnic group. But black households are making gains. Between 1990 and 2005, the median income of black households grew 14 percent, after adjusting for inflation—more than the 7 percent gain for all households during those years.

Since 2000, black households have fallen behind. The median income of black households fell 8 percent between 2000 and 2005, after adjusting for inflation. This loss was greater than the 3 percent decline in the median income of all households during those years. Despite the loss, black households are still better off than they once were. Their median income has grown from just 62 percent of the all-household median in 1990 to 67 percent in 2005.

■ Black households have lower incomes than Asian, Hispanic, and non-Hispanic white households because they are less likely to be headed by married couples—the most affluent household type.

The median income of black households is below average

(median income of total and black households, 2005)

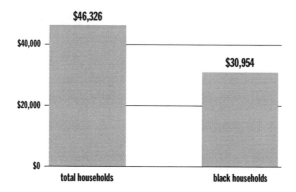

Table 4.1 Median Income of Total and Black Households, 1990 to 2005

(median income of total and black households, and index of black to total, 1990 to 2005; percent change in income for selected years; in 2005 dollars)

	median income		index, black to total
	total households	black households	
2005	$46,326	$30,954	67
2004	45,817	31,246	68
2003	45,970	31,506	69
2002	46,036	31,672	69
2001	46,569	32,499	70
2000	47,599	33,630	71
1999	47,671	32,694	69
1998	46,508	30,321	65
1997	44,883	30,383	68
1996	43,967	29,089	66
1995	43,346	28,485	66
1994	42,038	27,397	65
1993	41,562	25,986	63
1992	41,774	25,573	61
1991	42,108	26,287	62
1990	43,366	27,048	62
Percent change			
2000 to 2005	–2.7%	–8.0%	–
1990 to 2005	6.8	14.4	–

Note: Beginning in 2002, data for blacks are for those who identify themselves as being of the race alone or as being of the race in combination with other races. "–" means not applicable.
Source: Bureau of the Census, Historical Income Tables—Households, Internet site http://www.census.gov/hhes/www/income/histinc/h05.html; calculations by New Strategist

Most Black Married Couples Have Incomes above $50,000

The median income of black female-headed families was less than half the income of black married couples.

Among black households, married couples have the highest median income by far, at $56,539 in 2005. In contrast, black female-headed families had a median income of just $22,690. Because female-headed families are almost as numerous as married couples among black households, the median income of black households was just $30,954 in 2005—lower than that of any other racial or ethnic group.

Black household income rises with age to a peak of $41,331 among householders aged 45 to 54. Median household income drops rapidly after retirement age. Black householders aged 65 or older had a median income of just $17,141.

Education greatly increases household income. Black householders with a college degree had a median income of $61,471. By region, blacks have the highest household income in the West ($35,607) and the lowest in the Midwest ($27,495).

■ More than 1 million black households had an income of $100,000 or more in 2005, or 6 percent of all households with incomes that high.

Black household incomes peak in middle age

(median income of black households, by age of householder, 2005)

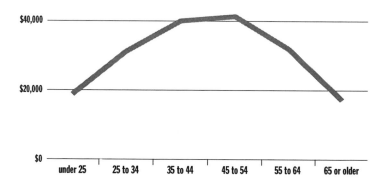

Table 4.2 Income of Black Households by Household Type, 2005

(number and percent distribution of black households by household income and household type, 2005; households in thousands as of 2006)

| | | family households | | | nonfamily households | | | |
| | | | female hh, no spouse present | male hh, no spouse present | female householder | | male householder | |
	total	married couples			total	living alone	total	living alone
Total black households	14,399	4,249	4,215	831	2,932	2,597	2,172	1,807
Under $5,000	975	81	430	45	263	245	154	147
$5,000 to $9,999	1,482	74	502	44	582	562	278	263
$10,000 to $14,999	1,276	150	443	57	401	371	226	214
$15,000 to $19,999	1,229	196	488	66	284	255	197	171
$20,000 to $24,999	1,090	190	393	58	235	217	213	195
$25,000 to $29,999	931	229	303	77	188	166	135	107
$30,000 to $34,999	872	235	280	49	154	136	153	136
$35,000 to $39,999	789	215	223	56	148	127	146	115
$40,000 to $44,999	732	247	192	45	118	105	129	106
$45,000 to $49,999	638	219	158	47	116	92	100	67
$50,000 to $54,999	608	232	152	32	102	85	91	71
$55,000 to $59,999	450	187	122	28	66	54	46	35
$60,000 to $64,999	474	213	100	43	49	28	70	54
$65,000 to $69,999	346	159	72	36	41	27	39	27
$70,000 to $74,999	311	159	51	14	38	28	50	26
$75,000 to $79,999	249	137	45	25	23	17	19	11
$80,000 to $84,999	259	168	35	13	22	20	21	11
$85,000 to $89,999	221	137	40	11	20	17	11	5
$90,000 to $94,999	164	99	32	10	7	7	16	11
$95,000 to $99,999	169	121	16	6	7	5	20	6
$100,000 or more	1,136	804	137	68	70	32	58	31
Median income	$30,954	$56,539	$22,690	$36,710	$18,684	$17,058	$25,476	$22,103

PERCENT DISTRIBUTION								
Total black households	100.0%	100.0%	100.0%	100.0%	100.0%	100.0%	100.0%	100.0%
Under $25,000	42.0	16.3	53.5	32.5	60.2	63.5	49.2	54.8
$25,000 to $49,999	27.5	26.9	27.4	33.0	24.7	24.1	30.5	29.4
$50,000 to $74,999	15.2	22.4	11.8	18.4	10.1	8.5	13.6	11.8
$75,000 to $99,999	7.4	15.6	4.0	7.8	2.7	2.5	4.0	2.4
$100,000 or more	7.9	18.9	3.3	8.2	2.4	1.2	2.7	1.7

Note: Blacks are those who identify themselves as being of the race alone or as being of the race in combination with other races.
Source: Bureau of the Census, 2006 Current Population Survey Annual Social and Economic Supplement, Internet site http://pubdb3.census.gov/macro/032006/hhinc/new01_000.htm; calculations by New Strategist

Table 4.3 Income of Black Households by Age of Householder, 2005

(number and percent distribution of black households by household income and age of householder, 2005; households in thousands as of 2006)

| | total | 15 to 24 | 25 to 34 | 35 to 44 | 45 to 54 | 55 to 64 | 65 or older | | |
							total	65 to 74	75 or older
Total black households	**14,399**	**1,206**	**2,853**	**3,129**	**3,027**	**2,049**	**2,136**	**1,198**	**938**
Under $5,000	975	189	216	186	161	129	94	46	49
$5,000 to $9,999	1,482	156	214	211	243	226	432	202	230
$10,000 to $14,999	1,276	162	232	161	153	160	407	196	210
$15,000 to $19,999	1,229	131	275	197	202	145	279	170	108
$20,000 to $24,999	1,090	98	240	236	194	156	167	96	71
$25,000 to $29,999	931	80	185	194	154	151	166	107	60
$30,000 to $34,999	872	76	203	200	173	114	107	60	47
$35,000 to $39,999	789	67	191	177	167	115	73	39	34
$40,000 to $44,999	732	48	173	161	178	105	67	40	27
$45,000 to $49,999	638	32	137	181	137	96	55	34	21
$50,000 to $54,999	608	20	124	170	153	94	47	27	20
$55,000 to $59,999	450	23	80	112	125	76	34	22	13
$60,000 to $64,999	474	25	109	155	97	52	35	28	8
$65,000 to $69,999	346	21	52	105	107	45	16	9	7
$70,000 to $74,999	311	12	70	71	97	50	12	8	4
$75,000 to $79,999	249	4	49	64	73	35	23	17	5
$80,000 to $84,999	259	8	39	72	85	32	22	18	4
$85,000 to $89,999	221	9	38	69	61	32	11	9	2
$90,000 to $94,999	164	4	34	52	47	20	7	3	4
$95,000 to $99,999	169	9	25	67	44	17	8	6	2
$100,000 or more	1,136	34	169	288	373	198	73	61	12
Median income	$30,954	$18,768	$31,180	$40,038	$41,331	$31,895	$17,141	$19,453	$14,447

PERCENT DISTRIBUTION

Total black households	100.0%	100.0%	100.0%	100.0%	100.0%	100.0%	100.0%	100.0%	100.0%
Under $25,000	42.0	61.0	41.3	31.7	31.5	39.8	64.6	59.3	71.2
$25,000 to $49,999	27.5	25.1	31.2	29.2	26.7	28.4	21.9	23.4	20.1
$50,000 to $74,999	15.2	8.4	15.2	19.6	19.1	15.5	6.7	7.8	5.5
$75,000 to $99,999	7.4	2.8	6.5	10.4	10.2	6.6	3.3	4.4	1.8
$100,000 or more	7.9	2.8	5.9	9.2	12.3	9.7	3.4	5.1	1.3

Note: Blacks are those who identify themselves as being of the race alone or as being of the race in combination with other races.
Source: Bureau of the Census, 2006 Current Population Survey Annual Social and Economic Supplement, Internet site http://pubdb3.census.gov/macro/032006/hhinc/new01_000.htm; calculations by New Strategist

Table 4.4 Income of Black Households by Educational Attainment of Householder, 2005

(number and percent distribution of black households headed by people aged 25 or older by household income and educational attainment of householder, 2005; households in thousands as of 2006)

	total	less than 9th grade	9th–12th grade, no diploma	high school graduate	some college, no degree	associate's degree	bachelor's degree or more total	bachelor's degree	master's degree	professional degree	doctoral degree
Total black households	13,194	778	1,838	4,356	2,636	1,069	2,516	1,683	649	101	84
Under $5,000	786	64	190	304	138	31	60	40	16	0	4
$5,000 to $9,999	1,326	215	350	492	154	57	58	50	5	4	0
$10,000 to $14,999	1,114	137	254	413	173	50	86	65	15	3	5
$15,000 to $19,999	1,098	87	263	429	177	71	72	50	18	4	0
$20,000 to $24,999	993	50	186	392	206	76	82	57	20	2	3
$25,000 to $29,999	851	56	112	322	174	84	101	84	15	0	3
$30,000 to $34,999	796	35	113	285	171	57	133	102	24	5	3
$35,000 to $39,999	723	24	56	262	194	71	115	90	24	0	2
$40,000 to $44,999	684	27	56	211	175	65	150	102	45	0	2
$45,000 to $49,999	606	6	52	186	173	69	120	85	28	4	3
$50,000 to $54,999	588	13	47	197	134	61	138	98	24	7	9
$55,000 to $59,999	427	13	23	122	101	65	102	59	37	2	4
$60,000 to $64,999	448	9	28	135	104	43	128	87	35	4	2
$65,000 to $69,999	325	4	14	105	70	37	96	63	28	4	2
$70,000 to $74,999	299	9	13	85	67	37	88	53	35	0	0
$75,000 to $79,999	245	7	9	74	52	23	80	51	20	6	4
$80,000 to $84,999	251	4	11	46	61	27	102	64	31	2	5
$85,000 to $89,999	212	4	13	47	44	18	86	68	13	2	2
$90,000 to $94,999	160	0	10	23	47	18	60	44	10	6	0
$95,000 to $99,999	161	5	9	28	45	20	53	37	15	0	1
$100,000 or more	1,102	10	27	197	175	90	602	332	193	48	30
Median income	$32,076	$13,852	$17,252	$26,839	$37,591	$42,436	$61,471	$56,054	$68,257	$91,626	$67,393

PERCENT DISTRIBUTION

Total black households	100.0%	100.0%	100.0%	100.0%	100.0%	100.0%	100.0%	100.0%	100.0%	100.0%	100.0%
Under $25,000	40.3	71.1	67.6	46.6	32.2	26.7	14.2	15.6	11.4	12.9	14.3
$25,000 to $49,999	27.7	19.0	21.2	29.1	33.6	32.4	24.6	27.5	21.0	8.9	15.5
$50,000 to $74,999	15.8	6.2	6.8	14.8	18.1	22.7	21.9	21.4	24.5	16.8	20.2
$75,000 to $99,999	7.8	2.6	2.8	5.0	9.4	9.9	15.1	15.7	13.7	15.8	14.3
$100,000 or more	8.4	1.3	1.5	4.5	6.6	8.4	23.9	19.7	29.7	47.5	35.7

Note: Blacks are those who identify themselves as being of the race alone or as being of the race in combination with other races.
Source: Bureau of the Census, 2006 Current Population Survey Annual Social and Economic Supplement, Internet site http://pubdb3.census.gov/macro/032006/hhinc/new01_000.htm; calculations by New Strategist

Table 4.5 Income of Black Households by Region, 2005

(number and percent distribution of black households by household income and region, 2005; households in thousands as of 2006)

	total	Northeast	Midwest	South	West
Total black households	**14,399**	**2,604**	**2,627**	**7,800**	**1,369**
Under $5,000	975	174	195	536	70
$5,000 to $9,999	1,482	265	314	780	122
$10,000 to $14,999	1,276	211	259	692	112
$15,000 to $19,999	1,229	202	252	684	92
$20,000 to $24,999	1,090	224	172	618	75
$25,000 to $29,999	931	155	187	502	88
$30,000 to $34,999	872	107	121	531	113
$35,000 to $39,999	789	139	155	417	79
$40,000 to $44,999	732	112	156	399	64
$45,000 to $49,999	638	131	96	363	49
$50,000 to $54,999	608	128	100	304	77
$55,000 to $59,999	450	89	76	249	35
$60,000 to $64,999	474	92	79	251	51
$65,000 to $69,999	346	69	58	190	30
$70,000 to $74,999	311	35	53	174	48
$75,000 to $79,999	249	33	46	146	24
$80,000 to $84,999	259	45	46	127	42
$85,000 to $89,999	221	57	41	109	14
$90,000 to $94,999	164	32	34	83	15
$95,000 to $99,999	169	35	27	91	17
$100,000 or more	1,136	268	161	554	153
Median income	$30,954	$32,108	$27,495	$30,646	$35,607

PERCENT DISTRIBUTION

Total black households	**100.0%**	**100.0%**	**100.0%**	**100.0%**	**100.0%**
Under $25,000	42.0	41.3	45.4	42.4	34.4
$25,000 to $49,999	27.5	24.7	27.2	28.4	28.7
$50,000 to $74,999	15.2	15.9	13.9	15.0	17.6
$75,000 to $99,999	7.4	7.8	7.4	7.1	8.2
$100,000 or more	7.9	10.3	6.1	7.1	11.2

Note: Blacks are those who identify themselves as being of the race alone or as being of the race in combination with other races.
Source: Bureau of the Census, 2006 Current Population Survey Annual Social and Economic Supplement, Internet site http:// pubdb3.census.gov/macro/032006/hhinc/new01_000.htm; calculations by New Strategist

Table 4.6 High-Income Total and Black Households, 2005

(number and percent distribution of total and black households with incomes of $100,000 or more, 2005; households in thousands as of 2006)

	total		black		
	number	percent distribution	number	percent distribution	share of total
Total households	**114,384**	**100.0%**	**14,399**	**100.0%**	**12.6%**
$100,000 or more	19,715	17.2	1,136	7.9	5.8
$100,000 to $149,999	12,132	10.6	798	5.5	6.6
$150,000 to $199,999	4,031	3.5	211	1.5	5.2
$200,000 to $249,999	1,529	1.3	50	0.3	3.3
$250,000 or more	2,023	1.8	77	0.5	3.8

Note: Blacks are those who identify themselves as being of the race alone or as being of the race in combination with other races.
Source: Bureau of the Census, 2006 Current Population Survey Annual Social and Economic Supplement, Internet stie http://pubdb3.census.gov/macro/032006/hhinc/new06_000.htm; calculations by New Strategist

Black Men and Women Have Made Gains

The median income of black women has grown 46 percent since 1990, after adjusting for inflation.

The median income of black men stood at $22,609 in 2005, up a hefty 21 percent since 1990, after adjusting for inflation. The median income of black women grew more than twice as fast during those years, up 46 percent. In 2005, the median income of black men was 72 percent as high as the median income of all men, up from 63 percent in 1990. Black women have seen their median income rise from 83 to 95 percent of the median for all women.

Since 2000, blacks have not fared as well as the average man or woman. The median income of black men fell 7 percent between 2000 and 2005, after adjusting for inflation. Black women saw their median fall 2 percent during those years.

■ The sluggish economy following the terrorist attacks of 2001 hurt blacks more than Asians, Hispanics, or non-Hispanic whites.

Black men have lost ground since 2000

(median income of black men for selected years 1990 to 2005; in 2005 dollars)

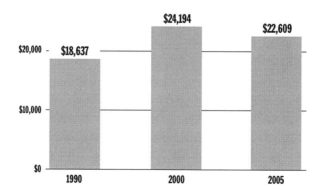

Table 4.7 Median Income of Total and Black Men, 1990 to 2005

(median income of total and black men aged 15 or older with income, and index of black to total, 1990 to 2005; percent change in income for selected years; in 2005 dollars)

	median income		index, black to total
	total men	black men	
2005	$31,275	$22,609	72
2004	31,537	23,473	74
2003	31,763	23,278	73
2002	31,739	23,349	74
2001	32,092	23,673	74
2000	32,129	24,194	75
1999	31,971	23,945	75
1998	31,686	23,109	73
1997	30,579	21,948	72
1996	29,525	20,429	69
1995	28,700	20,360	71
1994	28,300	19,521	69
1993	28,073	19,430	69
1992	27,891	17,813	64
1991	28,610	18,117	63
1990	29,390	18,637	63
Percent change			
2000 to 2005	2.7%	−6.6%	–
1990 to 2005	6.4	21.3	–

Note: Beginning in 2002, data for blacks are for those who identify themselves as being of the race alone or as being of the race in combination with other races. "–" means not applicable.
Source: Bureau of the Census, Current Population Survey Annual Demographic Supplements, Internet site http://www.census.gov/hhes/www/income/histinc/incpertoc.html; calculations by New Strategist

Table 4.8 Median Income of Total and Black Women, 1990 to 2005

(median income of total and black women aged 15 or older with income, and index of black to total, 1990 to 2005; percent change in income for selected years; in 2005 dollars)

	median income		index, black to total
	total women	black women	
2005	$18,576	$17,595	95
2004	18,258	17,927	98
2003	18,316	17,553	96
2002	18,250	18,097	99
2001	18,322	17,956	98
2000	18,209	18,002	99
1999	17,927	17,309	97
1998	17,259	15,712	91
1997	16,620	15,826	95
1996	15,875	14,583	92
1995	15,430	13,943	90
1994	14,939	13,738	92
1993	14,695	12,649	86
1992	14,609	12,118	83
1991	14,643	12,322	84
1990	14,584	12,061	83
Percent change			
2000 to 2005	2.0%	−2.3%	−
1990 to 2005	27.4	45.9	−

Note: Beginning in 2002, data for blacks are for those who identify themselves as being of the race alone or as being of the race in combination with other races. "−" means not applicable.
Source: Bureau of the Census, Current Population Survey Annual Demographic Supplements, Internet site http://www.census .gov/hhes/www/income/histinc/incpertoc.html; calculations by New Strategist

The Income of Black Men Peaks in the 35-to-44 Age Group

The percentage of men who work full-time also peaks in the 35-to-44 age group.

The median income of black men peaks at $31,568 in the 35-to-44 age group. Behind the income peak is labor force participation. Sixty-eight percent of black men aged 35 to 44 work full-time, more than in any other age group. Among those who work full-time, median income is $36,666. Median income rises above $40,000 among black men aged 45 or older who work full-time.

The median income of black women also peaks in the 35-to-44 age group, at $25,849, well below the median of black men. The labor force participation of black women is highest among those aged 35-to-44, with 62 percent working full-time. Among full-time workers, women's median income is above $30,000 for those aged 35 or older.

Black men working full-time have a median income 81 percent as high as the average man with a full-time job, up from only 74 percent in 1990. Black women who work full-time have a median income 91 percent as high as the average woman who works full-time—about the same as in 1990. Among blacks working full-time, women earn 89 percent as much as men.

■ Black incomes are below average in part because their educational attainment is less than that of non-Hispanic whites or Asians.

Black men are catching up to the average

(index of the median income of black men who work full-time to the median income of all men with full-time jobs, for selected years, 1990 to 2005)

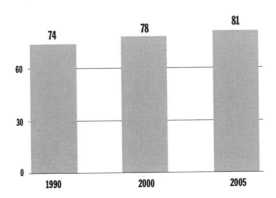

Table 4.9 Income of Black Men by Age, 2005

(number and percent distribution of black men aged 15 or older by income and age, 2005; median income of men with income and of men working full-time, year-round; percent working full-time, year-round; men in thousands as of 2006)

	total	15 to 24	25 to 34	35 to 44	45 to 54	55 to 64	65 or older total	65 to 74	75 or older
Total black men	**12,959**	**3,151**	**2,449**	**2,474**	**2,324**	**1,376**	**1,185**	**742**	**443**
Without income	2,308	1,407	267	200	223	129	81	52	29
With income	10,651	1,744	2,182	2,274	2,101	1,247	1,104	690	414
Under $5,000	1,073	546	163	106	133	72	54	31	23
$5,000 to $9,999	1,363	363	228	161	185	151	277	168	109
$10,000 to $14,999	1,183	224	185	190	151	141	292	153	139
$15,000 to $19,999	1,040	141	290	211	180	104	114	79	35
$20,000 to $24,999	1,041	162	278	182	212	105	101	63	39
$25,000 to $29,999	848	102	207	193	168	117	61	43	18
$30,000 to $34,999	741	85	185	216	129	74	51	36	16
$35,000 to $39,999	636	44	152	185	153	70	32	25	7
$40,000 to $44,999	580	28	121	173	157	84	16	11	5
$45,000 to $49,999	377	4	75	115	102	56	25	19	5
$50,000 to $54,999	421	4	75	146	117	62	16	9	6
$55,000 to $59,999	182	5	39	50	44	30	15	13	2
$60,000 to $64,999	245	18	39	76	65	35	12	10	3
$65,000 to $69,999	53	6	26	51	46	13	2	2	0
$70,000 to $74,999	152	0	39	44	43	20	6	6	0
$75,000 to $79,999	117	7	10	43	33	18	5	4	0
$80,000 to $84,999	80	0	16	3	34	24	2	1	0
$85,000 to $89,999	28	0	2	6	9	5	6	6	0
$90,000 to $94,999	63	0	5	20	26	10	2	0	2
$95,000 to $99,999	35	0	3	10	15	6	2	2	0
$100,000 or more	305	3	43	93	102	49	15	11	5
Median income									
Men with income	$22,609	$9,291	$23,750	$31,568	$30,641	$26,907	$13,605	$14,750	$12,506
Men working full-time	34,144	21,459	30,270	36,666	40,238	40,996	41,095	41,050	–
Percent working full-time	**44.8%**	**16.0%**	**60.1%**	**68.4%**	**61.7%**	**45.3%**	**7.1%**	**10.1%**	**1.8%**
PERCENT DISTRIBUTION									
Total black men	**100.0%**	**100.0%**	**100.0%**	**100.0%**	**100.0%**	**100.0%**	**100.0%**	**100.0%**	**100.0%**
Without income	17.8	44.7	10.9	8.1	9.6	9.4	6.8	7.0	6.5
With income	82.2	55.3	89.1	91.9	90.4	90.6	93.2	93.0	93.5
Under $15,000	27.9	36.0	23.5	18.5	20.2	26.5	52.6	47.4	61.2
$15,000 to $24,999	16.1	9.6	23.2	15.9	16.9	15.2	18.1	19.1	16.7
$25,000 to $34,999	12.3	5.9	16.0	16.5	12.8	13.9	9.5	10.6	7.7
$35,000 to $49,999	12.3	2.4	14.2	19.1	17.7	15.3	6.2	7.4	3.8
$50,000 to $74,999	8.1	1.0	8.9	14.8	13.6	11.6	4.3	5.4	2.5
$75,000 or more	4.8	0.3	3.2	7.1	9.4	8.1	2.7	3.2	1.6

Note: Blacks are those who identify themselves as being of the race alone or as being of the race in combination with other races. "–" means sample is too small to make a reliable estimate.
Source: Bureau of the Census, 2006 Current Population Survey Annual Social and Economic Supplement, Internet site http:// pubdb3.census.gov/macro/032006/perinc/new01_000.htm; calculations by New Strategist

Table 4.10 Income of Black Women by Age, 2005

(number and percent distribution of black women aged 15 or older by income and age, 2005; median income of women with income and of women working full-time, year-round; percent working full-time, year-round; women in thousands as of 2006)

	total	15 to 24	25 to 34	35 to 44	45 to 54	55 to 64	65 or older total	65 to 74	75 or older
Total black women	15,627	3,298	2,917	3,031	2,757	1,756	1,868	981	888
Without income	2,390	1,321	294	246	241	179	109	68	42
With income	13,237	1,977	2,623	2,785	2,516	1,577	1,759	913	846
Under $5,000	1,600	680	261	220	171	129	140	63	77
$5,000 to $9,999	2,417	438	361	293	340	313	670	313	356
$10,000 to $14,999	1,713	323	296	239	259	182	415	196	219
$15,000 to $19,999	1,448	190	368	265	261	167	197	114	83
$20,000 to $24,999	1,251	133	298	312	264	162	81	51	29
$25,000 to $29,999	1,003	69	218	276	229	120	93	60	33
$30,000 to $34,999	860	70	251	239	170	78	53	36	17
$35,000 to $39,999	619	19	150	182	155	91	22	11	10
$40,000 to $44,999	515	17	121	138	151	77	12	7	5
$45,000 to $49,999	373	25	63	134	83	53	17	14	3
$50,000 to $54,999	345	4	54	126	101	49	12	6	6
$55,000 to $59,999	220	3	50	54	71	32	8	5	4
$60,000 to $64,999	183	1	34	59	57	23	10	10	0
$65,000 to $69,999	126	2	17	45	42	21	0	0	0
$70,000 to $74,999	106	0	9	32	47	15	3	2	1
$75,000 to $79,999	72	0	12	30	22	4	4	4	0
$80,000 to $84,999	66	0	13	22	11	15	6	5	0
$85,000 to $89,999	65	0	12	32	11	3	7	4	2
$90,000 to $94,999	50	2	7	24	9	9	0	0	0
$95,000 to $99,999	17	0	1	6	9	2	0	0	0
$100,000 or more	185	2	28	58	55	33	10	10	0
Median income									
Women with income	$17,595	$8,061	$20,391	$25,849	$24,122	$19,888	$10,695	$11,626	$9,859
Women working full-time	30,366	20,529	29,310	32,412	31,926	31,189	30,873	31,636	—
Percent working full-time	**40.4%**	**15.6%**	**50.8%**	**62.1%**	**57.9%**	**41.2%**	**5.7%**	**8.4%**	**2.7%**
PERCENT DISTRIBUTION									
Total black women	100.0%	100.0%	100.0%	100.0%	100.0%	100.0%	100.0%	100.0%	100.0%
Without income	15.3	40.1	10.1	8.1	8.7	10.2	5.8	6.9	4.7
With income	84.7	59.9	89.9	91.9	91.3	89.8	94.2	93.1	95.3
Under $15,000	36.7	43.7	31.5	24.8	27.9	35.5	65.6	58.3	73.4
$15,000 to $24,999	17.3	9.8	22.8	19.0	19.0	18.7	14.9	16.8	12.6
$25,000 to $34,999	11.9	4.2	16.1	17.0	14.5	11.3	7.8	9.8	5.6
$35,000 to $49,999	9.6	1.8	11.5	15.0	14.1	12.6	2.7	3.3	2.0
$50,000 to $74,999	6.3	0.3	5.6	10.4	11.5	8.0	1.8	2.3	1.2
$75,000 or more	2.9	0.1	2.5	5.7	4.2	3.8	1.4	2.3	0.2

Note: Blacks are those who identify themselves as being of the race alone or as being of the race in combination with other races. "–" means sample is too small to make a reliable estimate.
Source: Bureau of the Census, 2006 Current Population Survey Annual Social and Economic Supplement, Internet site http:// pubdb3.census.gov/macro/032006/perinc/new01_000.htm; calculations by New Strategist

Table 4.11 Median Income of Total and Black Men Who Work Full-Time, 1990 to 2005

(median income of total and black men who work full-time, year-round, and index of black to total, 1990 to 2005; percent change in income for selected years; in 2005 dollars)

	median income of full-time workers		index, black
	total men	black men	to total
2005	$42,188	$34,144	81
2004	43,060	32,771	76
2003	44,044	35,513	81
2002	43,972	34,700	79
2001	44,262	35,202	80
2000	44,086	34,561	78
1999	43,869	35,323	81
1998	43,359	32,858	76
1997	42,752	32,623	76
1996	41,546	33,616	81
1995	40,958	31,544	77
1994	41,188	31,798	77
1993	41,344	31,351	76
1992	42,041	31,349	75
1991	42,395	31,628	75
1990	41,970	31,111	74
Percent change			
2000 to 2005	−4.3%	−1.2%	–
1990 to 2005	0.5	9.7	–

Note: Beginning in 2002, data for blacks are for those who identify themselves as being of the race alone or being of the race in combination with other races. The black/total indexes are calculated by dividing the median income of black men by the median income of total men and multiplying by 100. "–" means not applicable.
Source: Bureau of the Census, Current Population Surveys, Historical Income Tables—People, Internet site http://www.census .gov/hhes/www/income/histinc/incpertoc.html; calculations by New Strategist

Table 4.12 Median Income of Total and Black Women Who Work Full-Time, 1990 to 2005

(median income of total and black women who work full-time, year-round, and index of black to total, 1990 to 2005; percent change in income for selected years; in 2005 dollars)

	median income of full-time workers		index, black to total
	total women	black women	
2005	$33,256	$30,366	91
2004	33,190	30,169	91
2003	33,591	29,369	87
2002	33,619	30,072	89
2001	33,547	30,103	90
2000	33,013	29,189	88
1999	32,057	29,450	92
1998	32,120	28,542	89
1997	31,570	27,610	87
1996	30,889	27,241	88
1995	30,245	26,813	89
1994	30,313	26,877	89
1993	29,892	27,026	90
1992	30,125	27,623	92
1991	29,695	26,744	90
1990	29,822	26,857	90
Percent change			
2000 to 2005	0.7%	4.0%	–
1990 to 2005	11.5	13.1	–

Note: Beginning in 2002, data for blacks are for those who identify themselves as being of the race alone or as being of the race in combination with other races. The black/total indexes are calculated by dividing the median income of black women by the median income of total women and multiplying by 100. "–" means not applicable.
Source: Bureau of the Census, Current Population Surveys, Historical Income Tables—People, Internet site http://www.census.gov/hhes/www/income/histinc/incpertoc.html; calculations by New Strategist

Table 4.13   Median Income of Blacks Who Work Full-Time by Sex, 1990 to 2005

(median income of blacks who work full-time, year-round by sex, and black women's income as a percent of black men's income, 1990 to 2005; percent change in income for selected years; in 2005 dollars)

	median income of full-time workers		women's income as a percent of men's income
	black men	black women	
2005	$34,144	$30,366	88.9%
2004	32,771	30,169	92.1
2003	35,513	29,369	82.7
2002	34,700	30,072	86.7
2001	35,202	30,103	85.5
2000	34,561	29,189	84.5
1999	35,323	29,450	83.4
1998	32,858	28,542	86.9
1997	32,623	27,610	84.6
1996	33,616	27,241	81.0
1995	31,544	26,813	85.0
1994	31,798	26,877	84.5
1993	31,351	27,026	86.2
1992	31,349	27,623	88.1
1991	31,628	26,744	84.6
1990	31,111	26,857	86.3
Percent change			
2000 to 2005	−1.2%	4.0%	–
1990 to 2005	9.7	13.1	–

Note: Beginning in 2002, data for blacks are for those who identify themselves as being of the race aloneor as being of the race in combination with other races. "–" means not applicable.
Source: Bureau of the Census, Current Population Surveys, Historical Income Tables—People, Internet site http://www.census .gov/hhes/www/income/histinc/incpertoc.html; calculations by New Strategist

Black Earnings Rise with Education

The median earnings of black men with a professional degree exceed $100,000.

The earnings of black men and women who work full-time increase with educational attainment. Among black men with no more than a high school diploma who work full-time, median earnings were just $28,953 in 2005. College graduates earned a much larger $50,083. Twenty-one percent of black men with a master's degree who worked full-time earned $100,000 or more, as did the 55 percent majority of those with a professional degree (doctors and lawyers).

The pattern is the same for black women, although their earnings are less than those of black men. Black women who graduated from high school and work full-time earned a median of $23,969 in 2005. Those with a college degree earned a much larger $46,636. Thirty-one percent of black women with a professional degree who work full-time earned $100,000 or more.

■ As black educational attainment increases, so will black earnings.

Many highly educated black men earn $100,000 or more

(percent of black men aged 25 or older who work full-time, year-round and earn $100,000 or more, by educational attainment, 2005)

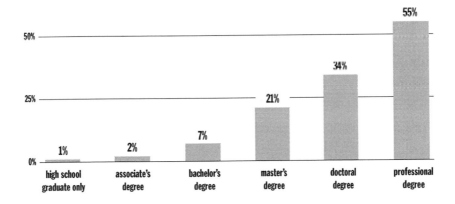

Table 4.14 Earnings of Black Men Who Work Full-Time by Education, 2005

(number and percent distribution of black men aged 25 or older who work full-time, year-round, by earnings and educational attainment, 2005; median earnings of men with earnings; men in thousands as of 2006)

	total	less than 9th grade	9th–12th grade, no diploma	high school graduate	some college, no degree	associate's degree	bachelor's degree or more total	bachelor's degree	master's degree	professional degree	doctoral degree
Black men working full-time	**5,306**	**148**	**420**	**2,009**	**1,069**	**430**	**1,230**	**845**	**287**	**51**	**47**
Under $5,000	62	4	7	29	10	1	9	8	2	0	0
$5,000 to $9,999	46	7	18	9	7	0	5	5	0	0	0
$10,000 to $14,999	256	21	42	130	36	6	22	20	2	0	0
$15,000 to $19,999	505	23	64	277	71	31	40	26	11	0	3
$20,000 to $24,999	618	25	91	310	121	33	39	35	4	0	0
$25,000 to $29,999	567	23	53	292	99	36	63	55	8	0	0
$30,000 to $34,999	528	17	46	204	121	38	102	80	20	2	0
$35,000 to $39,999	475	6	19	177	122	44	108	91	17	0	0
$40,000 to $44,999	472	12	28	171	101	39	121	83	31	3	3
$45,000 to $49,999	316	0	24	79	59	52	103	85	15	0	3
$50,000 to $54,999	372	1	4	95	97	48	125	88	24	11	3
$55,000 to $59,999	123	0	1	22	27	20	53	35	15	0	3
$60,000 to $64,999	221	3	14	58	60	20	66	49	11	2	4
$65,000 to $69,999	117	0	3	24	31	18	41	23	13	0	5
$70,000 to $74,999	130	2	0	37	39	10	42	27	14	0	2
$75,000 to $79,999	92	0	1	26	19	11	35	23	10	0	2
$80,000 to $84,999	69	0	0	15	17	6	32	13	14	3	2
$85,000 to $89,999	28	0	1	8	1	1	17	9	5	2	1
$90,000 to $94,999	54	0	0	12	7	6	30	24	5	0	0
$95,000 to $99,999	27	0	0	9	2	1	15	7	7	0	0
$100,000 or more	228	5	2	25	21	10	166	60	61	28	16
Median earnings	$35,521	$23,683	$23,913	$28,953	$36,998	$42,228	$50,083	$46,106	$57,292	–	–

PERCENT DISTRIBUTION

	total	less than 9th grade	9th–12th grade, no diploma	high school graduate	some college, no degree	associate's degree	bachelor's degree or more total	bachelor's degree	master's degree	professional degree	doctoral degree
Black men working full-time	100.0%	100.0%	100.0%	100.0%	100.0%	100.0%	100.0%	100.0%	100.0%	100.0%	100.0%
Under $15,000	6.9	21.6	16.0	8.4	5.0	1.6	2.9	3.9	1.4	0.0	0.0
$15,000 to $24,999	21.2	32.4	36.9	29.2	18.0	14.9	6.4	7.2	5.2	0.0	6.4
$25,000 to $34,999	20.6	27.0	23.6	24.7	20.6	17.2	13.4	16.0	9.8	3.9	0.0
$35,000 to $49,999	23.8	12.2	16.9	21.3	26.4	31.4	27.0	30.7	22.0	5.9	12.8
$50,000 to $74,999	18.1	4.1	5.2	11.7	23.8	27.0	26.6	26.3	26.8	25.5	36.2
$75,000 to $99,999	5.1	0.0	0.5	3.5	4.3	5.8	10.5	9.0	14.3	9.8	10.6
$100,000 or more	4.3	3.4	0.5	1.2	2.0	2.3	13.5	7.1	21.3	54.9	34.0

Note: Blacks are those who identify themselves as being of the race alone or as being of the race in combination with other races. Earnings include wages and salary only. "–" means sample is too small to make a reliable estimate.
Source: Bureau of the Census, 2006 Current Population Survey Annual Social and Economic Supplement, Internet site http://pubdb3.census.gov/macro/032006/perinc/new03_000.htm; calculations by New Strategist

Table 4.15 Earnings of Black Women Who Work Full-Time by Education, 2005

(number and percent distribution of black women aged 25 or older who work full-time, year-round, by earnings and educational attainment, 2005; median earnings of women with earnings; women in thousands as of 2006)

	total	less than 9th grade	9th–12th grade, no diploma	high school graduate	some college, no degree	associate's degree	bachelor's degree or more				
							total	bachelor's degree	master's degree	professional degree	doctoral degree
Black women working full-time	**5,791**	**74**	**370**	**1,860**	**1,241**	**594**	**1,653**	**1,135**	**417**	**72**	**28**
Under $5,000	72	0	7	37	15	5	8	4	2	2	0
$5,000 to $9,999	111	5	22	53	22	3	5	4	1	0	0
$10,000 to $14,999	387	20	66	198	58	22	22	16	2	2	2
$15,000 to $19,999	680	20	108	330	118	61	42	35	5	0	2
$20,000 to $24,999	799	13	72	369	181	77	87	70	16	2	0
$25,000 to $29,999	733	4	36	301	204	96	91	84	7	0	0
$30,000 to $34,999	650	2	27	186	177	83	175	134	32	8	2
$35,000 to $39,999	475	2	3	129	128	57	156	110	42	4	0
$40,000 to $44,999	422	0	6	83	105	56	171	106	58	4	3
$45,000 to $49,999	290	0	10	38	63	28	150	105	43	2	0
$50,000 to $54,999	314	0	4	69	66	27	148	118	19	7	4
$55,000 to $59,999	154	0	3	18	27	13	94	55	37	1	1
$60,000 to $64,999	167	2	5	11	30	31	89	53	32	1	2
$65,000 to $69,999	85	0	0	10	7	5	63	32	27	4	0
$70,000 to $74,999	82	0	0	7	9	6	60	35	20	5	0
$75,000 to $79,999	75	2	0	0	8	7	58	43	12	2	2
$80,000 to $84,999	62	0	0	3	17	4	38	29	4	3	2
$85,000 to $89,999	44	0	0	4	0	4	37	22	11	2	1
$90,000 to $94,999	40	0	0	5	2	0	32	18	15	0	0
$95,000 to $99,999	17	0	0	0	0	0	17	12	3	2	0
$100,000 or more	132	0	0	7	5	10	109	53	28	22	7
Median earnings	$30,570	–	$19,122	$23,969	$30,406	$31,277	$46,636	$45,189	$49,933	–	–

PERCENT DISTRIBUTION

	total	less than 9th grade	9th–12th grade, no diploma	high school graduate	some college, no degree	associate's degree	total	bachelor's degree	master's degree	professional degree	doctoral degree
Black women working full-time	100.0%	100.0%	100.0%	100.0%	100.0%	100.0%	100.0%	100.0%	100.0%	100.0%	100.0%
Under $15,000	9.8	33.8	25.7	15.5	7.7	5.1	2.1	2.1	1.2	5.6	7.1
$15,000 to $24,999	25.5	44.6	48.6	37.6	24.1	23.2	7.8	9.3	5.0	2.8	7.1
$25,000 to $34,999	23.9	8.1	17.0	26.2	30.7	30.1	16.1	19.2	9.4	11.1	7.1
$35,000 to $49,999	20.5	2.7	5.1	13.4	23.9	23.7	28.9	28.3	34.3	13.9	10.7
$50,000 to $74,999	13.8	2.7	3.2	6.2	11.2	13.8	27.5	25.8	32.4	25.0	25.0
$75,000 to $99,999	4.1	2.7	0.0	0.6	2.2	2.5	11.0	10.9	10.8	12.5	17.9
$100,000 or more	2.3	0.0	0.0	0.4	0.4	1.7	6.6	4.7	6.7	30.6	25.0

Note: Blacks are those who identify themselves as being of the race alone or as being of the race in combination with other races. Earnings include wages and salary only. "–" means sample is too small to make a reliable estimate.
Source: Bureau of the Census, 2006 Current Population Survey Annual Social and Economic Supplement, Internet site http:// pubdb3.census.gov/macro/032006/perinc/new03_000.htm; calculations by New Strategist

One in Four Blacks Is Poor

The black poverty rate has fallen since 1990.

Twenty-five percent of blacks were poor in 2005, down from 32 percent in 1990. The black share of the poverty population fell from 29 to 26 percent during those years. Between 2000 and 2005, the black poverty rate grew slightly, as did the black share of the poor.

One-third of black children are poor. The black poverty rate falls to a low of 17 percent in the 35-to-54 age group, then rises to 25 percent among blacks aged 75 or older. Black women are more likely than black men to be poor.

Family type has a strong effect on black poverty. Only 8 percent of black married couples were poor in 2005. This compares with a poverty rate of 36 percent among black female-headed families. Fully 42 percent of black female-headed families with children are poor. This is a lower poverty rate than in 1990, however, when the 56 percent majority of black female-headed families with children were poor.

■ If black educational attainment continues to grow, the black poverty rate should resume its decline.

The black poverty rate bottomed out in 2000

(percent of blacks below poverty level for selected years, 1990 to 2005)

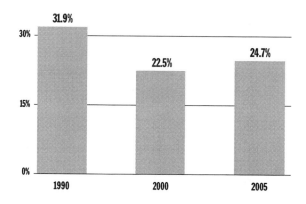

Table 4.16 Total People and Blacks below Poverty Level, 1990 to 2005

(number and percent of total and blacks below poverty level, and black share of poor, 1990 to 2005; people in thousands as of the following year)

| | total people in poverty | | blacks in poverty | | |
	number	percent	number	percent	black share of total
2005	36,950	12.6%	9,517	24.7%	25.8%
2004	37,040	12.7	9,411	24.7	25.4
2003	35,861	12.5	9,108	24.3	25.4
2002	34,570	12.1	8,884	23.9	25.7
2001	32,907	11.7	8,136	22.7	24.7
2000	31,581	11.3	7,982	22.5	25.3
1999	32,791	11.9	8,441	23.6	25.7
1998	34,476	12.7	9,091	26.1	26.4
1997	35,574	13.3	9,116	26.5	25.6
1996	36,529	13.7	9,694	28.4	26.5
1995	36,425	13.8	9,872	29.3	27.1
1994	38,059	14.5	10,196	30.6	26.8
1993	39,265	15.1	10,877	33.1	27.7
1992	38,014	14.8	10,827	33.4	28.5
1991	35,708	14.2	10,242	32.7	28.7
1990	33,585	13.5	9,837	31.9	29.3

Note: Beginning in 2002, data for blacks are for those who identify themselves as being of the race alone or as being of the race in combination with other races.
Source: Bureau of the Census, Current Population Survey Annual Demographic Supplements, Internet site http://www.census.gov/hhes/www/poverty/histpov/histpov2.html, calculations by New Strategist

Table 4.17   Total People and Blacks below Poverty Level by Age, 2005

(number and percent of total people and blacks below poverty level by age, and black share of total, 2005; numbers in thousands)

	total		black		
	number	percent	number	percent	share of total
Total people in poverty	**36,950**	**12.6%**	**9,517**	**24.7%**	**25.8%**
Under age 18	12,896	17.6	4,074	33.5	31.6
Under age 5	4,107	20.4	1,224	36.9	29.8
Aged 5 to 17	8,789	16.5	2,850	32.2	32.4
Aged 18 to 64	20,450	11.1	4,735	20.3	23.2
Aged 18 to 24	5,094	18.2	1,176	27.6	23.1
Aged 25 to 34	4,965	12.6	1,190	22.2	24.0
Aged 35 to 44	4,186	9.7	907	16.5	21.7
Aged 45 to 54	3,504	8.2	845	16.6	24.1
Aged 55 to 59	1,441	8.1	324	17.9	22.5
Aged 60 to 64	1,260	9.6	292	22.1	23.2
Aged 65 or older	3,603	10.1	708	23.2	19.7
Aged 65 to 74	1,648	8.9	371	21.6	22.5
Aged 75 or older	1,955	11.5	337	25.3	17.2

Note: Blacks are those who identify themselves as being of the race alone or as being of the race in combination with other races.
Source: Bureau of the Census, 2006 Current Population Survey Annual Social and Economic Supplement, Internet site http:// pubdb3.census.gov/macro/032006/pov/new01_100.htm

Table 4.18   Blacks below Poverty Level by Age and Sex, 2005

(number and percent of blacks below poverty level by age and sex, and female share of poor, 2005; numbers in thousands)

		males		females		
	total	number	percent	number	percent	share of poor
Total blacks in poverty	**9,517**	**4,006**	**22.2%**	**5,511**	**26.9%**	**57.9%**
Under age 18	4,074	2,050	33.2	2,024	33.8	49.7
Under age 5	1,224	611	36.2	613	37.6	50.1
Aged 5 to 17	2,850	1,439	32.1	1,411	32.4	49.5
Aged 18 to 64	4,735	1,719	16.1	3,016	23.8	63.7
Aged 18 to 24	1,176	434	21.1	742	33.7	63.1
Aged 25 to 34	1,190	401	16.4	789	27.1	66.3
Aged 35 to 44	907	280	11.3	628	20.7	69.2
Aged 45 to 54	845	372	16.0	473	17.1	56.0
Aged 55 to 59	324	130	16.1	194	19.4	59.9
Aged 60 to 64	292	102	18.0	190	25.2	65.1
Aged 65 or older	708	237	20.0	471	25.2	66.5
Aged 65 to 74	371	149	20.1	222	22.6	59.8
Aged 75 or older	337	88	19.8	249	28.1	73.9

Note: Blacks are those who identify themselves as being of the race alone or as being of the race in combination with other races.
Source: Bureau of the Census, 2006 Current Population Survey Annual Social and Economic Supplement, Internet site http:// pubdb3.census.gov/macro/032006/pov/new01_100.htm

Table 4.19 Number and Percent of Black Families below Poverty Level by Family Type, 1990 to 2005

(number and percent of black families below poverty level by family type, 1990 to 2005; families in thousands as of the following year)

	total black families in poverty		married couples		female householder, no spouse present		male householder, no spouse present	
	number	percent	number	percent	number	percent	number	percent
2005	2,050	22.0%	348	8.2%	1,524	36.2%	178	21.3%
2004	2,082	22.8	386	9.1	1,538	37.6	158	20.7
2003	2,021	22.1	331	7.8	1,496	36.8	194	24.1
2002	1,958	21.4	340	8.0	1,454	35.7	165	20.8
2001	1,829	20.7	328	7.8	1,351	35.2	150	19.4
2000	1,686	19.3	266	6.3	1,300	34.3	120	16.3
1999	1,887	21.8	295	7.1	1,487	39.2	105	14.8
1998	1,981	23.4	290	7.3	1,557	40.8	134	20.3
1997	1,985	23.6	312	8.0	1,563	39.8	111	19.7
1996	2,206	26.1	352	9.1	1,724	43.7	130	19.8
1995	2,127	26.4	314	8.5	1,701	45.1	112	19.5
1994	2,212	27.3	336	8.7	1,715	46.2	161	30.1
1993	2,499	31.3	458	12.3	1,908	49.9	133	29.6
1992	2,484	31.1	490	13.0	1,878	50.2	116	24.8
1991	2,343	30.4	399	11.0	1,834	51.2	110	21.9
1990	2,193	29.3	448	12.6	1,648	48.1	97	20.6

Note: Beginning in 2002, data are for those who identify themselves as being of the race alone or as being of the race in combination with other races.
Source: Bureau of the Census, Current Population Survey Annual Demographic Supplements, Internet site http.//www.census.gov/hhes/www/poverty/histpov/hstpov4.html; calculations by New Strategist

Table 4.20 Number and Percent of Black Families with Children below Poverty Level by Family Type, 1990 to 2005

(number and percent of black families with related children under age 18 below poverty level by family type, 1990 to 2005; families in thousands as of the following year)

	total black families with children in poverty		married couples		female householder, no spouse present		male householder, no spouse present	
	number	percent	number	percent	number	percent	number	percent
2005	1,679	28.3%	213	9.2%	1,335	42.0%	131	29.6%
2004	1,655	28.6	213	9.3	1,339	43.3	102	25.3
2003	1,698	28.6	210	9.1	1,341	42.7	146	30.7
2002	1,597	27.2	199	8.5	1,288	41.3	110	26.3
2001	1,524	26.6	205	8.7	1,220	40.8	99	24.6
2000	1,411	25.3	157	6.7	1,177	41.0	76	21.7
1999	1,603	28.9	199	8.7	1,320	46.0	84	21.7
1998	1,673	30.5	189	8.6	1,397	47.5	88	24.8
1997	1,721	30.5	205	9.0	1,436	46.9	81	25.8
1996	1,941	34.1	239	11.0	1,593	51.0	109	27.2
1995	1,821	34.1	209	9.9	1,533	53.2	79	23.4
1994	1,954	35.9	245	11.4	1,591	53.9	118	34.6
1993	2,171	39.3	298	13.9	1,780	57.7	93	31.6
1992	2,132	39.1	343	15.4	1,706	57.4	83	33.5
1991	2,016	39.2	263	12.4	1,676	60.5	77	31.7
1990	1,887	37.2	301	14.3	1,513	56.1	73	27.3

Note: Beginning in 2002, data are for those who identify themselves as being of the race alone or as being of the race in combination with other races.
Source: Bureau of the Census, Current Population Survey Annual Demographic Supplements, Internet site http://www.census .gov/hhes/www/poverty/histpov/hstpov4.html; calculations by New Strategist

5

Labor Force

■ In 2006, the labor force participation rate of black men stood at 67.0 percent, well below the 73.5 percent rate for all men. Conversely, black women are more likely to work than the average woman—61.7 percent compared with 59.4 percent for all women.

■ Blacks make up 11 percent of the workforce in 2006, but are 14 percent of education administrators, 21 percent of dieticians, 23 percent of social workers, 24 percent of taxi drivers and chauffeurs, and 30 percent of security guards.

■ The 54 percent majority of black workers has at least some college, and nearly one in four has a college degree.

■ Although black households have fewer earners than average, black couples are more likely than the average married couple to be dual earner—57 percent compared with 54 percent for all married couples.

■ Among the 16 percent of blacks represented by a union, median weekly earnings ($694) are more than 30 percent higher than the earnings of those not represented by a union ($520).

■ The black labor force is projected to grow by nearly 3 million workers between 2004 and 2014, a 17 percent rise compared with a 10 percent increase for the total labor force.

Two-Thirds of Black Men Are in the Labor Force

The labor force participation rate of black men is below average.

In 2006, the labor force participation rate of black men stood at 67.0 percent, well below the 73.5 percent rate for all men. At every age, black men are less likely than average to work, but the gap is most pronounced among the young and the old.

Black women are more likely to work than the average woman. In 2006, 61.7 percent of black women were in the labor force—a higher proportion than the 59.4 percent rate for all women.

■ The high unemployment rate of black men—particularly teenagers—discourages many from even looking for a job.

Black women are almost as likely as black men to work

(percent of blacks aged 16 or older in the labor force, by sex, 2006)

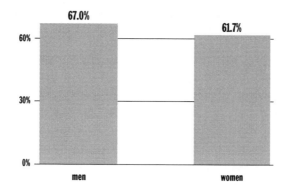

Table 5.1 Total and Black Labor Force by Age and Sex, 2006

(number of total people and blacks aged 16 or older in the civilian labor force, and black share of total, by age and sex, 2006)

	men			women		
	total	black	black share of total	total	black	black share of total
Total in labor force	**81,255**	**8,128**	**10.0%**	**70,173**	**9,186**	**13.1%**
Aged 16 to 17	1,453	152	10.5	1,499	166	11.1
Aged 18 to 19	2,240	256	11.4	2,089	297	14.2
Aged 20 to 24	8,116	971	12.0	6,997	989	14.1
Aged 25 to 34	17,944	1,986	11.1	14,628	2,211	15.1
Aged 35 to 44	19,407	1,999	10.3	16,441	2,349	14.3
Aged 45 to 54	18,489	1,792	9.7	16,656	1,993	12.0
Aged 55 to 64	10,509	777	7.4	9,475	963	10.2
Aged 65 or older	3,096	195	6.3	2,388	218	9.1

Note: The civilian labor force equals the number of employed plus the number of unemployed.
Source: Bureau of Labor Statistics, 2006 Current Population Survey, Internet site http://www.bls.gov/cps/home.htm; calculations by New Strategist

Table 5.2 Labor Force Participation Rate of Total People and Blacks by Age and Sex, 2006

(percent of total people and blacks aged 16 or older in the civilian labor force, and index of black to total, by age and sex, 2006)

	men			women		
	total	black	index, black to total	total	black	index, black to total
Total people	**73.5%**	**67.0%**	**91**	**59.4%**	**61.7%**	**104**
Aged 16 to 17	31.5	21.4	68	33.5	23.9	71
Aged 18 to 19	58.2	46.4	80	55.8	49.0	88
Aged 20 to 24	79.6	71.6	90	69.5	66.2	95
Aged 25 to 34	91.7	85.7	93	74.4	78.6	106
Aged 35 to 44	92.1	84.4	92	75.9	80.1	106
Aged 45 to 54	88.1	79.2	90	76.0	73.0	96
Aged 55 to 64	69.6	55.9	80	58.2	55.1	95
Aged 65 or older	20.3	16.7	82	11.7	11.8	101

Note: The civilian labor force equals the number of employed plus the number of unemployed. The index is calculated by dividing the black rate by the total rate and multiplying by 100.
Source: Bureau of Labor Statistics, 2006 Current Population Survey, Internet site http://www.bls.gov/cps/home.htm; calculations by New Strategist

Table 5.3 Labor Force Participation Rate of Blacks by Age and Sex, 2006

(percent of blacks aged 16 or older in the civilian labor force, by age and sex, 2006)

	total	men	women
Total blacks	**64.1%**	**67.0%**	**61.7%**
Aged 16 to 19	34.0	32.3	35.6
Aged 16 to 17	22.6	21.4	23.9
Aged 18 to 19	47.8	46.4	49.0
Aged 20 to 24	68.8	71.6	66.2
Aged 25 to 34	81.8	85.7	78.6
Aged 25 to 29	80.6	84.0	77.7
Aged 30 to 34	83.1	87.6	79.5
Aged 35 to 44	82.0	84.4	80.1
Aged 35 to 39	82.5	85.7	79.9
Aged 40 to 44	81.6	83.1	80.3
Aged 45 to 54	75.8	79.2	73.0
Aged 45 to 49	77.4	81.0	74.4
Aged 50 to 54	74.0	77.2	71.3
Aged 55 to 64	55.4	55.9	55.1
Aged 55 to 59	63.8	63.9	63.7
Aged 60 to 64	43.9	44.5	43.4
Aged 65 or older	13.7	16.7	11.8
Aged 65 to 69	21.9	24.6	19.9
Aged 70 to 74	14.7	16.7	13.2
Aged 75 or older	6.3	8.7	5.0

Note: The civilian labor force equals the number of employed plus the number of unemployed.
Source: Bureau of Labor Statistics, 2006 Current Population Survey, Internet site http://www.bls.gov/cps/home.htm

Table 5.4 Employment Status of Blacks by Sex and Age, 2006

(number and percent of blacks aged 16 or older in the civilian labor force by sex, age, and employment status, 2006; numbers in thousands)

	civilian noninstitutional population	civilian labor force			unemployed	
		total	percent of population	employed	number	percent of labor force
Total blacks	**27,007**	**17,314**	**64.1%**	**15,765**	**1,549**	**8.9%**
Aged 16 to 19	2,565	871	34.0	618	253	29.1
Aged 20 to 24	2,851	1,960	68.8	1,643	318	16.2
Aged 25 to 34	5,133	4,197	81.8	3,809	388	9.3
Aged 35 to 44	5,302	4,348	82.0	4,072	276	6.3
Aged 45 to 54	4,992	3,785	75.8	3,570	214	5.7
Aged 55 to 64	3,137	1,739	55.4	1,659	81	4.6
Aged 65 or older	3,027	414	13.7	394	19	4.7
Total black men	**12,130**	**8,128**	**67.0**	**7,354**	**774**	**9.5**
Aged 16 to 19	1,266	409	32.3	275	134	32.7
Aged 20 to 24	1,355	971	71.6	804	167	17.2
Aged 25 to 34	2,318	1,986	85.7	1,797	189	9.5
Aged 35 to 44	2,369	1,999	84.4	1,882	118	5.9
Aged 45 to 54	2,261	1,792	79.2	1,680	112	6.3
Aged 55 to 64	1,390	777	55.9	734	43	5.5
Aged 65 or older	1,170	195	16.7	184	11	5.8
Total black women	**14,877**	**9,186**	**61.7**	**8,410**	**775**	**8.4**
Aged 16 to 19	1,299	462	35.6	343	120	25.9
Aged 20 to 24	1,495	989	66.2	839	150	15.2
Aged 25 to 34	2,815	2,211	78.6	2,012	199	9.0
Aged 35 to 44	2,933	2,349	80.1	2,191	158	6.7
Aged 45 to 54	2,731	1,993	73.0	1,890	102	5.1
Aged 55 to 64	1,747	963	55.1	925	38	3.9
Aged 65 or older	1,857	218	11.8	210	8	3.7

Note: The civilian labor force equals the number of the employed plus the number of the unemployed. The civilian population equals the number in the labor force plus the number not in the labor force.
Source: Bureau of Labor Statistics, 2006 Current Population Survey, Internet site http://www.bls.gov/cps/home.htm

Nine Percent of Professional Workers Are Black

Blacks account for 23 percent of social workers.

Blacks accounted for 11 percent of the workforce in 2006, but the black share of workers by occupation varies widely. Blacks are a relatively large 16 percent of service workers and 14 percent of production workers. Blacks account for 9 percent of professional workers, including 11 percent of registered nurses.

Blacks account for 21 percent of dietitians, 24 percent of taxi drivers and chauffeurs, 28 percent of garbage collectors, and 30 percent of security guards. Among the nation's education administrators, a substantial 14 percent are black.

■ Although blacks are underrepresented in many managerial and professional occupations, they have been making gains over the past few years.

Blacks account for a larger-than-average share of employment in some rapidly growing industries

(black share of employed people aged 16 or older by selected industry, 2006)

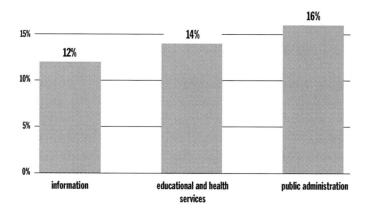

Table 5.5 Total and Black Workers by Occupation, 2006

(total number of employed persons aged 16 or older in the civilian labor force, number and percent distribution of employed blacks, and black share of total, by occupation, 2006; numbers in thousands)

	total	black number	percent distribution	share of total
TOTAL EMPLOYED	**144,427**	**15,765**	**100.0%**	**10.9%**
Management, professional, and related occupations	**50,420**	**4,252**	**27.0**	**8.4**
Management, business, and financial operations	21,233	1,547	9.8	7.3
Management occupations	15,249	950	6.0	6.2
Business and financial operations occupations	5,983	597	3.8	10.0
Professional and related occupations	29,187	2,704	17.2	9.3
Computer and mathematical occupations	3,209	233	1.5	7.3
Architecture and engineering occupations	2,830	158	1.0	5.6
Life, physical, and social science occupations	1,434	81	0.5	5.6
Community and social services occupations	2,156	402	2.5	18.6
Legal occupations	1,637	107	0.7	6.5
Education, training, and library occupations	8,126	795	5.0	9.8
Arts, design, entertainment, sports, and media occupations	2,735	183	1.2	6.7
Health care practitioner and technical occupations	7,060	746	4.7	10.6
Service occupations	**23,811**	**3,797**	**24.1**	**15.9**
Health care support occupations	3,132	774	4.9	24.7
Protective service occupations	2,939	578	3.7	19.7
Food preparation and serving-related occupations	7,606	892	5.7	11.7
Building and grounds cleaning and maintenance occupations	5,381	840	5.3	15.6
Personal care and service occupations	4,754	714	4.5	15.0
Sales and office occupations	**36,141**	**4,051**	**25.7**	**11.2**
Sales and related occupations	16,641	1,503	9.5	9.0
Office and administrative support occupations	19,500	2,548	16.2	13.1
Natural resources, construction, maintenance occupations	**15,830**	**1,079**	**6.8**	**6.8**
Farming, fishing, and forestry occupations	961	47	0.3	4.9
Construction and extraction occupations	9,507	624	4.0	6.6
Installation, maintenance, and repair occupations	5,362	408	2.6	7.6
Production, transportation, material-moving occupations	**18,224**	**2,586**	**16.4**	**14.2**
Production occupations	9,378	1,148	7.3	12.2
Transportation and material-moving occupations	8,846	1,438	9.1	16.3

Source: Bureau of Labor Statistics, 2006 Current Population Survey, Internet site http://www.bls.gov/cps/home.htm; calculations by New Strategist

Table 5.6 Total and Black Workers by Detailed Occupation, 2006

(total number of employed workers agd 16 or older and percent black, by detailed occupation, 2006; numbers in thousands)

	total	percent black
TOTAL EMPLOYED	**144,427**	**10.9%**
Management, professional, and related occupations	**50,420**	**8.4**
Management, business, and financial operations occupations	21,233	7.3
Management occupations	15,249	6.2
Chief executives	1,689	3.1
General and operations managers	998	5.7
Advertising and promotions managers	75	5.4
Marketing and sales managers	888	4.8
Administrative services managers	87	7.3
Computer and information systems managers	401	6.4
Financial managers	1,083	7.0
Human resources managers	280	11.0
Industrial production managers	298	3.0
Purchasing managers	165	8.7
Transportation, storage, and distribution managers	249	9.8
Farm, ranch, and other agricultural managers	242	2.4
Farmers and ranchers	784	0.8
Construction managers	1,010	3.7
Education administrators	796	14.2
Engineering managers	103	2.9
Food service managers	900	5.8
Lodging managers	174	6.5
Medical and health services managers	511	10.3
Property, real estate, and community association managers	618	7.2
Social and community service managers	315	15.0
Business and financial operations occupations	5,983	10.0
Wholesale and retail buyers, except farm products	222	3.2
Purchasing agents, except wholesale, retail, and farm products	290	7.9
Claims adjusters, appraisers, examiners, and investigators	283	14.1
Compliance officers, excl. agriculture, construction, health and safety, and transportation	149	17.4
Cost estimators	114	1.0
Human resources, training, and labor relations specialists	765	14.5
Management analysts	572	5.9
Accountants and auditors	1,779	10.2
Appraisers and assessors of real estate	134	1.5
Budget analysts	52	18.1
Financial analysts	103	4.0
Personal financial advisors	389	7.0
Insurance underwriters	92	16.2
Loan counselors and officers	468	11.1
Tax examiners, collectors, and revenue agents	67	21.4
Tax preparers	98	10.6

(continued)

	total	percent black
Professional and related occupations	29,187	9.3%
Computer and mathematical occupations	3,209	7.3
Computer scientists and systems analysts	715	9.5
Computer programmers	562	3.9
Computer software engineers	846	5.8
Computer support specialists	314	10.5
Database administrators	90	8.9
Network and computer systems administrators	180	4.4
Network systems and data communications analysts	356	7.9
Operations research analysts	85	18.1
Architecture and engineering occupations	2,830	5.6
Architects, except naval	221	3.2
Aerospace engineers	110	5.6
Chemical engineers	70	4.2
Civil engineers	304	5.0
Computer hardware engineers	80	3.8
Electrical and electronics engineers	382	5.9
Industrial engineers, including health and safety	174	7.0
Mechanical engineers	322	4.3
Drafters	181	3.0
Engineering technicians, except drafters	396	9.3
Surveying and mapping technicians	96	3.0
Life, physical, and social science occupations	1,434	5.7
Biological scientists	116	3.5
Medical scientists	164	5.3
Chemists and materials scientists	116	7.4
Environmental scientists and geoscientists	101	2.9
Market and survey researchers	129	9.0
Psychologists	189	2.6
Chemical technicians	76	11.4
Community and social services occupations	2,156	18.6
Counselors	614	17.9
Social workers	698	22.7
Miscellaneous community and social service specialists	293	23.9
Clergy	416	12.4
Legal occupations	1,637	6.5
Lawyers	965	5.0
Judges, magistrates, and other judicial workers	66	11.3
Paralegals and legal assistants	345	8.4
Miscellaneous legal support workers	261	8.7
Education, training, and library occupations	8,126	9.8
Postsecondary teachers	1,194	6.7
Preschool and kindergarten teachers	690	13.9
Elementary and middle school teachers	2,701	9.7
Secondary school teachers	1,098	7.3
Special education teachers	401	9.0
Other teachers and instructors	705	9.4
Librarians	229	8.8
Teacher assistants	942	14.9

(continued)

	total	percent black
Arts, design, entertainment, sports, and media occupations	2,735	6.7%
Artists and related workers	223	5.1
Designers	821	3.2
Producers and directors	134	6.4
Athletes, coaches, umpires, and related workers	270	9.5
Musicians, singers, and related workers	203	9.0
Announcers	62	21.6
News analysts, reporters, and correspondents	78	4.0
Public relations specialists	141	8.8
Editors	157	5.1
Technical writers	60	8.9
Writers and authors	174	5.7
Miscellaneous media and communication workers	67	7.5
Broadcast and sound engineering technicians and radio operators	89	11.7
Photographers	127	7.1
Health care practitioner and technical occupations	7,060	10.6
Chiropractors	69	3.3
Dentists	196	3.1
Dietitians and nutritionists	96	21.2
Pharmacists	245	6.0
Physicians and surgeons	863	5.2
Physician assistants	85	10.9
Registered nurses	2,529	10.9
Occupational therapists	78	3.1
Physical therapists	198	5.8
Respiratory therapists	85	15.3
Speech-language pathologists	114	8.1
Veterinarians	67	0.4
Clinical laboratory technologists and technicians	321	14.2
Dental hygienists	144	1.4
Diagnostic related technologists and technicians	281	7.5
Emergency medical technicians and paramedics	156	11.9
Health diagnosing and treating practitioner support technicians	425	11.8
Licensed practical and licensed vocational nurses	556	23.2
Medical records and health information technicians	98	20.5
Service occupations	**23,811**	**15.9**
Health care support occupations	3,132	24.7
Nursing, psychiatric, and home health aides	1,906	34.8
Physical therapist assistants and aides	61	2.7
Massage therapists	124	5.4
Dental assistants	274	5.4
Protective service occupations	2,939	19.7
First-line supervisors/managers of police and detectives	103	5.5
Firefighters	253	9.9
Bailiffs, correctional officers, and jailers	451	24.2
Detectives and criminal investigators	144	17.6
Police and sheriff's patrol officers	655	14.9
Private detectives and investigators	85	11.4
Security guards and gaming surveillance officers	835	29.8

(continued)

	total	percent black
Food preparation and serving related occupations	7,606	11.7%
Chefs and head cooks	313	14.1
First-line supervisors/managers of food preparation and serving workers	652	14.7
Cooks	1,868	17.4
Food preparation workers	698	12.3
Bartenders	389	2.5
Combined food preparation and serving workers, including fast food	344	12.5
Counter attendants, cafeteria, food concession, and coffee shop	308	12.1
Waiters and waitresses	1,960	7.0
Food servers, nonrestaurant	155	23.7
Dining room and cafeteria attendants and bartender helpers	380	8.4
Dishwashers	279	10.0
Hosts and hostesses, restaurant, lounge, and coffee shop	257	6.3
Building and grounds cleaning and maintenance occupations	5,381	15.6
First-line supervisors/managers of housekeeping and janitorial workers	305	16.2
First-line supervisors/managers of landscaping, lawn service, and groundskeeping workers	235	5.8
Janitors and building cleaners	2,082	18.7
Maids and housekeeping cleaners	1,423	19.9
Pest control workers	78	7.7
Grounds maintenance workers	1,259	7.8
Personal care and service occupations	4,754	15.0
First-line supervisors/managers of gaming workers	124	5.8
First-line supervisors/managers of personal service workers	176	11.2
Nonfarm animal caretakers	137	3.6
Gaming services workers	106	7.6
Barbers	100	36.7
Hairdressers, hairstylists, and cosmetologists	767	11.9
Miscellaneous personal appearance workers	230	6.5
Baggage porters, bellhops, and concierges	78	14.8
Transportation attendants	134	21.8
Child care workers	1,401	17.0
Personal and home care aides	703	22.4
Recreation and fitness workers	322	11.3
Residential advisors	62	25.6
Sales and office occupations	**36,141**	**11.2**
Sales and related occupations	16,641	9.0
First-line supervisors/managers of retail sales workers	3,435	7.4
First-line supervisors/managers of nonretail sales workers	1,433	5.6
Cashiers	3,063	15.3
Counter and rental clerks	146	11.1
Parts salespersons	149	3.0
Retail salespersons	3,386	11.1
Advertising sales agents	220	6.7
Insurance sales agents	548	6.9

(continued)

	total	percent black
Securities, commodities, and financial services sales agents	398	9.3%
Travel agents	82	7.1
Sales representatives, services, all other	563	5.9
Sales representatives, wholesale and manufacturing	1,422	2.9
Models, demonstrators, and product promoters	75	3.2
Real estate brokers and sales agents	1,046	5.8
Telemarketers	142	19.5
Door-to-door sales workers, news and street vendors, related workers	261	6.5
Office and administrative support occupations	19,500	13.1
First-line supervisors/managers of office and admin. support workers	1,543	9.0
Bill and account collectors	213	25.1
Billing and posting clerks and machine operators	422	13.3
Bookkeeping, accounting, and auditing clerks	1,511	7.8
Payroll and timekeeping clerks	158	11.0
Tellers	432	10.6
Court, municipal, and license clerks	114	12.4
Credit authorizers, checkers, and clerks	56	10.8
Customer service representatives	1,916	18.3
Eligibility interviewers, government programs	61	25.4
File clerks	363	13.9
Hotel, motel, and resort desk clerks	117	18.1
Interviewers, except eligibility and loan	141	17.3
Library assistants, clerical	119	8.2
Loan interviewers and clerks	190	12.0
Order clerks	128	8.8
Human resources assistants, except payroll and timekeeping	56	17.9
Receptionists and information clerks	1,403	10.8
Reservation and transportation ticket agents and travel clerks	156	19.3
Couriers and messengers	273	15.3
Dispatchers	303	11.7
Postal service clerks	153	22.7
Postal service mail carriers	329	15.7
Postal service mail sorters, processors, processing machine operators	98	28.2
Production, planning, and expediting clerks	296	7.5
Shipping, receiving, and traffic clerks	543	14.0
Stock clerks and order fillers	1,462	17.8
Weighers, measurers, checkers, and samplers, recordkeeping	81	15.3
Secretaries and administrative assistants	3,455	9.8
Computer operators	185	15.2
Data entry keyers	475	15.2
Word processors and typists	256	18.1
Insurance claims and policy processing clerks	274	11.4
Mail clerks and mail machine operators, except postal service	123	25.8
Office clerks, general	1,035	12.4
Office machine operators, except computer	52	20.3

(continued)

	total	percent black
Natural resources, construction, and maintenance occupations	**15,830**	**6.8%**
Farming, fishing, and forestry occupations	961	4.9
Graders and sorters, agricultural products	68	11.5
Logging workers	78	7.5
Construction and extraction occupations	9,507	6.6
First-line supervisors/managers of construction trades, extraction workers	976	4.6
Brickmasons, blockmasons, and stonemasons	244	7.1
Carpenters	1,843	4.5
Carpet, floor, and tile installers and finishers	279	5.3
Cement masons, concrete finishers, and terrazzo workers	107	13.8
Construction laborers	1,693	7.5
Operating engineers and other construction equipment operators	451	8.3
Drywall installers, ceiling tile installers, and tapers	295	3.8
Electricians	882	7.5
Painters, construction and maintenance	713	7.0
Pipelayers, plumbers, pipefitters, and steamfitters	662	8.5
Roofers	242	7.0
Sheet metal workers	125	2.2
Structural iron and steel workers	59	2.6
Helpers, construction trades	132	9.9
Construction and building inspectors	102	10.1
Highway maintenance workers	103	10.5
Installation, maintenance, and repair occupations	5,362	7.6
First-line supervisors/managers of mechanics, installers, and repairers	357	7.8
Computer, automated teller, and office machine repairers	371	8.4
Radio and telecommunications equipment installers and repairers	205	11.2
Electric motor, power tool, and related repairers	69	4.2
Security and fire alarm systems installers	141	6.6
Aircraft mechanics and service technicians	162	4.1
Automotive body and related repairers	875	6.1
Automotive service technicians and mechanics	367	6.3
Bus and truck mechanics and diesel engine specialists	237	2.6
Heavy vehicle and mobile equipment service technicians and mechanics	61	6.0
Small engine mechanics	405	4.8
Heating, air conditioning, and refrigeration mechanics and installers	56	5.3
Industrial and refractory machinery mechanics	436	9.1
Maintenance and repair workers, general	435	11.3
Millwrights	67	6.2
Electrical power-line installers and repairers	109	12.0
Telecommunications line installers and repairers	210	11.3
Precision instrument and equipment repairers	73	5.3
Coin, vending, and amusement machine servicers and repairers	62	8.2
Production, transportation, and material-moving occupations	**18,224**	**14.2**
Production occupations	9,378	12.2
First-line supervisors/managers of production and operating workers	868	9.8
Electrical, electronics, and electromechanical assemblers	213	14.0

(continued)

	total	percent black
Bakers	186	9.4%
Butchers and other meat, poultry, and fish processing workers	292	12.8
Food batchmakers	81	10.5
Computer control programmers and operators	54	4.8
Cutting, punching, and press machine setters, operators, and tenders, metal and plastic	119	13.8
Grinding, lapping, polishing, and buffing machine tool setters, operators, and tenders, metal and plastic	62	12.6
Machinists	415	5.2
Molders and molding machine setters, operators, tenders, metal and plastic	70	9.8
Tool and die makers	105	3.0
Welding, soldering, and brazing workers	546	7.5
Printing machine operators	208	9.5
Laundry and dry-cleaning workers	190	18.3
Pressers, textile, garment, and related materials	63	21.7
Sewing machine operators	292	10.7
Tailors, dressmakers, and sewers	111	7.6
Upholsterers	54	10.9
Cabinetmakers and bench carpenters	113	1.8
Sawing machine setters, operators, and tenders, wood	58	8.6
Stationary engineers and boiler operators	94	8.5
Water and liquid waste treatment plant and system operators	95	13.4
Chemical processing machine setters, operators, and tenders	57	12.1
Crushing, grinding, polishing, mixing, and blending workers	105	19.3
Cutting workers	78	5.8
Inspectors, testers, sorters, samplers, and weighers	702	11.4
Medical, dental, and ophthalmic laboratory technicians	95	9.7
Packaging and filling machine operators and tenders	275	21.5
Painting workers	173	9.0
Photographic process workers and processing machine operators	62	15.2
Helpers—production workers	53	16.1
Transportation and material-moving occupations	8,846	16.3
Supervisors, transportation and material-moving workers	228	13.0
Aircraft pilots and flight engineers	115	0.0
Bus drivers	565	29.4
Driver/sales workers and truck drivers	3,475	13.9
Taxi drivers and chauffeurs	282	23.8
Railroad conductors and yardmasters	50	14.8
Parking lot attendants	65	16.6
Service station attendants	96	5.9
Crane and tower operators	54	13.5
Dredge, excavating, and loading machine operators	63	4.7
Industrial truck and tractor operators	574	20.1
Cleaners of vehicles and equipment	401	16.9
Laborers and freight, stock, and material movers, hand	1,899	16.2
Packers and packagers, hand	432	18.9
Refuse and recyclable material collectors	91	28.0

Source: Bureau of Labor Statistics, 2006 Current Population Survey, Internet site http://www.bls.gov/cps/home.htm

Table 5.7 Total and Black Workers by Industry, 2006

(total number of employed people aged 16 or older in the civilian labor force, number and percent distribution of employed blacks, and black share of total, by industry, 2006; numbers in thousands)

	total	black number	black percent distribution	black share of total
Total employed	**144,428**	**15,765**	**100.0%**	**10.9%**
Agriculture, forestry, fishing, hunting	2,206	60	0.4	2.7
Mining	687	33	0.2	4.8
Construction	11,749	647	4.1	5.5
Manufacturing	16,377	1,557	9.9	9.5
Wholesale/retail trade	21,328	1,992	12.6	9.3
Transportation and utilities	7,455	1,230	7.8	16.5
Information	3,573	420	2.7	11.8
Financial activities	10,490	1,068	6.8	10.2
Professional and business services	14,868	1,463	9.3	9.8
Educational and health services	29,938	4,265	27.1	14.2
Leisure and hospitality	12,145	1,280	8.1	10.5
Other services	7,088	692	4.4	9.8
Public administration	6,524	1,056	6.7	16.2

Source: Bureau of Labor Statistics, 2006 Current Population Survey, Internet site http://www.bls.gov/cps/home.htm; calculations by New Strategist

Most Black Workers Have College Experience

Twenty-three percent have at least a bachelor's degree.

Among the 14 million blacks in the labor force in 2006, only 11 percent were not high school graduates. The 54 percent majority of black workers has at least some college, and nearly one in four has a college degree. Black labor force participation increases sharply with education, from a low of 40 percent among blacks aged 25 or older without a high school diploma to 82 percent among those with a bachelor's degree.

Black job tenure is about average, with 26 percent of blacks having worked for their current employer for 12 months or less. Among all workers, a slightly smaller 24 percent had one year or less job tenure. Blacks are slightly less likely than the average worker to have held their current job for 20 or more years—8 percent of blacks versus 9 percent of all workers.

■ Among employed blacks, 89 percent of men and 83 percent of women work full-time.

Few black workers are high school dropouts

(percent distribution of black workers aged 25 or older by educational attainment, 2006)

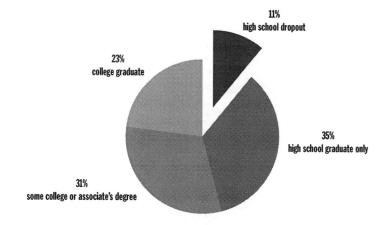

11%
high school dropout

23%
college graduate

35%
high school graduate only

31%
some college or associate's degree

Table 5.8 Total and Black Workers by Educational Attainment, 2006

(number of total people and blacks aged 25 or older in the civilian labor force, black labor force participation rate, distribution of blacks in labor force, and black share of total labor force, by educational attainment, 2006; numbers in thousands)

	total labor force	black labor force			
		number	participation rate	percent distribution	share of total
Total aged 25 or older	**129,034**	**14,482**	**70.0%**	**100.0%**	**11.2%**
Not a high school graduate	12,758	1,593	40.1	11.0	12.5
High school graduate only	38,354	5,105	66.8	35.3	13.3
Some college	22,504	3,015	74.0	20.8	13.4
Associate's degree	12,906	1,413	77.9	9.8	10.9
Bachelor's degree or more	42,512	3,356	82.1	23.2	7.9

Source: Bureau of Labor Statistics, 2006 Current Population Survey, Internet site http://www.bls.gov/cps/home.htm; calculations by New Strategist

Table 5.9 Total and Black Workers by Job Tenure, 2006

(number of total and black employed wage-and-salary workers aged 16 or older, percent distribution by tenure with current employer, and index of black to total, 2006; numbers in thousands)

	total	black	index black to total
Total workers, number	**125,668**	**14,265**	**–**
Total workers, percent	**100.0%**	**100.0%**	**100**
12 months or less	24.4	26.2	107
13 to 23 months	7.0	6.6	94
2 years	5.2	5.7	110
3 to 4 years	16.9	17.2	102
5 to 9 years	20.9	21.1	101
10 to 14 years	9.5	8.4	88
15 to 19 years	6.7	6.5	97
20 or more years	9.4	8.2	87

Note: The index is calculated by dividing the black figure by the total figure and multiplying by 100. "–" means not applicable.
Source: Bureau of Labor Statistics, 2006 Current Population Survey, Internet site http://www.bls.gov/cps/home.htm; calculations by New Strategist

Table 5.10   Black Workers by Full-Time and Part-Time Status, Age, and Sex, 2006

(number and percent distribution of employed blacks aged 16 or older by age, sex, and full- and part-time employment status, 2006; numbers in thousands)

	men			women		
	total	full-time	part-time	total	full-time	part-time
Total employed blacks	**7,354**	**6,529**	**825**	**8,411**	**7,001**	**1,410**
Aged 16 to 19	275	105	170	343	108	235
Aged 20 to 24	804	602	202	840	584	256
Aged 25 to 54	5,358	5,034	324	6,093	5,404	689
Aged 55 or older	918	788	130	1,135	905	230
PERCENT DISTRIBUTION BY EMPLOYMENT STATUS						
Total employed blacks	**100.0%**	**88.8%**	**11.2%**	**100.0%**	**83.2%**	**16.8%**
Aged 16 to 19	100.0	38.2	61.8	100.0	31.5	68.5
Aged 20 to 24	100.0	74.9	25.1	100.0	69.5	30.5
Aged 25 to 54	100.0	94.0	6.0	100.0	88.7	11.3
Aged 55 or older	100.0	85.8	14.2	100.0	79.7	20.3
PERCENT DISTRIBUTION BY AGE						
Total employed blacks	**100.0%**	**100.0%**	**100.0%**	**100.0%**	**100.0%**	**100.0%**
Aged 16 to 19	3.7	1.6	20.6	4.1	1.5	16.7
Aged 20 to 24	10.9	9.2	24.5	10.0	8.3	18.2
Aged 25 to 54	72.9	77.1	39.3	72.4	77.2	48.9
Aged 55 or older	12.5	12.1	15.8	13.5	12.9	16.3

Source: Bureau of Labor Statistics, 2006 Current Population Survey, Internet site http://www.bls.gov/cps/home.htm; calculations by New Strategist

Black Households Have Fewer Earners

Among black couples, most are dual earners.

The average black household has only 1.23 earners, less than the 1.36 earners in the typical American household. Behind the lower figure for blacks is the fact that female-headed families head a large share of black households, and many female-headed families have only one earner. Consequently, blacks account for a disproportionately large share of the nation's one-earner households and for a much smaller share of households with two or more earners.

Although black households have fewer earners than average, black couples are more likely than the average married couple to be dual earners. Fifty-seven percent of black couples are dual earners. Among all married couples, the figure is a smaller 54 percent. Only 18 percent of black husbands are the family's sole provider compared with 23 percent of husbands nationally.

■ Among black couples aged 55 to 64, husbands and wives are almost equally likely to be the sole provider.

Among black households, single earners are more common than dual earners

(percent distribution of black households by number of earners, 2006)

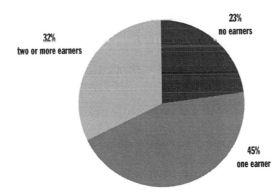

32%
two or more earners

23%
no earners

45%
one earner

Table 5.11 Total and Black Households by Number of Earners, 2006

(number of total households, number and percent distribution of black households and black share of total, by number of earners per household, 2006; numbers in thousands)

		black		
	total	number	percent distribution	share of total
Total households	**114,384**	**14,399**	**100.0%**	**12.6%**
No earners	24,224	3,295	22.9	13.6
One earner	42,066	6,523	45.3	15.5
Two or more earners	48,095	4,581	31.8	9.5
Two earners	38,327	3,735	25.9	9.7
Three earners	7,337	700	4.9	9.5
Four or more earners	2,430	146	1.0	6.0
Average number of earners per household	1.36	1.23	–	–

Note: Blacks include those who identify themselves as being of the race alone or as being of the race in combination with other races. "–" means not applicable.
Source: Bureau of the Census, 2006 Current Population Survey, Annual Social and Economic Supplement, Internet site http://pubdb3.census.gov/macro/032006/hhinc/new01_000.htm; calculations by New Strategist

Table 5.12 Labor Force Status of Black Married Couples, 2005

(number and percent distribution of black married-couple family groups aged 20 or older by age of householder and labor force status of husband and wife, 2005; numbers in thousands)

	total	husband and wife	husband only	wife only	neither husband nor wife in labor force
		husband and/or wife in labor force			
Total black couples	**4,362**	**2,488**	**802**	**423**	**650**
Under age 25	120	78	33	6	2
Aged 25 to 29	298	204	56	23	15
Aged 30 to 34	484	339	105	29	11
Aged 35 to 39	484	353	100	17	14
Aged 40 to 44	583	440	88	33	21
Aged 45 to 54	1,099	738	203	98	59
Aged 55 to 64	776	295	161	154	167
Aged 65 or older	517	38	56	61	362
Total black couples	**100.0%**	**57.0%**	**18.4%**	**9.7%**	**14.9%**
Under age 25	100.0	65.0	27.5	5.0	1.7
Aged 25 to 29	100.0	68.5	18.8	7.7	5.0
Aged 30 to 34	100.0	70.0	21.7	6.0	2.3
Aged 35 to 39	100.0	72.9	20.7	3.5	2.9
Aged 40 to 44	100.0	75.5	15.1	5.7	3.6
Aged 45 to 54	100.0	67.2	18.5	8.9	5.4
Aged 55 to 64	100.0	38.0	20.7	19.8	21.5
Aged 65 or older	100.0	7.4	10.8	11.8	70.0

Note: Blacks include those who identify themselves as being of the race alone or as being of the race in combination with other races.
Source: Bureau of the Census, America's Families and Living Arrangements: 2005, Internet site http://www.census.gov/population/www/socdemo/hh-fam/cps2005.html; calculations by New Strategist

Most Black Workers Drive to Work Alone

Union representation is higher than average among blacks.

Sixteen percent of blacks are represented by a union, more than the 13 percent share among all workers. Among blacks represented by a union, median weekly earnings ($694) are more than 30 percent higher than the earnings of those not represented by a union ($520).

Although blacks have lower earnings than the average American worker, few earn the minimum wage or less. In 2006, just 1.7 percent of black wage and salary workers earned at or below the minimum wage. Blacks account for 10 percent of the nation's minimum wage workers.

Three of four black workers drive themselves to work alone, while 10 percent carpool. Their median travel time to work is 23 minutes, and they cover a median distance of 11 miles.

■ Only 5 percent of black workers hold more than one job.

Ten percent of blacks use mass transportation to get to work

(percent distribution of black workers aged 16 or older by selected means of transportation to work, 2005)

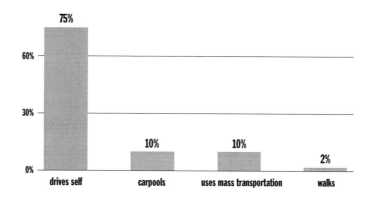

Table 5.13 Total and Black Minimum Wage Workers, 2006

(number and percent distribution of total and black wage and salary workers aged 16 or older paid hourly rates and those paid at or below minimum wage, by sex, 2006; numbers in thousands)

	total paid hourly rates	at or below minimum wage		
		total	at $5.15/hour	below $5.15/hour
Total workers aged 16 or older	**76,514**	**1,692**	**409**	**1,283**
Black workers aged 16 or older	**9,903**	**173**	**62**	**111**
Black men	4,485	68	28	40
Black women	5,419	106	34	72
PERCENT DISTRIBUTION BY RACE/SEX				
Total workers aged 16 or older	**100.0%**	**100.0%**	**100.0%**	**100.0%**
Black workers aged 16 or older	**12.9**	**10.2**	**15.2**	**8.7**
Black men	5.9	4.0	6.8	3.1
Black women	7.1	6.3	8.3	5.6
PERCENT DISTRIBUTION BY WAGE STATUS				
Total workers aged 16 or older	**100.0%**	**2.2%**	**0.5%**	**1.7%**
Black workers aged 16 or older	**100.0**	**1.7**	**0.6**	**1.1**
Black men	100.0	1.5	0.6	0.9
Black women	100.0	2.0	0.6	1.3

Source: Bureau of Labor Statistics, 2006 Current Population Survey, Internet site http://www.bls.gov/cps/home.htm

Table 5.14 Total and Black Multiple Job Holders by Sex, 2006

(total number and percent of employed people aged 16 or older who hold more than one job, number and percent of blacks holding more than one job, and black share of total, by sex, 2006; numbers in thousands)

	total		black		
	number	percent of total employed	number	percent of employed blacks	share of total
Total multiple job holders	**7,576**	**5.2%**	**818**	**5.2%**	**10.8%**
Men	3,822	4.9	404	5.5	10.6
Women	3,753	5.6	415	4.9	11.1

Source: Bureau of Labor Statistics, 2006 Current Population Survey, Internet site http://www.bls.gov/cps/home.htm; calculations by New Strategist

Table 5.15 Union Representation of Total and Black Workers, 2006

(number of total and black employed wage and salary workers aged 16 or older, number and percent represented by unions, and median weekly earnings of those working full-time by union representation status, 2006; number in thousands)

	total	blacks
Total employed	**128,237**	**14,878**
Number represented by unions	16,860	2,391
Percent represented by unions	13.1%	16.1%
Median weekly earnings of full-time workers	**$671**	**$554**
Workers represented by unions	827	694
Workers not represented by unions	642	520

Note: Workers represented by unions are either members of a labor union or similar employee association or workers who report no union affiliation but whose jobs are covered by a union or an employee association contract.
Source: Bureau of Labor Statistics, 2006 Current Population Survey, Internet site http://www.bls.gov/cps/home.htm

Table 5.16 Journey to Work by Black Workers, 2005

(number and percent distribution of black workers aged 16 or older by principal means of transportation to work, travel time from home to work, distance from home to work, and departure time to work, 2005; numbers in thousands)

	number	percent distribution
Total black workers	**13,051**	**100.0%**
Principal means of transportation to work		
Drives self	9,796	75.1
Carpools	1,269	9.7
Uses mass transportation	1,353	10.4
Uses taxicab	47	0.4
Bicycles or ride motorcycle	26	0.2
Walks only	291	2.2
Uses other means	109	0.8
Works at home	160	1.2
Travel time from home to work		
Less than 15 minutes	3,498	26.8
15 to 29 minutes	4,577	35.1
30 to 44 minutes	2,295	17.6
45 to 59 minutes	901	6.9
1 hour or more	839	6.4
Works at home	160	1.2
No fixed place of work	781	6.0
Median travel time (minutes)	23	–
Distance from home to work		
Less than 1 mile	372	2.9
1 to 4 miles	2,503	19.2
5 to 9 miles	2,831	21.7
10 to 19 miles	3,520	27.0
20 to 29 miles	1,699	13.0
30 to 49 miles	981	7.5
50 miles or more	203	1.6
Works at home	160	1.2
No fixed place of work	781	6.0
Median distance (miles)	11	–
Departure time to work		
12:00 a.m. to 2:59 a.m.	85	0.7
3:00 a.m. to 5:59 a.m.	1,543	11.8
6:00 a.m. to 6:59 a.m.	2,248	17.2
7:00 a.m. to 7:29 a.m.	1,738	13.3
7:30 a.m. to 7:59 a.m.	1,361	10.4
8:00 a.m. to 8:29 a.m.	1,270	9.7
8:30 a.m. to 8:59 a.m.	538	4.1
9:00 a.m. to 9:59 a.m.	659	5.0
10:00 a.m. to 3:59 p.m.	1,607	12.3
4:00 p.m. to 11:59 p.m.	966	7.4

Note: Departure time numbers may not add to total because not reported is not shown and those who work at home are not included. "–" means not applicable.
Source: Bureau of the Census, American Housing Survey for the United States: 2005, Internet site http://www.census.gov/hhes/ www/housing/ahs/ahs05/ahs05.html; calculations by New Strategist

The Black Labor Force Will Grow by Nearly 3 Million

Blacks will account for 12 percent of the labor force in 2014.

The black labor force will grow by nearly 3 million workers between 2004 and 2014, a 17 percent rise. At the same time, the total labor force will increase by a smaller 10 percent. The labor force participation rate of black women is projected to rise by 0.8 percentage points between 2004 and 2014, to 62.3 percent. The rate for black men is projected to fall by 2.0 percentage points during those years, to 64.7 percent.

Blacks will account for a larger share of workers entering than exiting the labor force during the next decade. Between 2004 and 2014, blacks will account for 15 percent of labor force entrants and for a smaller 12 percent of those exiting the labor force. Consequently, the black share of the labor force will climb from 11 to 12 percent over those years.

■ Black women outnumber black men in the labor force, and the gap will grow slightly during the next decade.

The black labor force is growing faster than average

(projected percent change in total and black workers aged 16 or older, 2004–14)

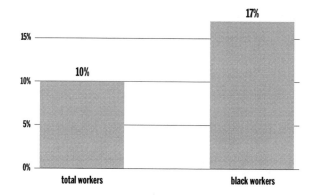

Table 5.17 Total and Black Labor Force Projections, 2004 and 2014

(projected number and percent of total people and blacks aged 16 or older in the civilian labor force by sex, 2004 and 2014; percent change in number and percentage point change in rate, 2004–14; numbers in thousands)

	2004	2014	percent change
NUMBER			
Total labor force	**147,401**	**162,100**	**10.0%**
Black labor force	16,638	19,433	16.8
Total men in labor force	**78,980**	**86,194**	**9.1**
Black men in labor force	7,773	9,075	16.8
Total women in labor force	**68,421**	**75,906**	**10.9**
Black women in labor force	8,865	10,358	16.8

	2004	2014	percentage point change
PARTICIPATION RATE			
Total people	**66.0%**	**65.6%**	**–0.4**
Total blacks	63.8	63.4	–0.4
Total men	**73.3**	**71.8**	**–1.5**
Black men	66.7	64.7	–2.0
Total women	**59.2**	**59.7**	**0.5**
Black women	61.5	62.3	0.8

Note: Blacks include only those who identified their race as black alone.
Source: Bureau of Labor Statistics, Employment Projections, Internet site http://www.bls.gov/emp/home.htm; calculations by New Strategist

Table 5.18 Total and Black Labor Force Entrants and Leavers, 2004 to 2014

(projected number and percent distribution of total people and blacks aged 16 or older in the civilian labor force in 2004 and 2014, and number and percent distribution of entrants, leavers, and stayers, 2004–14; numbers in thousands)

	2004 labor force	2004–2014 entrants	2004–2014 leavers	2004–2014 stayers	2014 labor force
NUMBER					
Total labor force	**147,401**	**39,048**	**24,352**	**123,049**	**162,100**
Black labor force	16,638	5,795	2,999	13,639	19,433
PERCENT DISTRIBUTION					
Total labor force	**100.0%**	**100.0%**	**100.0%**	**100.0%**	**100.0%**
Black labor force	11.3	14.8	12.3	11.1	12.0

Note: Blacks include only those who identify their race as black alone.
Source: Bureau of Labor Statistics, Employment Projections, Internet site http://www.bls.gov/emp/home.htm; calculations by New Strategist

6

Living Arrangements

■ Married couples head only 30 percent of black households—well below their 51 percent share of all households. Female-headed families are almost as numerous, accounting for 29 percent of total black households.

■ Black households are only slightly larger than the average household, with 2.64 people on average in black households versus 2.57 people in households nationally.

■ Black children are much less likely than the average American child to live with both parents. Among black children under age 18, only 35 percent live with mom and dad.

■ Fewer than half of blacks are married. Among black men, only 38 percent are currently married. The figure is a smaller 29 percent among black women.

Few Black Households Are Headed by Married Couples

Female-headed families are almost as numerous.

In 2006, the number of black households in the United States numbered more than 14 million and account for 13 percent of the total. Black householders have an average age of 46, a few years younger than the average of 49 for all householders.

Married couples head only 30 percent of black households—well below their 51 percent share of all households. Female-headed families are almost as numerous and account for 29 percent of the total, a much higher proportion than their 12 percent share of households nationally.

Female-headed families outnumber married couples among black householders under age 40. Between ages 40 and 74, married couples outnumber female-headed families. Among black householders aged 75 or older, women living alone are the most common household type and account for 44 percent of households in the age group.

■ Black household incomes will remain well below average as long as female-headed families account for so many black households.

Black households are diverse

(percent distribution of black households by household type, 2006)

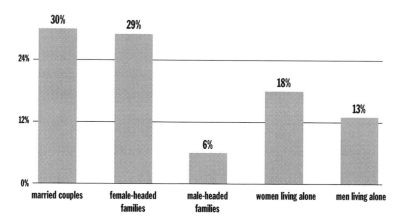

Table 6.1 Total and Black Households by Age of Householder, 2006

(number and percent distribution of total and black households, and black share of total, by age of householder, 2006, numbers in thousands)

| | total | | black | | |
	number	percent distribution	number	percent distribution	share of total
Total households	**114,384**	**100.0%**	**14,399**	**100.0%**	**12.6%**
Under age 25	6,795	5.9	1,206	8.4	17.7
Aged 25 to 29	9,223	8.1	1,372	9.5	14.9
Aged 30 to 34	9,896	8.7	1,481	10.3	15.0
Aged 35 to 39	10,976	9.6	1,497	10.4	13.6
Aged 40 to 44	12,040	10.5	1,632	11.3	13.6
Aged 45 to 49	12,470	10.9	1,677	11.6	13.4
Aged 50 to 54	11,262	9.8	1,350	9.4	12.0
Aged 55 to 64	18,264	16.0	2,049	14.2	11.2
Aged 65 to 74	11,687	10.2	1,198	8.3	10.3
Aged 75 or older	11,772	10.3	938	6.5	8.0
Avg. age of householder	49.2 yrs.	–	45.9 yrs.	–	–

Note: Blacks include those who identify themselves as being of the race alone or as being of the race in combination with other races. "–" means not applicable.
Source: Bureau of the Census, America's Families and Living Arrangements: 2006, Internet site http://www.census.gov/ population/www/socdemo/hh-fam/cps2006.html; calculations by New Strategist

Table 6.2 Total and Black Households by Household Type, 2006

(number and percent distribution of total and black households, and black share of total, by household type, 2006; numbers in thousands)

| | total | | black | | |
	number	percent distribution	number	percent distribution	share of total
Total households	**114,384**	**100.0%**	**14,399**	**100.0%**	**12.6%**
Family households	77,402	67.7	9,295	64.6	12.0
Married couples	58,179	50.9	4,249	29.5	7.3
Female hh, no spouse	14,093	12.3	4,215	29.3	29.9
Male hh, no spouse	5,130	4.5	831	5.8	16.2
Nonfamily households	36,982	32.3	5,104	35.4	13.8
Female householder	20,230	17.7	2,932	20.4	14.5
Living alone	17,392	15.2	2,597	18.0	14.9
Male householder	16,753	14.6	2,172	15.1	13.0
Living alone	13,061	11.4	1,807	12.5	13.8

Note: Blacks include those who identify themselves as being of the race alone or as being of the race in combination with other races.
Source: Bureau of the Census, America's Families and Living Arrangements: 2006, Internet site http://www.census.gov/ population/www/socdemo/hh-fam/cps2006.html; calculations by New Strategist

Table 6.3 Black Households by Age of Householder and Household Type, 2006

(number and percent distribution of black households by age of householder and household type, 2006; numbers in thousands)

| | | family households | | | nonfamily households | | | |
| | | | female hh, no spouse present | male hh, no spouse present | female householder | | male householder | |
	total	married couples			total	living alone	total	living alone
Total black households	**14,399**	**4,249**	**4,215**	**831**	**2,932**	**2,597**	**2,172**	**1,807**
Under age 25	1,206	114	448	145	282	196	217	147
Aged 25 to 29	1,372	266	530	121	217	168	237	178
Aged 30 to 34	1,481	431	568	81	178	148	223	161
Aged 35 to 39	1,497	489	564	74	191	158	180	149
Aged 40 to 44	1,632	575	548	94	183	165	232	208
Aged 45 to 49	1,677	623	447	95	229	203	283	231
Aged 50 to 54	1,350	468	317	58	317	286	190	164
Aged 55 to 64	2,049	742	397	82	539	506	290	262
Aged 65 to 74	1,198	374	213	50	370	359	191	180
Aged 75 or older	938	168	182	32	426	410	130	128

PERCENT DISTRIBUTION BY AGE

Total black households	**100.0%**	**100.0%**	**100.0%**	**100.0%**	**100.0%**	**100.0%**	**100.0%**	**100.0%**
Under age 25	8.4	2.7	10.6	17.4	9.6	7.5	10.0	8.1
Aged 25 to 29	9.5	6.3	12.6	14.6	7.4	6.5	10.9	9.9
Aged 30 to 34	10.3	10.1	13.5	9.7	6.1	5.7	10.3	8.9
Aged 35 to 39	10.4	11.5	13.4	8.9	6.5	6.1	8.3	8.2
Aged 40 to 44	11.3	13.5	13.0	11.3	6.2	6.4	10.7	11.5
Aged 45 to 49	11.6	14.7	10.6	11.4	7.8	7.8	13.0	12.8
Aged 50 to 54	9.4	11.0	7.5	7.0	10.8	11.0	8.7	9.1
Aged 55 to 64	14.2	17.5	9.4	9.9	18.4	19.5	13.4	14.5
Aged 65 to 74	8.3	8.8	5.1	6.0	12.6	13.8	8.8	10.0
Aged 75 or older	6.5	4.0	4.3	3.9	14.5	15.8	6.0	7.1

PERCENT DISTRIBUTION BY HOUSEHOLD TYPE

Total black households	**100.0%**	**29.5%**	**29.3%**	**5.8%**	**20.4%**	**18.0%**	**15.1%**	**12.5%**
Under age 25	100.0	9.5	37.1	12.0	23.4	16.3	18.0	12.2
Aged 25 to 29	100.0	19.4	38.6	8.8	15.8	12.2	17.3	13.0
Aged 30 to 34	100.0	29.1	38.4	5.5	12.0	10.0	15.1	10.9
Aged 35 to 39	100.0	32.7	37.7	4.9	12.8	10.6	12.0	10.0
Aged 40 to 44	100.0	35.2	33.6	5.8	11.2	10.1	14.2	12.7
Aged 45 to 49	100.0	37.1	26.7	5.7	13.7	12.1	16.9	13.8
Aged 50 to 54	100.0	34.7	23.5	4.3	23.5	21.2	14.1	12.1
Aged 55 to 64	100.0	36.2	19.4	4.0	26.3	24.7	14.2	12.8
Aged 65 to 74	100.0	31.2	17.8	4.2	30.9	30.0	15.9	15.0
Aged 75 or older	100.0	17.9	19.4	3.4	45.4	43.7	13.9	13.6

Note: Blacks include those who identify themselves as being of the race alone or as being of the race in combination with other races.
Source: Bureau of the Census, America's Families and Living Arrangements: 2006, Internet site http://www.census.gov/ population/www/socdemo/hh-fam/cps2006.html; calculations by New Strategist

People Who Live Alone Account for Nearly One-Third of Black Households

The percentage of blacks who live alone rises with age.

Black households are only slightly larger than the average household, with 2.64 people on average in black households versus 2.57 people in households nationally. Although black households are larger than average, blacks are more likely to live alone. Thirty-one percent of black households are people who live alone versus 27 percent of households nationally. Blacks account for 14 percent of the nation's single-person households.

The percentage of blacks who live alone rises from just 5 percent of those under age 25 to 40 percent of those aged 75 or older. Older women are far more likely than older men to live alone. Among blacks aged 75 or older, 29 percent of men and 46 percent of women live by themselves.

■ Because many blacks are not married, the percentage who live alone in old age may rise.

Most black households are home to only one or two people

(percent distribution of black households, by size, 2006)

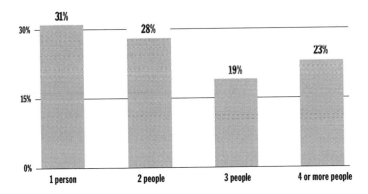

Table 6.4 Total and Black Households by Size, 2006

(number and percent distribution of total and black households, and black share of total, by size, 2006; numbers in thousands)

	total		black		
	number	percent distribution	number	percent distribution	share of total
Total households	**114,384**	**100.0%**	**14,399**	**100.0%**	**12.6%**
One person	30,453	26.6	4,404	30.6	14.5
Two people	37,775	33.0	4,060	28.2	10.7
Three people	18,924	16.5	2,689	18.7	14.2
Four people	15,998	14.0	1,770	12.3	11.1
Five people	7,306	6.4	887	6.2	12.1
Six people	2,562	2.2	385	2.7	15.0
Seven or more people	1,366	1.2	205	1.4	15.0
Average number of persons per household	2.57	–	2.64	–	–

Note: Blacks include those who identify themselves as being of the race alone or as being of the race in combination with other races. "–" means not applicable.
Source: Bureau of the Census, 2006 Current Population Survey Annual Social and Economic Supplement, Internet site http:// pubdb3.census.gov/macro/032006/hhinc/new01_007.htm; calculations by New Strategist

Table 6.5 Blacks Who Live Alone by Sex and Age, 2006

(total number of blacks aged 15 or older, number and percent living alone, and percent distribution of blacks living alone, by sex and age, 2006; numbers in thousands)

		living alone		
	total	number	percent distribution	share of total
Total blacks	**28,586**	**4,404**	**100.0%**	**15.4%**
Under age 25	6,449	343	7.8	5.3
Aged 25 to 34	5,366	655	14.9	12.2
Aged 35 to 44	5,505	679	15.4	12.3
Aged 45 to 54	5,081	884	20.1	17.4
Aged 55 to 64	3,132	768	17.4	24.5
Aged 65 to 74	1,723	539	12.2	31.3
Aged 75 or older	1,331	538	12.2	40.4
Black men	**12,959**	**1,807**	**100.0**	**13.9**
Under age 25	3,151	147	8.1	4.7
Aged 25 to 34	2,449	340	18.8	13.9
Aged 35 to 44	2,474	356	19.7	14.4
Aged 45 to 54	2,324	395	21.9	17.0
Aged 55 to 64	1,376	262	14.5	19.0
Aged 65 to 74	742	180	10.0	24.3
Aged 75 or older	443	128	7.1	28.9
Black women	**15,627**	**2,597**	**100.0**	**16.6**
Under age 25	3,298	196	7.5	5.9
Aged 25 to 34	2,917	315	12.1	10.8
Aged 35 to 44	3,031	323	12.4	10.7
Aged 45 to 54	2,757	489	18.8	17.7
Aged 55 to 64	1,756	506	19.5	28.8
Aged 65 to 74	981	359	13.8	36.6
Aged 75 or older	888	410	15.8	46.2

Note: Blacks include those who identify themselves as being of the race alone or as being of the race in combination with other races.
Source: Bureau of the Census, 2006 Current Population Survey Annual Social and Economic Supplement, Internet site http://pubdb3.census.gov/macro/032006/hhinc/new01_007.htm; calculations by New Strategist

Black Households Are More Likely to Include Children

Most black children live with only their mother.

Thirty-six percent of black households include children under age 18, a significantly greater proportion than the 32 percent share among all U.S. households. Among black households with children, married couples head only 41 percent of the total, while female-headed families head a larger 53 percent.

Black children are much less likely than the average American child to live with both parents. Among black children under age 18, only 35 percent live with mom and dad. Among all children, the figure is a much larger 67 percent.

Blacks are almost as likely as the average American to live in a family household—76 percent of blacks and 79 percent of all Americans aged 15 or older are part of a family household. But only 15 percent of blacks are married-couple householders versus 25 percent of the population as a whole.

■ The poverty rate among black children is well above average because most live in a female-headed family—the poorest family type.

Few black children live with both parents

(percent distribution of blacks under age 18 by living arrangement, 2006)

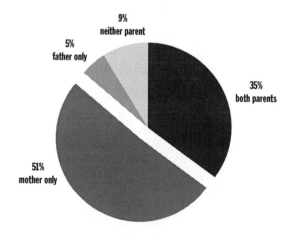

Table 6.6 Total and Black Households with Children by Age of Householder, 2006

(number of total and black households, number and percent with children under age 18, and number and percent distribution of total and black households with children under age 18 by age of householder and black share of total, 2006, numbers in thousands)

| | total | | black | | |
	number	percent distribution	number	percent distribution	share of total
TOTAL HOUSEHOLDS	**114,384**	**100.0%**	**14,399**	**100.0%**	**12.6%**
Total households with children under age 18	**36,466**	**31.9**	**5,138**	**35.7**	**14.1**
Total households with children under age 18	**36,466**	**100.0%**	**5,138**	**100.0%**	**14.1%**
Under age 25	2,003	5.5	450	8.8	22.5
Aged 25 to 29	4,242	11.6	757	14.7	17.8
Aged 30 to 34	6,128	16.8	929	18.1	15.2
Aged 35 to 39	7,309	20.0	982	19.1	13.4
Aged 40 to 44	7,353	20.2	909	17.7	12.4
Aged 45 to 49	5,359	14.7	605	11.8	11.3
Aged 50 to 54	2,642	7.2	294	5.7	11.1
Aged 55 to 64	1,225	3.4	173	3.4	14.1
Aged 65 or older	205	0.6	40	0.8	19.5

Note: Blacks include those who identify themselves as being of the race alone or as being of the race in combination with other races.
Source: Bureau of the Census, America's Families and Living Arrangements: 2006, Internet site http://www.census.gov/population/www/socdemo/hh-fam/cps2006.html; calculations by New Strategist

Table 6.7 Total and Black Households with Children by Type of Household, 2006

(number and percent distribution of total and black households with children under age 18, and black share of total, by type of household, 2006; numbers in thousands)

| | total | | black | | |
	number	percent distribution	number	percent distribution	share of total
Total households with children under age 18	**36,466**	**100.0%**	**5,138**	**100.0%**	**14.1%**
Married couples	25,982	71.2	2,100	40.9	8.1
Female-headed families	8,389	23.0	2,712	52.8	32.3
Male-headed families	2,095	5.7	327	6.4	15.6

Note: Blacks include those who identify themselves as being of the race alone or as being of the race in combination with other races.
Source: Bureau of the Census, America's Families and Living Arrangements: 2006, Internet site http://www.census.gov/population/www/socdemo/hh-fam/cps2006.html; calculations by New Strategist

Table 6.8 Black Households by Age of Householder, Type of Household, and Presence of Children, 2006

(number and percent distribution of black households by age of householder, type of household, and presence of own children under age 18, and average age of householder, 2006; numbers in thousands)

	total		married couples		female-headed families		male-headed families	
	total	with children	total	with children	total	with children	total	with children
Total black households	**14,399**	**5,138**	**4,249**	**2,100**	**4,215**	**2,712**	**831**	**327**
Under age 25	1,206	450	114	83	448	336	145	31
Aged 25 to 29	1,372	757	266	206	530	487	121	64
Aged 30 to 34	1,481	929	431	325	568	544	81	60
Aged 35 to 39	1,497	982	489	413	564	517	74	51
Aged 40 to 44	1,632	909	575	424	548	436	94	48
Aged 45 to 49	1,677	605	623	345	447	223	95	38
Aged 50 to 54	1,350	294	468	182	317	91	58	20
Aged 55 to 64	2,049	173	742	100	397	67	82	7
Aged 65 or older	2,136	40	542	22	395	12	82	7
Average age of householder	45.9 yrs.	37.1 yrs.	47.6 yrs.	39.9 yrs.	41.7 yrs.	35.0 yrs.	40.6 yrs.	36.6 yrs.

PERCENT OF HOUSEHOLDS WITH CHILDREN BY TYPE

	total		married couples		female-headed families		male-headed families	
Total black households	**100.0%**	**35.7%**	**100.0%**	**49.4%**	**100.0%**	**64.3%**	**100.0%**	**39.4%**
Under age 25	100.0	37.3	100.0	72.8	100.0	75.0	100.0	21.4
Aged 25 to 29	100.0	55.2	100.0	77.4	100.0	91.9	100.0	52.9
Aged 30 to 34	100.0	62.7	100.0	75.4	100.0	95.8	100.0	74.1
Aged 35 to 39	100.0	65.6	100.0	84.5	100.0	91.7	100.0	68.9
Aged 40 to 44	100.0	55.7	100.0	73.7	100.0	79.6	100.0	51.1
Aged 45 to 49	100.0	36.1	100.0	55.4	100.0	49.9	100.0	40.0
Aged 50 to 54	100.0	21.8	100.0	38.9	100.0	28.7	100.0	34.5
Aged 55 to 64	100.0	8.4	100.0	13.5	100.0	16.9	100.0	8.5
Aged 65 or older	100.0	1.9	100.0	4.1	100.0	3.0	100.0	8.5

Note: Blacks include those who identify themselves as being of the race alone or as being of the race in combination with other races.

Source: Bureau of the Census, America's Families and Living Arrangements: 2006, Internet site http://www.census.gov/population/www/socdemo/hh-fam/cps2006.html; calculations by New Strategist

Table 6.9 Living Arrangements of Total and Black Children, 2006

(number and percent distribution of total and black children under age 18, and black share of total, by living arrangement, 2006; numbers in thousands)

	total		black		
	number	percent distribution	number	percent distribution	share of total
Total children	**73,664**	**100.0%**	**12,261**	**100.0%**	**16.6%**
Living with both parents	49,661	67.4	4,338	35.4	8.7
Living with mother only	17,161	23.3	6,199	50.6	36.1
Never married	7,443	10.1	3,847	31.4	51.7
Married, spouse absent	789	1.1	228	1.9	28.9
Divorced or separated	8,308	11.3	1,966	16.0	23.7
Widowed	621	0.8	158	1.3	25.4
Living with father only	3,459	4.7	608	5.0	17.6
Never married	1,255	1.7	325	2.7	25.9
Married, spouse absent	243	0.3	32	0.3	13.2
Divorced or separated	1,823	2.5	222	1.8	12.2
Widowed	138	0.2	29	0.2	21.0
Living with neither parent	3,383	4.6	1,116	9.1	33.0

Note: Blacks include those who identify themselves as being of the race alone or as being of the race in combination with other races.
Source: Bureau of the Census, America's Families and Living Arrangements: 2006, Internet site http://www.census.gov/population/www/socdemo/hh-fam/cps2006.html; calculations by New Strategist

Table 6.10 Living Arrangements of Total and Black Adults, 2006

(number and percent distribution of total people and blacks aged 15 or older by living arrangement, and black share of total, 2006; numbers in thousands)

	total		black		
	number	percent distribution	number	percent distribution	share of total
Total people	**233,039**	**100.0%**	**28,554**	**100.0%**	**12.3%**
Living in family household	182,981	78.5	21,759	76.2	11.9
Living in nonfamily household	50,058	21.5	6,795	23.8	13.6
Householder	**114,384**	**49.1**	**14,399**	**50.4**	**12.6**
Family householder	77,402	33.2	9,295	32.6	12.0
Married couple householder	58,179	25.0	4,216	14.8	7.2
Other family householder	19,223	8.2	5,079	17.8	26.4
Nonfamily householder	36,982	15.9	5,104	17.9	13.8
Living alone	30,453	13.1	4,404	15.4	14.5
Living with nonrelatives	6,529	2.8	700	2.5	10.7
Not a householder	**118,655**	**50.9**	**14,155**	**49.6**	**11.9**
In family household	105,579	45.3	12,464	43.7	11.8
Spouse of householder	58,179	25.0	4,216	14.8	7.2
Child of householder	34,579	14.8	5,592	19.6	16.2
Other relative of householder	12,821	5.5	2,656	9.3	20.7
In nonfamily household	13,076	5.6	1,691	5.9	12.9

Note: Blacks include those who identify themselves as being of the race alone or as being of the race in combination with other races.

Source: Bureau of the Census, America's Families and Living Arrangements: 2006, Internet site http://www.census.gov/ population/www/socdemo/hh-fam/cps2006.html; calculations by New Strategist

Table 6.11 Living Arrangements of Black Adults by Sex, 2006

(number and percent distribution of blacks aged 15 or older by living arrangement and sex, 2006; numbers in thousands)

	men		women	
	number	percent distribution	number	percent distribution
Total blacks	**12,939**	**100.0%**	**15,615**	**100.0%**
Living in family household	9,712	75.1	12,046	77.1
Living in nonfamily household	3,226	24.9	3,569	22.9
Householder	**5,564**	**43.0**	**8,835**	**56.6**
Family householder	3,392	26.2	5,903	37.8
Married couple householder	2,561	19.8	1,688	10.8
Other family householder	831	6.4	4,215	27.0
Nonfamily householder	2,172	16.8	2,932	18.8
Living alone	1,807	14.0	2,597	16.6
Living with nonrelatives	365	2.8	335	2.1
Not a householder	**7,374**	**57.0**	**6,780**	**43.4**
In family household	6,321	48.9	6,143	39.3
Spouse of householder	2,561	19.8	1,688	10.8
Child of householder	3,139	24.3	2,453	15.7
Other relative of householder	621	4.8	2,002	12.8
In nonfamily household	1,054	8.1	637	4.1

Note: Blacks include those who identify themselves as being of the race alone or as being of the race in combination with other races.
Source: Bureau of the Census, America's Families and Living Arrangements: 2006, Internet site http://www.census.gov/population/www/socdemo/hh-fam/cps2006.html; calculations by New Strategist

The Largest Share of Blacks Has Never Married

Only 30 percent of blacks are currently married.

Fewer than half of blacks are married. Among black men, only 38 percent are currently married. The figure is a smaller 29 percent among black women. A larger share of both men and women has never married.

A study of martial history by the Census Bureau reveals that only 30 percent of black men and 24 percent of black women have married once and are still married. About one in five black men and women have ever divorced. The figure tops 30 percent among black men and women aged 50 to 69. Among black women aged 70 or older, 60 percent of women have been widowed.

■ Because many blacks are not married, and married couples are the most affluent household type, black household incomes are well below average.

Many blacks have yet to marry

(percent distribution of blacks aged 15 or older by marital history and sex, 2004)

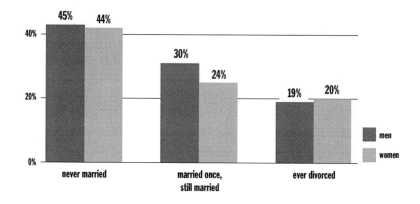

Table 6.12 Total and Black Marital Status, 2006

(number and percent distribution of total people and blacks aged 15 or older by marital status, and black share of total, 2006; numbers in thousands)

| | total | | black | | |
	number	percent distribution	number	percent distribution	share of total
Total people	**233,039**	**100.0%**	**28,554**	**100.0%**	**12.3%**
Never married	68,515	29.4	12,964	45.4	18.9
Married, spouse present	119,055	51.1	8,670	30.4	7.3
Married, spouse absent	3,785	1.6	544	1.9	14.4
Separated	4,963	2.1	1,388	4.9	28.0
Divorced	22,806	9.8	3,198	11.2	14.0
Widowed	13,914	6.0	1,790	6.3	12.9

Note: Blacks include those who identify themselves as being of the race alone or as being of the race in combination with other races.
Source: Bureau of the Census, America's Families and Living Arrangements: 2006, Internet site http://www.census.gov/population/www/socdemo/hh-fam/cps2006.html; calculations by New Strategist

Table 6.13 Marital Status of Black Men by Age, 2006

(number and percent distribution of black men aged 18 or older by age and current marital status, 2006; numbers in thousands)

	total	never married	married, spouse present	married, spouse absent	separated	divorced	widowed
Total black men	**11,841**	**5,060**	**4,444**	**266**	**539**	**1,196**	**336**
Aged 18 to 19	601	591	2	0	8	0	0
Aged 20 to 24	1,452	1,313	104	8	12	8	8
Aged 25 to 29	1,297	990	224	18	47	18	1
Aged 30 to 34	1,151	580	444	20	34	72	2
Aged 35 to 39	1,199	452	515	33	43	146	10
Aged 40 to 44	1,269	395	595	37	59	168	15
Aged 45 to 49	1,258	305	636	34	81	192	10
Aged 50 to 54	1,058	212	518	29	95	188	16
Aged 55 to 64	1,369	140	785	49	90	253	52
Aged 65 or older	1,185	82	620	38	72	150	223
Total black men	**100.0%**	**42.7%**	**37.5%**	**2.2%**	**4.6%**	**10.1%**	**2.8%**
Aged 18 to 19	100.0	98.3	0.3	0.0	1.3	0.0	0.0
Aged 20 to 24	100.0	90.4	7.2	0.6	0.8	0.6	0.6
Aged 25 to 29	100.0	76.3	17.3	1.4	3.6	1.4	0.1
Aged 30 to 34	100.0	50.4	38.6	1.7	3.0	6.3	0.2
Aged 35 to 39	100.0	37.7	43.0	2.8	3.6	12.2	0.8
Aged 40 to 44	100.0	31.1	46.9	2.9	4.6	13.2	1.2
Aged 45 to 49	100.0	24.2	50.6	2.7	6.4	15.3	0.8
Aged 50 to 54	100.0	20.0	49.0	2.7	9.0	17.8	1.5
Aged 55 to 64	100.0	10.2	57.3	3.6	6.6	18.5	3.8
Aged 65 or older	100.0	6.9	52.3	3.2	6.1	12.7	18.8

Note: Blacks include those who identify themselves as being of the race alone or as being of the race in combination with other races.
Source: Bureau of the Census, America's Families and Living Arrangements: 2006, Internet site http://www.census.gov/ population/www/socdemo/hh-fam/cps2006.html; calculations by New Strategist

Table 6.14 Marital Status of Black Women by Age, 2006

(number and percent distribution of black women aged 18 or older by age and current marital status, 2006; numbers in thousands)

	total	never married	married, spouse present	married, spouse absent	separated	divorced	widowed
Total black women	**14,521**	**5,755**	**4,220**	**275**	**833**	**1,989**	**1,449**
Aged 18 to 19	639	616	12	2	6	2	1
Aged 20 to 24	1,555	1,389	119	12	19	12	2
Aged 25 to 29	1,499	1,014	340	24	71	45	5
Aged 30 to 34	1,418	684	464	40	98	129	3
Aged 35 to 39	1,475	546	515	33	119	243	19
Aged 40 to 44	1,556	458	599	27	111	322	40
Aged 45 to 49	1,485	411	600	32	110	266	66
Aged 50 to 54	1,270	259	495	24	94	320	77
Aged 55 to 64	1,756	244	643	38	141	417	272
Aged 65 or older	1,868	133	431	43	64	234	964
Total black women	**100.0%**	**39.6%**	**29.1%**	**1.9%**	**5.7%**	**13.7%**	**10.0%**
Aged 18 to 19	100.0	96.4	1.9	0.3	0.9	0.3	0.2
Aged 20 to 24	100.0	89.3	7.7	0.8	1.2	0.8	0.1
Aged 25 to 29	100.0	67.6	22.7	1.6	4.7	3.0	0.3
Aged 30 to 34	100.0	48.2	32.7	2.8	6.9	9.1	0.2
Aged 35 to 39	100.0	37.0	34.9	2.2	8.1	16.5	1.3
Aged 40 to 44	100.0	29.4	38.5	1.7	7.1	20.7	2.6
Aged 45 to 49	100.0	27.7	40.4	2.2	7.4	17.9	4.4
Aged 50 to 54	100.0	20.4	39.0	1.9	7.4	25.2	6.1
Aged 55 to 64	100.0	13.9	36.6	2.2	8.0	23.7	15.5
Aged 65 or older	100.0	7.1	23.1	2.3	3.4	12.5	51.6

Note: Blacks include those who identify themselves as being of the race alone or as being of the race in combination with other races.
Source: Bureau of the Census, America's Families and Living Arrangements: 2006, Internet site http://www.census.gov/ population/www/socdemo/hh-fam/cps2006.html; calculations by New Strategist

Table 6.15 Marital History of Black Men by Age, 2004

(number of black men aged 15 or older and percent distribution by marital history and age, 2004; numbers in thousands)

	total	15–19	20–24	25–29	30–34	35–39	40–49	50–59	60–69	70+
Total black men, number	11,985	1,527	1,326	1,120	1,122	1,141	2,415	1,650	991	693
Total black men, percent	100.0%	100.0%	100.0%	100.0%	100.0%	100.0%	100.0%	100.0%	100.0%	100.0%
Never married	44.5	98.4	89.8	70.7	43.6	32.1	24.7	14.6	10.2	7.5
Ever married	55.5	1.6	10.2	29.3	56.4	67.9	75.3	85.4	89.8	92.5
Married once	44.0	1.6	10.2	28.3	52.4	58.2	62.0	60.0	62.5	63.9
Still married	30.1	1.3	10.2	24.1	39.0	43.7	39.3	39.4	41.1	35.6
Married twice	9.7	0.0	0.0	1.0	4.0	8.6	12.3	20.7	21.8	22.7
Still married	7.1	0.0	0.0	1.0	3.0	8.1	9.8	13.7	13.5	16.3
Married three or more times	1.7	0.0	0.0	0.0	0.0	1.0	1.0	4.7	5.5	5.9
Still married	1.3	0.0	0.0	0.0	0.0	1.0	1.0	3.8	3.5	2.9
Ever divorced	19.1	0.1	0.0	2.6	11.9	17.9	29.7	39.2	36.0	28.1
Currently divorced	10.4	0.1	0.0	1.6	8.9	8.9	18.4	20.6	16.6	11.5
Ever widowed	3.6	0.0	0.0	0.0	0.2	0.3	1.6	3.9	10.6	31.0
Currently widowed	2.6	0.0	0.0	0.0	0.2	0.2	1.4	2.0	8.3	22.9

Note: Blacks are those identifying themselves as being of the race alone.
Source: Bureau of the Census, Number, Timing, and Duration of Marriages and Divorces: 2004, Detailed Tables; Internet site http://www.census.gov/population/www/socdemo/marr-div/2004detailed_tables.html

Table 6.16 Marital History of Black Women by Age, 2004

(number of black women aged 15 or older and percent distribution by marital history and age, 2004; numbers in thousands)

	total	15–19	20–24	25–29	30–34	35–39	40–49	50–59	60–69	70+
Total black women, number	14,735	1,555	1,495	1,371	1,407	1,431	2,937	2,135	1,227	1,177
Total black women, percent	100.0%	100.0%	100.0%	100.0%	100.0%	100.0%	100.0%	100.0%	100.0%	100.0%
Never married	43.5	98.1	88.1	66.3	47.0	39.0	29.4	17.5	8.7	8.4
Ever married	56.5	1.9	11.9	33.7	53.0	61.0	70.6	82.5	91.3	91.6
Married once	45.5	1.9	11.8	32.3	49.2	50.9	57.0	60.0	70.7	69.7
Still married	24.3	1.8	10.2	24.4	36.3	32.8	34.1	27.4	26.9	14.5
Married twice	9.6	0.0	0.1	1.4	3.3	9.4	12.1	19.6	17.6	18.6
Still married	5.0	0.0	0.1	1.4	2.5	7.8	6.4	11.1	7.0	5.1
Married three or more times	1.3	0.0	0.0	0.0	0.5	0.7	1.6	2.9	3.0	3.3
Still married	0.7	0.0	0.0	0.0	0.2	0.4	0.9	2.0	1.0	1.3
Ever divorced	19.6	0.0	0.9	3.7	10.6	22.6	27.5	39.4	34.0	24.4
Currently divorced	12.2	0.0	0.8	2.5	7.5	13.0	18.6	24.5	21.8	10.6
Ever widowed	10.1	0.1	0.0	0.8	1.4	0.9	3.0	12.5	30.6	60.0
Currently widowed	9.2	0.1	0.0	0.5	1.4	0.7	2.5	10.8	27.7	57.6

Note: Blacks are those identifying themselves as being of the race alone.
Source: Bureau of the Census, Number, Timing, and Duration of Marriages and Divorces: 2004, Detailed Tables; Internet site http://www.census.gov/population/www/socdemo/marr-div/2004detailed_tables.html

7

Population

■ The number of blacks in the U.S. population grew 7 percent between 2000 and 2006, much less than the growth rate of Asians and Hispanics. But the black growth rate greatly exceeded the small 1.5 percent increase for non-Hispanic whites.

■ The nation's 40 million blacks account for more than one in ten Americans. Seventeen percent of Americans under age 20 are black, a share that falls to just 9 percent of people aged 65 or older.

■ The 54 percent majority of blacks live in the South, where they account for a substantial 20 percent of the population. Although New York is the state with the largest black population, only 9 percent of blacks live there.

The Black Population Is Growing Slowly

The growth rate of the black population is well below that of Asians or Hispanics.

The number of blacks in the U.S. population grew 7 percent between 2000 and 2006, much less than the 23 to 24 percent growth rate for Asians and Hispanics. But the black growth rate greatly exceeded the small 1.5 percent increase for non-Hispanic whites.

The count of blacks ranges from 38 million who identify themselves as black and no other race (called black alone) to 40 million who identify themselves as black alone or black in combination with other races. Beginning in 2000, Americans could identify themselves as more than one race, increasing the complexity of racial identification. Adding to the complexity is the fact that Hispanic is an ethnic identity rather than a race, meaning blacks can also be Hispanic. Five percent of the nation's blacks also identify themselves as Hispanic.

■ Unlike Hispanics or Asians, most of whom live in only a few states, blacks are an important segment of the population throughout the country. This relatively even distribution adds to their cultural influence and political power.

Blacks are outnumbered by Hispanics

(population by race and Hispanic origin, 2006; numbers in millions; American Indians, Asians, and blacks are those who identify themselves as being of the race alone)

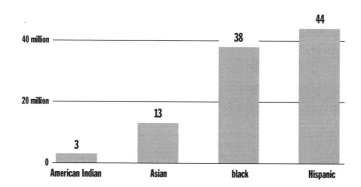

Table 7.1 Population by Race and Hispanic Origin, 2000 and 2006

(number and percent distribution of people by race and Hispanic origin, 2000 and 2006, and percent change in number, 2000–06; numbers in thousands)

	2006 number	2006 percent distribution	2000 number	2000 percent distribution	percent change in number 2000–06
RACE					
Total population	299,398,484	100.0%	282,216,952	100.0%	6.1%
One race	294,679,815	98.4	278,288,359	98.6	5.9
American Indian	2,902,851	1.0	2,673,624	0.9	8.6
Asian	13,159,343	4.4	10,697,440	3.8	23.0
Black	38,342,549	12.8	35,814,967	12.7	7.1
Native Hawaiian	528,818	0.2	465,124	0.2	13.7
White	239,746,254	80.1	228,637,204	81.0	4.9
Two or more races	4,718,669	1.6	3,928,593	1.4	20.1
HISPANIC ORIGIN					
Total population	299,398,484	100.0	282,216,952	100.0	6.1
Hispanic	44,321,038	14.8	35,659,724	12.6	24.3
Non-Hispanic	255,077,446	85.2	246,557,228	87.4	3.5
Non-Hispanic white	198,744,494	66.4	195,774,391	69.4	1.5

Note: Native Hawaiians include other Pacific Islanders. Hispanics may be of any race.
Source: Bureau of the Census, National Population Estimates, Internet site http://www.census.gov/popest/national/index.html; calculations by New Strategist

Table 7.2 Blacks by Racial Identification, 2000 and 2006

(total number of people, and number and percent distribution of blacks by racial identification, 2000 and 2006 percent change, 2000–06)

	2006 number	2006 percent distribution	2000 number	2000 percent distribution	percent change 2000–06
Total people	299,398,484	100.0%	282,216,952	100.0%	6.1%
Black alone or in combination with one or more other races	40,240,898	13.4	37,233,421	13.2	8.1
Black alone	38,342,549	12.8	35,814,967	12.7	7.1
Black in combination	1,898,349	0.6	1,418,454	0.5	33.8

Source: Bureau of the Census, National Population Estimates, Internet site http://www.census.gov/popest/national/asrh/NC-EST2006-srh.html; calculations by New Strategist

Table 7.3 Blacks by Hispanic Origin, 2006

(number and percent distribution of blacks by Hispanic origin and racial identifcation, 2006)

	black alone or in combination		black alone	
	number	percent distribution	number	percent distribution
Total blacks	**40,240,898**	**100.0%**	**38,342,549**	**100.0%**
Not Hispanic	38,294,161	95.2	36,689,680	95.7
Hispanic	1,946,737	4.8	1,652,869	4.3

Source: Bureau of the Census, National Population Estimates, Internet site http://www.census.gov/popest/national/asrh/NC-EST2006-srh.html; calculations by New Strategist

Thirteen Percent of Americans Are Black

The black population grew 8 percent between 2000 and 2006.

The nation's 40 million blacks account for more than 1 in 10 Americans. The black share of the population is largest among children and young adults. Seventeen percent of Americans under age 20 are black. The share falls with age to just 9 percent of people aged 65 or older.

The black population, like the non-Hispanic white population, has been affected by baby boom and baby bust over the decades. Consequently, some age groups are growing while others are shrinking. The number of blacks aged 55 to 59 expanded by 42 percent between 2000 and 2006 as boomers entered the age group. But the number of blacks aged 35 to 39 fell 5 percent as the small generation X aged into its late thirties.

Black females outnumber black males beginning in the 25-to-29 age group. By age 65 or older, only 62 black males are left for every 100 black females.

■ The diversity of older Americans will increase greatly as today's young adults become the nation's elderly.

The black share of the population decreases with age

(black share of the total population for selected age groups, 2006)

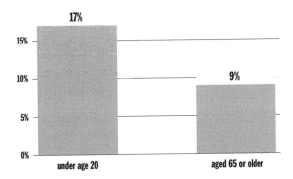

Table 7.4 Black Share of Total Population by Age, 2006

(total number of people, number and percent distribution of blacks, and black share of total, by age, 2006)

	total	black number	black percent distribution	black share of total
Total people	**299,398,484**	**40,240,898**	**100.0%**	**13.4%**
Under age 5	20,417,636	3,470,662	8.6	17.0
Aged 5 to 9	19,709,887	3,301,967	8.2	16.8
Aged 10 to 14	20,627,397	3,508,741	8.7	17.0
Aged 15 to 19	21,324,186	3,553,270	8.8	16.7
Aged 20 to 24	21,111,240	3,240,737	8.1	15.4
Aged 25 to 29	20,709,480	3,014,732	7.5	14.6
Aged 30 to 34	19,706,499	2,710,943	6.7	13.8
Aged 35 to 39	21,185,785	2,813,164	7.0	13.3
Aged 40 to 44	22,481,165	2,939,909	7.3	13.1
Aged 45 to 49	22,797,569	2,838,933	7.1	12.5
Aged 50 to 54	20,480,605	2,384,972	5.9	11.6
Aged 55 to 59	18,224,445	1,940,678	4.8	10.6
Aged 60 to 64	13,362,238	1,299,383	3.2	9.7
Aged 65 to 69	10,375,554	1,009,580	2.5	9.7
Aged 70 to 74	8,541,290	801,880	2.0	9.4
Aged 75 to 79	7,381,027	599,470	1.5	8.1
Aged 80 to 84	5,665,664	424,322	1.1	7.5
Aged 85 or older	5,296,817	387,555	1.0	7.3
Aged 18 to 24	29,454,784	4,590,762	11.4	15.6
Aged 18 or older	225,662,922	27,756,283	69.0	12.3
Aged 65 or older	37,260,352	3,222,807	8.0	8.6
Median age (years)	36.4	30.1	–	–

Note: Blacks are those who identify themselves as being of the race alone or as being of the race in combination with one or more other races. "–" means not applicable.
Source: Bureau of the Census, National Population Estimates, Internet site http://www.census.gov/popest/national/asrh/ NC-EST2006-asrh.html; calculations by New Strategist

Table 7.5 Blacks by Age, 2000 and 2006

(number of blacks by age, 2000 and 2006; percent change, 2000–06)

	2006	2000	percent change
Total blacks	**40,240,898**	**37,233,421**	**8.1%**
Under age 5	3,470,662	3,242,170	7.0
Aged 5 to 9	3,301,967	3,547,396	−6.9
Aged 10 to 14	3,508,741	3,423,039	2.5
Aged 15 to 19	3,553,270	3,165,108	12.3
Aged 20 to 24	3,240,737	2,861,079	13.3
Aged 25 to 29	3,014,732	2,720,841	10.8
Aged 30 to 34	2,710,943	2,777,611	−2.4
Aged 35 to 39	2,813,164	2,970,829	−5.3
Aged 40 to 44	2,939,909	2,842,171	3.4
Aged 45 to 49	2,838,933	2,390,813	18.7
Aged 50 to 54	2,384,972	1,908,280	25.0
Aged 55 to 59	1,940,678	1,363,040	42.4
Aged 60 to 64	1,299,383	1,104,101	17.7
Aged 65 to 69	1,009,580	911,855	10.7
Aged 70 to 74	801,880	752,932	6.5
Aged 75 to 79	599,470	569,465	5.3
Aged 80 to 84	424,322	358,438	18.4
Aged 85 or older	387,555	324,253	19.5
Aged 18 to 24	4,590,762	4,126,555	11.2
Aged 18 or older	27,756,283	25,121,184	10.5
Aged 65 or older	3,222,807	2,916,943	10.5

Note: Blacks are those who identify themselves as being of the race alone or as being of the race in combination with one or more other races.
Source: Bureau of the Census, National Population Estimates, Internet site http://www.census.gov/popest/national/asrh/ NC-EST2006-asrh.html; calculations by New Strategist

Table 7.6 Blacks by Age and Sex, 2006

(number of blacks by age and sex, and sex ratio by age, 2006)

	total	females	males	sex ratio
Total blacks	**40,240,898**	**21,030,677**	**19,210,221**	**91**
Under age 5	3,470,662	1,706,545	1,764,117	103
Aged 5 to 9	3,301,967	1,627,339	1,674,628	103
Aged 10 to 14	3,508,741	1,729,382	1,779,359	103
Aged 15 to 19	3,553,270	1,754,333	1,798,937	103
Aged 20 to 24	3,240,737	1,601,729	1,639,008	102
Aged 25 to 29	3,014,732	1,547,831	1,466,901	95
Aged 30 to 34	2,710,943	1,423,637	1,287,306	90
Aged 35 to 39	2,813,164	1,487,231	1,325,933	89
Aged 40 to 44	2,939,909	1,563,041	1,376,868	88
Aged 45 to 49	2,838,933	1,518,571	1,320,362	87
Aged 50 to 54	2,384,972	1,292,541	1,092,431	85
Aged 55 to 59	1,940,678	1,064,129	876,549	82
Aged 60 to 64	1,299,383	730,440	568,943	78
Aged 65 to 69	1,009,580	580,738	428,842	74
Aged 70 to 74	801,880	475,417	326,463	69
Aged 75 to 79	599,470	375,062	224,408	60
Aged 80 to 84	424,322	277,707	146,615	53
Aged 85 or older	387,555	275,004	112,551	41
Aged 18 to 24	4,590,762	2,269,569	2,321,193	102
Aged 18 or older	27,756,283	14,880,918	12,875,365	87
Aged 65 or older	3,222,807	1,983,928	1,238,879	62

Note: Blacks are those who identify themselves as being of the race alone or as being of the race in combination with one or more other races. The sex ratio is the number of males divided by the number of females multiplied by 100.
Source: Bureau of the Census, National Population Estimates, Internet site http://www.census.gov/popest/national/asrh/ NC-EST2006-asrh.html; calculations by New Strategist

Most Blacks Live in the South

Blacks account for one in five Southerners.

The 54 percent majority of blacks live in the South, where they account for a substantial 20 percent of the population. The Northeast and Midwest are each home to 18 percent of the black population, while only 10 percent of blacks live in the West.

Although most blacks live in the South, no single state is home to more than 9 percent of the black population. New York has the largest black population among the 50 states, but only 9 percent of blacks live in New York state. Blacks account for the largest share of state populations in the South. They are more than 30 percent of the populations of Georgia, Louisiana, Maryland, and Mississippi.

Seven metropolitan areas are home to more than 1 million blacks: Atlanta, Chicago, Detroit, Miami, New York, Philadelphia, and Washington, D.C. In 10 metropolitan areas, blacks account for more than 40 percent of the population: Albany, Georgia; Columbus, Georgia–Alabama; Florence, South Carolina; Jackson, Mississippi; Macon, Georgia; Memphis, Tennessee–Mississippi–Arkansas; Montgomery, Alabama; Pine Bluff, Arkansas; Rocky Mount, North Carolina; and Sumter, South Carolina.

■ The number of blacks in Louisiana fell 6 percent between 2000 and 2006 because of the effects of Hurricane Katrina on the New Orleans metropolitan area and other parts of the state.

Few blacks live in the West

(percent distribution of blacks by region, 2006)

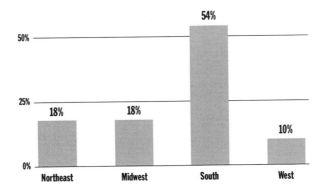

Table 7.7 Total and Black Population by Region, 2006

(total number of people, number and percent distribution of blacks, and black share of total, by region, 2006)

	total	black		
		number	percent distribution	share of total
Total people	**299,398,484**	**40,240,898**	**100.0%**	**13.4%**
Northeast	54,741,353	7,249,439	18.0	13.2
Midwest	66,217,736	7,292,743	18.1	11.0
South	109,083,752	21,697,542	53.9	19.9
West	69,355,643	4,001,174	9.9	5.8

Note: Blacks are those who identify themselves as being of the race alone or as being of the race in combination with one or more other races.
Source: Bureau of the Census, State Population Estimates, Internet site http://www.census.gov/popest/states/asrh/ SC-EST2006-04.html; calculations by New Strategist

Table 7.8 Blacks by Region, 2000 and 2006

(number of blacks by region, 2000 and 2006; percent change, 2000–06)

	2006	2000	percent change
Total blacks	**40,240,898**	**36,419,434**	**10.5%**
Northeast	7,249,439	6,556,909	10.6
Midwest	7,292,743	6,838,669	6.6
South	21,697,542	19,528,231	11.1
West	4,001,174	3,495,625	14.5

Note: Blacks are those who identify themselves as being of the race alone or as being of the race in combination with one or more other races. Total number of blacks in 2000 differs from the total in previous tables of this chapter because these are census counts from April 1, 2000.
Source: Bureau of the Census, 2000 Census, The Black Population 2000, Internet site http://www.census.gov/population/www/ cen2000/briefs.html; and State Population Estimates, Internet site http://www.census.gov/popest/states/asrh/SC-EST2006-04.html; calculations by New Strategist

Table 7.9 Total and Black Population by State, 2006

(total number of people, number and percent distribution of blacks, and black share of total, by state, 2006)

	total	black number	black percent distribution	black share of total
Total people	299,398,484	40,240,898	100.0%	13.4%
Alabama	4,599,030	1,228,083	3.1	26.7
Alaska	670,053	33,120	0.1	4.9
Arizona	6,166,318	269,202	0.7	4.4
Arkansas	2,810,872	453,662	1.1	16.1
California	36,457,549	2,706,205	6.7	7.4
Colorado	4,753,377	227,497	0.6	4.8
Connecticut	3,504,809	385,748	1.0	11.0
Delaware	853,476	185,493	0.5	21.7
District of Columbia	581,530	334,267	0.8	57.5
Florida	18,089,888	2,971,181	7.4	16.4
Georgia	9,363,941	2,854,474	7.1	30.5
Hawaii	1,285,498	44,669	0.1	3.5
Idaho	1,466,465	13,855	0.0	0.9
Illinois	12,831,970	1,997,141	5.0	15.6
Indiana	6,313,520	599,813	1.5	9.5
Iowa	2,982,085	88,242	0.2	3.0
Kansas	2,764,075	185,582	0.5	6.7
Kentucky	4,206,074	337,894	0.8	8.0
Louisiana	4,287,768	1,375,461	3.4	32.1
Maine	1,321,574	14,864	0.0	1.1
Maryland	5,615,727	1,705,728	4.2	30.4
Massachusetts	6,437,193	491,336	1.2	7.6
Michigan	10,095,643	1,518,332	3.8	15.0
Minnesota	5,167,101	268,943	0.7	5.2
Mississippi	2,910,540	1,091,110	2.7	37.5
Missouri	5,842,713	706,546	1.8	12.1
Montana	944,632	6,999	0.0	0.7
Nebraska	1,768,331	87,462	0.2	4.9
Nevada	2,495,529	217,490	0.5	8.7
New Hampshire	1,314,895	18,336	0.0	1.4
New Jersey	8,724,560	1,326,160	3.3	15.2
New Mexico	1,954,599	58,766	0.1	3.0
New York	19,306,183	3,519,135	8.7	18.2
North Carolina	8,856,505	1,972,357	4.9	22.3
North Dakota	635,867	7,570	0.0	1.2
Ohio	11,478,006	1,460,770	3.6	12.7
Oklahoma	3,579,212	311,770	0.8	8.7
Oregon	3,700,758	91,260	0.2	2.5
Pennsylvania	12,440,621	1,410,946	3.5	11.3
Rhode Island	1,067,610	76,759	0.2	7.2
South Carolina	4,321,249	1,274,166	3.2	29.5
South Dakota	781,919	10,702	0.0	1.4
Tennessee	6,038,803	1,046,674	2.6	17.3
Texas	23,507,783	2,908,563	7.2	12.4
Utah	2,550,063	36,674	0.1	1.4
Vermont	623,908	6,155	0.0	1.0
Virginia	7,642,884	1,579,160	3.9	20.7
Washington	6,395,798	288,828	0.7	4.5
West Virginia	1,818,470	67,499	0.2	3.7
Wisconsin	5,556,506	361,640	0.9	6.5
Wyoming	515,004	6,609	0.0	1.3

Note: Blacks are those who identify themselves as being of the race alone or as being of the race in combination with one or more other races.
Source: Bureau of the Census, State Population Estimates, Internet site http://www.census.gov/popest/states/asrh/
SC-EST2006-04.html; calculations by New Strategist

Table 7.10 Blacks by State, 2000 and 2006

(number of blacks by state, 2000 and 2006; percent change, 2000–06)

	2006	2000	percent change
Total blacks	**40,240,898**	**36,419,434**	**10.5%**
Alabama	1,228,083	1,168,998	5.1
Alaska	33,120	27,147	22.0
Arizona	269,202	185,599	45.0
Arkansas	453,662	427,152	6.2
California	2,706,205	2,513,041	7.7
Colorado	227,497	190,717	19.3
Connecticut	385,748	339,078	13.8
Delaware	185,493	157,152	18.0
District of Columbia	334,267	350,455	–4.6
Florida	2,971,181	2,471,730	20.2
Georgia	2,854,474	2,393,425	19.3
Hawaii	44,669	33,343	34.0
Idaho	13,855	8,127	70.5
Illinois	1,997,141	1,937,671	3.1
Indiana	599,813	538,015	11.5
Iowa	88,242	72,512	21.7
Kansas	185,582	170,610	8.8
Kentucky	337,894	311,878	8.3
Louisiana	1,375,461	1,468,317	–6.3
Maine	14,864	9,553	55.6
Maryland	1,705,728	1,525,036	11.8
Massachusetts	491,336	398,479	23.3
Michigan	1,518,332	1,474,613	3.0
Minnesota	268,943	202,972	32.5
Mississippi	1,091,110	1,041,708	4.7
Missouri	706,546	655,377	7.8
Montana	6,999	4,441	57.6
Nebraska	87,462	75,833	15.3
Nevada	217,490	150,508	44.5
New Hampshire	18,336	12,218	50.1
New Jersey	1,326,160	1,211,750	9.4
New Mexico	58,766	42,412	38.6
New York	3,519,135	3,234,165	8.8
North Carolina	1,972,357	1,776,283	11.0
North Dakota	7,570	5,372	40.9
Ohio	1,460,770	1,372,501	6.4
Oklahoma	311,770	284,766	9.5
Oregon	91,260	72,647	25.6
Pennsylvania	1,410,946	1,289,123	9.5
Rhode Island	76,759	58,051	32.2
South Carolina	1,274,166	1,200,901	6.1
South Dakota	10,702	6,687	60.0
Tennessee	1,046,674	953,349	9.8
Texas	2,908,563	2,493,057	16.7
Utah	36,674	24,382	50.4
Vermont	6,155	4,492	37.0
Virginia	1,579,160	1,441,207	9.6
Washington	288,828	238,398	21.2
West Virginia	67,499	62,817	7.5
Wisconsin	361,640	326,506	10.8
Wyoming	6,609	4,863	35.9

Note: Blacks are those who identify themselves as being of the race alone or as being of the race in combination with one or more other races. Total number of blacks in 2000 differs from the total in previous tables of this chapter because these are census counts from April 1, 2000.
Source: Bureau of the Census, 2000 Census, The Black Population 2000, Internet site http://www.census.gov/population/www/ cen2000/briefs.html; and State Population Estimates, Internet site http://www.census.gov/popest/states/asrh/SC-EST2006-04.html; calculations by New Strategist

Table 7.11 Total and Black Population by Metropolitan Area, 2005

(total number of people, number of blacks, and black share of total, for selected metropolitan areas, 2005)

	total population	black number	black share of total
Abilene, TX	146,427	9,357	6.4%
Akron, OH	684,459	83,253	12.2
Albany, GA	158,772	76,381	48.1
Albany–Schenectady–Troy, NY	816,044	60,124	7.4
Albuquerque, NM	783,920	24,171	3.1
Alexandria, LA	142,353	40,525	28.5
Allentown–Bethlehem–Easton, PA–NJ	766,822	31,945	4.2
Altoona, PA	122,717	1,629	1.3
Amarillo, TX	227,799	12,035	5.3
Ames, IA	70,480	1,402	2.0
Anchorage, AK	341,282	20,029	5.9
Anderson, IN	125,161	10,276	8.2
Anderson, SC	172,748	29,024	16.8
Ann Arbor, MI	319,791	40,878	12.8
Anniston–Oxford, AL	109,762	21,628	19.7
Appleton, WI	211,469	1,752	0.8
Asheville, NC	379,808	19,715	5.2
Athens–Clarke County, GA	167,582	33,928	20.2
Atlanta–Sandy Springs–Marietta, GA	4,828,838	1,502,745	31.1
Atlantic City, NJ	264,403	45,441	17.2
Auburn–Opelika, AL	118,664	27,997	23.6
Augusta–Richmond County, GA–SC	508,401	185,038	36.4
Austin–Round Rock, TX	1,406,364	106,330	7.6
Bakersfield, CA	724,206	40,738	5.6
Baltimore–Towson, MD	2,583,923	743,133	28.8
Bangor, ME	140,625	993	0.7
Barnstable Town, MA	220,838	4,972	2.3
Baton Rouge, LA	706,909	240,828	34.1
Battle Creek, MI	134,628	15,727	11.7
Bay City, MI	107,256	1,956	1.8
Beaumont–Port Arthur, TX	366,855	92,572	25.2
Bellingham, WA	178,425	2,276	1.3
Bend, OR	140,161	1,434	1.0
Billings, MT	143,977	1,066	0.7
Binghamton, NY	237,626	8,739	3.7
Birmingham–Hoover, AL	1,069,498	299,191	28.0
Bismarck, ND	96,068	551	0.6
Blacksburg–Christiansburg–Radford, VA	140,200	7,281	5.2
Bloomington, IN	161,204	3,636	2.3
Bloomington–Normal, IL	146,894	9,105	6.2
Boise City–Nampa, ID	530,359	4,764	0.9
Boston–Cambridge–Quincy, MA–NH	4,270,631	302,758	7.1
Boulder, CO	271,934	3,319	1.2
Bowling Green, KY	105,848	7,850	7.4

(continued)

	total population	black number	share of total
Bremerton–Silverdale, WA	231,902	7,539	3.3%
Bridgeport–Stamford–Norwalk, CT	884,050	93,460	10.6
Brownsville–Harlingen, TX	374,081	1,644	0.4
Brunswick, GA	92,964	24,023	25.8
Buffalo–Niagara Falls, NY	1,111,554	138,850	12.5
Burlington, NC	136,552	26,243	19.2
Burlington–South Burlington, VT	197,382	2,562	1.3
Canton–Massillon, OH	401,032	30,778	7.7
Cape Coral–Fort Myers, FL	539,097	40,949	7.6
Casper, WY	68,203	934	1.4
Cedar Rapids, IA	239,343	7,830	3.3
Champaign–Urbana, IL	198,091	21,000	10.6
Charleston, WV	301,716	15,932	5.3
Charleston–North Charleston, SC	575,297	174,565	30.3
Charlotte–Gastonia–Concord, NC–SC	1,491,330	352,030	23.6
Charlottesville, VA	177,569	24,928	14.0
Chattanooga, TN–GA	476,969	68,427	14.3
Cheyenne, WY	81,793	2,375	2.9
Chicago–Naperville–Joliet, IL–IN–WI	9,272,117	1,716,689	18.5
Chico, CA	207,937	4,559	2.2
Cincinnati–Middletown, OH–KY–IN	2,026,216	248,023	12.2
Clarksville, TN–KY	229,822	47,256	20.6
Cleveland, TN	104,259	4,013	3.8
Cleveland–Elyria–Mentor, OH	2,082,379	424,156	20.4
Coeur d'Alene, ID	126,079	403	0.3
College Station–Bryan, TX	181,896	22,870	12.6
Colorado Springs, CO	571,244	41,362	7.2
Columbia, MO	143,221	13,261	9.3
Columbia, SC	652,063	216,186	33.2
Columbus, GA–AL	274,086	118,449	43.2
Columbus, IN	72,650	1,665	2.3
Columbus, OH	1,665,428	246,829	14.8
Corpus Christi, TX	405,416	16,098	4.0
Corvallis, OR	74,075	1,043	1.4
Cumberland, MD–WV	93,637	2,861	3.1
Dallas–Fort Worth–Arlington, TX	5,727,391	821,443	14.3
Dalton, GA	130,351	3,290	2.5
Danville, IL	79,235	8,161	10.3
Danville, VA	106,853	34,926	32.7
Davenport–Moline–Rock Island, IA–IL	367,050	24,083	6.6
Dayton, OH	817,340	125,616	15.4
Decatur, AL	146,379	17,987	12.3
Decatur, IL	106,433	16,775	15.8
Deltona–Daytona Beach–Ormond Beach, FL	475,189	47,554	10.0
Denver–Aurora, CO	2,327,901	139,787	6.0
Des Moines, IA	511,565	22,158	4.3
Detroit–Warren–Livonia, MI	4,428,941	1,038,638	23.5
Dothan, AL	134,993	32,022	23.7

(continued)

	total population	black	
		number	share of total
Dover, DE	140,205	30,626	21.8%
Dubuque, IA	86,626	1,382	1.6
Duluth, MN–WI	261,976	2,944	1.1
Durham, NC	434,878	122,804	28.2
Eau Claire, WI	146,010	924	0.6
El Centro, CA	144,523	3,222	2.2
Elizabethtown, KY	105,570	10,613	10.1
Elkhart–Goshen, IN	192,562	11,489	6.0
Elmira, NY	84,117	4,154	4.9
El Paso, TX	708,319	22,328	3.2
Erie, PA	266,662	17,136	6.4
Eugene–Springfield, OR	327,762	4,965	1.5
Evansville, IN–KY	340,915	21,457	6.3
Fairbanks, AK	83,656	5,455	6.5
Fargo, ND–MN	175,563	3,233	1.8
Farmington, NM	124,994	1,087	0.9
Fayetteville, NC	324,076	124,202	38.3
Fayetteville–Springdale–Rogers, AR–MO	395,592	6,787	1.7
Flagstaff, AZ	120,776	2,189	1.8
Flint, MI	438,589	92,075	21.0
Florence, SC	193,365	78,738	40.7
Florence–Muscle Shoals, AL	139,966	17,811	12.7
Fond du Lac, WI	94,964	559	0.6
Fort Collins–Loveland, CO	264,807	3,016	1.1
Fort Smith, AR–OK	278,361	10,911	3.9
Fort Walton Beach–Crestview–Destin, FL	177,284	17,417	9.8
Fort Wayne, IN	395,458	43,244	10.9
Fresno, CA	858,948	49,391	5.8
Gadsden, AL	101,151	14,612	14.4
Gainesville, FL	224,719	44,101	19.6
Gainesville, GA	163,204	11,001	6.7
Gettysburg, PA	95,850	1,072	1.1
Glens Falls, NY	123,464	2,047	1.7
Goldsboro, NC	109,615	36,523	33.3
Grand Forks, ND–MN	89,111	1,117	1.3
Grand Junction, CO	126,588	1,627	1.3
Grand Rapids–Wyoming, MI	750,962	59,936	8.0
Great Falls, MT	77,462	673	0.9
Greeley, CO	223,966	1,495	0.7
Green Bay, WI	289,298	4,611	1.6
Greensboro–High Point, NC	657,975	157,761	24.0
Greenville, NC	154,987	55,606	35.9
Greenville, SC	570,538	100,591	17.6
Gulfport–Biloxi, MS	244,808	49,599	20.3
Hagerstown–Martinsburg, MD–WV	240,247	14,144	5.9
Hanford–Corcoran, CA	121,418	5,807	4.8
Harrisburg–Carlisle, PA	500,356	50,668	10.1
Harrisonburg, VA	102,997	3,078	3.0

(continued)

	total population	black number	black share of total
Hartford–West Hartford–East Hartford, CT	1,140,319	122,106	10.7%
Hattiesburg, MS	125,782	35,304	28.1
Hickory–Lenoir–Morganton, NC	347,698	23,793	6.8
Holland–Grand Haven, MI	245,075	4,095	1.7
Honolulu, HI	873,177	31,515	3.6
Hot Springs, AR	91,690	7,249	7.9
Houma–Bayou Cane–Thibodaux, LA	196,621	31,754	16.1
Houston–Sugar Land–Baytown, TX	5,193,448	866,016	16.7
Huntington–Ashland, WV–KY–OH	279,158	8,017	2.9
Huntsville, AL	358,646	75,563	21.1
Idaho Falls, ID	113,677	345	0.3
Indianapolis, IN	1,608,730	243,128	15.1
Iowa City, IA	129,932	4,254	3.3
Ithaca, NY	87,080	3,137	3.6
Jackson, MI	152,954	10,995	7.2
Jackson, MS	497,168	234,461	47.2
Jackson, TN	105,237	32,509	30.9
Jacksonville, FL	1,223,882	278,709	22.8
Jacksonville, NC	125,251	25,256	20.2
Janesville, WI	154,296	8,398	5.4
Jefferson City, MO	135,442	7,156	5.3
Johnson City, TN	181,670	4,800	2.6
Johnstown, PA	138,963	3,801	2.7
Jonesboro, AR	109,727	9,931	9.1
Joplin, MO	162,578	2,590	1.6
Kalamazoo–Portage, MI	307,353	29,640	9.6
Kankakee–Bradley, IL	103,593	16,474	15.9
Kansas City, MO–KS	1,909,666	245,939	12.9
Kennewick–Richland–Pasco, WA	219,224	4,358	2.0
Killeen–Temple–Fort Hood, TX	330,421	67,411	20.4
Kingsport–Bristol–Bristol, TN–VA	298,447	5,394	1.8
Kingston, NY	170,938	8,430	4.9
Knoxville, TN	635,635	43,791	6.9
Kokomo, IN	102,346	7,620	7.4
La Crosse, WI–MN	123,253	1,475	1.2
Lafayette, IN	171,344	4,610	2.7
Lafayette, LA	242,090	63,277	26.1
Lake Charles, LA	186,858	45,540	24.4
Lakeland, FL	530,126	76,933	14.5
Lancaster, PA	476,155	19,944	4.2
Lansing–East Lansing, MI	435,632	40,195	9.2
Laredo, TX	221,478	1,369	0.6
Las Cruces, NM	184,089	3,337	1.8
Las Vegas–Paradise, NV	1,691,213	177,190	10.5
Lawrence, KS	94,200	4,876	5.2
Lawton, OK	102,887	21,178	20.6
Lebanon, PA	121,054	2,558	2.1
Lewiston–Auburn, ME	104,298	896	0.9

(continued)

	total population	black	
		number	share of total
Lexington–Fayette, KY	410,876	45,054	11.0%
Lima, OH	101,619	11,430	11.2
Lincoln, NE	268,089	8,929	3.3
Little Rock–North Little Rock, AR	623,851	140,545	22.5
Logan, UT–ID	106,718	633	0.6
Longview, TX	199,417	34,683	17.4
Longview, WA	95,905	1,123	1.2
Los Angeles–Long Beach–Santa Ana, CA	12,703,423	988,235	7.8
Louisville, KY–IN	1,183,916	163,233	13.8
Lubbock, TX	250,628	19,050	7.6
Lynchburg, VA	227,858	39,826	17.5
Macon, GA	218,398	95,496	43.7
Madera, CA	134,159	4,001	3.0
Madison, WI	519,330	22,632	4.4
Manchester–Nashua, NH	393,207	7,132	1.8
Mansfield, OH	121,365	9,856	8.1
McAllen–Edinburg–Mission, TX	671,967	2,298	0.3
Medford, OR	191,465	1,095	0.6
Memphis, TN–MS–AR	1,236,181	559,809	45.3
Merced, CA	237,278	9,253	3.9
Miami–Fort Lauderdale–Miami Beach, FL	5,334,685	1,116,727	20.9
Michigan City–La Porte, IN	104,164	9,590	9.2
Midland, TX	119,720	8,220	6.9
Milwaukee–Waukesha–West Allis, WI	1,480,517	249,725	16.9
Minneapolis–St. Paul–Bloomington, MN–WI	3,076,239	215,563	7.0
Missoula, MT	96,467	548	0.6
Mobile, AL	393,585	137,711	35.0
Modesto, CA	497,804	15,885	3.2
Monroe, LA	165,220	56,175	34.0
Monroe, MI	152,392	3,908	2.6
Montgomery, AL	339,638	140,473	41.4
Morgantown, WV	106,899	3,371	3.2
Morristown, TN	131,585	4,192	3.2
Mount Vernon–Anacortes, WA	111,330	987	0.9
Muncie, IN	108,356	7,807	7.2
Muskegon–Norton Shores, MI	169,500	24,258	14.3
Myrtle Beach–Conway–North Myrtle Beach, SC	224,487	34,543	15.4
Napa, CA	127,445	2,282	1.8
Naples–Marco Island, FL	302,514	17,417	5.8
Nashville–Davidson–Murfreesboro, TN	1,384,347	212,243	15.3
New Haven–Milford, CT	817,828	104,149	12.7
New Orleans–Metairie–Kenner, LA	1,292,774	495,864	38.4
New York–Northern New Jersey– Long Island, NY–NJ–PA	18,351,099	3,336,148	18.2
Niles–Benton Harbor, MI	158,224	25,335	16.0
Norwich–New London, CT	253,468	15,337	6.1
Ocala, FL	295,555	33,035	11.2
Ocean City, NJ	96,630	5,658	5.9

(continued)

	total population	black	
		number	share of total
Odessa, TX	123,331	5,851	4.7%
Ogden–Clearfield, UT	481,703	7,052	1.5
Oklahoma City, OK	1,124,533	130,341	11.6
Olympia, WA	225,469	7,634	3.4
Omaha–Council Bluffs, NE–IA	795,707	66,227	8.3
Orlando–Kissimmee, FL	1,903,273	298,246	15.7
Oshkosh–Neenah, WI	150,687	1,337	0.9
Owensboro, KY	109,410	4,561	4.2
Oxnard–Thousand Oaks–Ventura, CA	782,759	23,766	3.0
Palm Bay–Melbourne–Titusville, FL	521,226	50,655	9.7
Panama City–Lynn Haven, FL	158,141	17,876	11.3
Parkersburg–Marietta–Vienna, WV–OH	161,018	1,349	0.8
Pascagoula, MS	155,942	31,277	20.1
Pensacola–Ferry Pass–Brent, FL	415,313	71,752	17.3
Peoria, IL	357,285	32,939	9.2
Philadelphia–Camden–Wilmington, PA–NJ–DE–MD	5,644,383	1,183,449	21.0
Phoenix–Mesa–Scottsdale, AZ	3,805,123	173,743	4.6
Pine Bluff, AR	95,402	44,206	46.3
Pittsburgh, PA	2,314,937	198,411	8.6
Pittsfield, MA	125,654	4,000	3.2
Plattsburgh, NY	75,053	959	1.3
Pocatello, ID	83,492	583	0.7
Portland–South Portland–Biddeford, ME	500,263	6,346	1.3
Portland–Vancouver–Beaverton, OR–WA	2,063,277	71,391	3.5
Port St. Lucie–Fort Pierce, FL	374,713	46,917	12.5
Poughkeepsie–Newburgh–Middletown, NY	635,978	63,276	9.9
Prescott, AZ	194,928	1,600	0.8
Providence–New Bedford–Fall River, RI–MA	1,565,972	87,512	5.6
Provo–Orem, UT	443,188	1,336	0.3
Pueblo, CO	147,187	3,474	2.4
Punta Gorda, FL	154,716	6,064	3.9
Racine, WI	190,368	20,626	10.8
Raleigh–Cary, NC	924,415	189,675	20.5
Rapid City, SD	114,805	1,869	1.6
Reading, PA	382,917	19,512	5.1
Redding, CA	176,570	2,227	1.3
Reno–Sparks, NV	387,750	10,852	2.8
Richmond, VA	1,132,036	340,910	30.1
Riverside–San Bernardino–Ontario, CA	3,827,946	313,886	8.2
Roanoke, VA	279,269	34,491	12.4
Rochester, MN	173,360	4,803	2.8
Rochester, NY	996,309	116,393	11.7
Rockford, IL	333,729	34,485	10.3
Rocky Mount, NC	141,985	64,509	45.4
Rome, GA	90,124	12,381	13.7
Sacramento–Arden-Arcade–Roseville, CA	2,004,476	165,384	8.3
Saginaw–Saginaw Township North, MI	202,037	40,341	20.0

(continued)

	total population	black number	black share of total
St. Cloud, MN	172,989	3,085	1.8%
St. Joseph, MO–KS	111,755	3,603	3.2
St. Louis, MO–IL	2,725,336	505,584	18.6
Salem, OR	360,857	3,699	1.0
Salinas, CA	389,004	11,530	3.0
Salisbury, MD	107,489	27,598	25.7
Salt Lake City, UT	1,017,572	15,059	1.5
San Angelo, TX	100,894	4,370	4.3
San Antonio, TX	1,844,018	118,087	6.4
San Diego–Carlsbad–San Marcos, CA	2,824,259	163,098	5.8
Sandusky, OH	76,797	6,870	8.9
San Francisco–Oakland–Fremont, CA	4,071,751	389,171	9.6
San Jose–Sunnyvale–Santa Clara, CA	1,726,057	50,757	2.9
San Luis Obispo–Paso Robles, CA	239,638	3,397	1.4
Santa Barbara–Santa Maria, CA	383,393	8,586	2.2
Santa Cruz–Watsonville, CA	240,367	3,208	1.3
Santa Fe, NM	137,758	1,069	0.8
Santa Rosa–Petaluma, CA	453,850	8,849	1.9
Sarasota–Bradenton–Venice, FL	660,611	42,252	6.4
Savannah, GA	302,925	106,202	35.1
Scranton Wilkes-Barre, PA	528,353	9,887	1.9
Seattle–Tacoma–Bellevue, WA	3,133,715	200,123	6.4
Sheboygan, WI	111,100	991	0.9
Sherman–Denison, TX	113,899	7,363	6.5
Shreveport–Bossier City, LA	375,139	148,534	39.6
Sierra Vista–Douglas, AZ	120,439	5,005	4.2
Sioux City, IA–NE–SD	139,910	3,175	2.3
Sioux Falls, SD	201,044	4,398	2.2
South Bend Mishawaka, IN–MI	303,925	36,690	12.1
Spartanburg, SC	259,224	53,760	20.7
Spokane, WA	425,684	10,677	2.5
Springfield, IL	202,317	21,219	10.5
Springfield, MA	653,913	44,359	6.8
Springfield, MO	382,521	8,157	2.1
Springfield, OH	139,053	13,709	9.9
State College, PA	124,263	2,547	2.0
Stockton, CA	646,259	54,571	8.4
Sumter, SC	102,146	48,928	47.9
Syracuse, NY	628,295	49,151	7.8
Tallahassee, FL	317,527	103,660	32.6
Tampa–St. Petersburg–Clearwater, FL	2,596,556	302,910	11.7
Terre Haute, IN	158,940	5,778	3.6
Texarkana, TX–AR	125,886	29,456	23.4
Toledo, OH	637,276	84,664	13.3
Topeka, KS	224,023	16,862	7.5
Trenton–Ewing, NJ	345,118	70,471	20.4
Tucson, AZ	902,720	35,002	3.9
Tulsa, OK	867,878	82,741	9.5

(continued)

	total population	black	
		number	share of total
Tuscaloosa, AL	189,393	66,599	35.2%
Tyler, TX	185,465	34,522	18.6
Utica–Rome, NY	281,918	11,100	3.9
Valdosta, GA	117,756	37,776	32.1
Vallejo–Fairfield, CA	395,426	63,704	16.1
Vero Beach, FL	126,258	10,557	8.4
Victoria, TX	117,233	6,613	5.6
Vineland–Millville–Bridgeton, NJ	139,968	23,584	16.8
Virginia Beach–Norfolk–Newport News, VA–NC	1,585,416	516,266	32.6
Visalia–Porterville, CA	404,909	7,638	1.9
Waco, TX	214,582	33,338	15.5
Warner Robins, GA	123,176	33,375	27.1
Washington–Arlington–Alexandria, DC–VA–MD–WV	5,119,490	1,378,998	26.9
Waterloo–Cedar Falls, IA	153,873	10,627	6.9
Weirton–Steubenville, WV–OH	123,066	5,314	4.3
Wenatchee, WA	103,393	460	0.4
Wheeling, WV–OH	141,860	3,896	2.7
Wichita, KS	575,506	46,996	8.2
Wichita Falls, TX	137,103	11,329	8.3
Williamsport, PA	112,735	4,959	4.4
Wilmington, NC	308,470	46,693	15.1
Winchester, VA–WV	114,482	4,482	3.9
Winston-Salem, NC	437,100	86,412	19.8
Worcester, MA	759,409	27,672	3.6
Yakima, WA	227,809	2,561	1.1
York–Hanover, PA	400,670	18,494	4.6
Youngstown–Warren–Boardman, OH–PA	569,009	63,518	11.2
Yuba City, CA	153,262	4,248	2.8
Yuma, AZ	175,793	3,639	2.1

Note: Blacks are those who identify themselves as being of the race alone or as being of the race in combination with one or more other races.

Source: Bureau of the Census, 2005 American Community Survey, Internet site http://www.census.gov/acs/www/; calculations by New Strategist

8

Spending

■ The nation's 14 million black households spent an average of $32,849 in 2005, less than the $46,409 spent by the average household.

■ The spending of blacks is below average because married couples—the most affluent householders—head relatively few black households. Nevertheless, blacks spend more than average on a such items as pork, poultry, fish, noncarbonated fruit-flavored drinks, clothes, and shoes.

■ Because homeownership is relatively low among blacks, they spend less than average on mortgage interest, but more on rent, residential phone service, and phone cards.

Black Households Spend Less than the Average Household

On some products and services, however, they spend more.

The nation's 14 million black households spent an average of $32,849 in 2005, according to the Bureau of Labor Statistics' Consumer Expenditure Survey. While the annual spending of black households (called consumer units by the Bureau of Labor Statistics) is less than the $46,409 spent by the average household, on some items blacks spend more.

One reason for the lower spending of blacks is that married couples head relatively few black households, and married couples are the most affluent household type. Nevertheless, blacks spend more than average on a number of foods such as pork, poultry, and fish. They spend 5 percent more than the average household on clothes and 7 percent more on telephone service.

■ Black spending will remain below average until married couples become a larger share of black households.

Black households spend 29 percent less than the average household

(average annual spending of total and black consumer units, 2005)

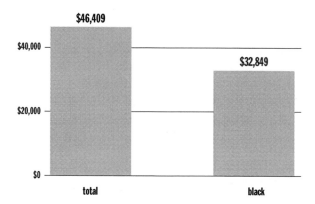

Table 8.1 Average Spending by Race and Hispanic Origin of Householder, 2005

(average annual spending of households by product and service category and by race and Hispanic origin of householder, 2005)

	total households	Asian	black	Hispanic	non-Hispanic white, other
Number of households (in 000s)	117,356	4,283	14,042	12,462	90,995
Average number of persons per household	2.5	2.9	2.6	3.4	2.3
Average before-tax household income	$58,712	$73,995	$39,385	$47,509	$63,203
Average annual household spending	**$46,409**	**$52,054**	**$32,849**	**$40,123**	**$49,331**
FOOD	**5,931**	**6,632**	**4,319**	**5,551**	**6,223**
Groceries	**3,297**	**3,580**	**2,663**	**3,344**	**3,384**
Cereals and bakery products	445	492	363	400	463
Cereals and cereal products	143	216	132	147	144
Bakery products	302	276	231	253	319
Meats, poultry, fish, and eggs	764	892	787	876	746
Beef	228	196	193	285	225
Pork	153	164	170	160	150
Other meats	103	82	90	99	106
Poultry	134	147	177	177	122
Fish and seafood	113	259	121	109	113
Eggs	33	45	35	46	30
Dairy products	378	303	245	364	400
Fresh milk and cream	146	137	98	162	151
Other dairy products	232	166	147	202	249
Fruits and vegetables	552	814	428	640	558
Fresh fruits	182	284	122	219	185
Fresh vegetables	175	312	122	210	178
Processed fruits	106	125	99	119	105
Processed vegetables	89	93	85	92	89
Other food at home	1,158	1,078	840	1,064	1,217
Sugar and other sweets	119	102	82	90	128
Fats and oils	85	86	79	84	86
Miscellaneous foods	609	567	432	535	645
Nonalcoholic beverages	303	279	230	321	312
Food prepared by consumer unit on trips	41	45	17	33	46
Restaurants and other food away from home	**2,634**	**3,052**	**1,657**	**2,207**	**2,838**
ALCOHOLIC BEVERAGES	**426**	**319**	**173**	**286**	**483**
HOUSING	**15,167**	**19,017**	**11,650**	**14,338**	**15,813**
Shelter	**8,805**	**12,659**	**6,524**	**8,937**	**9,134**
Owned dwellings	5,958	8,623	3,188	4,886	6,527
Mortgage interest and charges	3,317	5,354	1,998	3,166	3,538
Property taxes	1,541	2,203	734	1,058	1,730
Maintenance, repair, insurance, other expenses	1,101	1,066	456	662	1,259

(continued)

	total households	Asian	black	Hispanic	non-Hispanic white, other
Rented dwellings	$2,345	$3,479	$3,148	$3,876	$2,013
Other lodging	502	556	189	175	594
Utilities, fuels, and public services	**3,183**	**3,018**	**3,253**	**2,986**	**3,201**
Natural gas	473	454	549	378	475
Electricity	1,155	942	1,205	1,071	1,159
Fuel oil and other fuels	142	58	45	43	170
Telephone	1,048	1,166	1,124	1,130	1,025
Water and other public services	366	398	330	365	371
Household services	**801**	**948**	**530**	**605**	**868**
Personal services	322	449	289	336	324
Other household services	479	499	241	268	544
Housekeeping supplies	**611**	**439**	**352**	**508**	**663**
Laundry and cleaning supplies	134	91	119	156	133
Other household products	320	233	160	252	352
Postage and stationery	157	115	74	100	178
Household furnishings and equipment	**1,767**	**1,954**	**991**	**1,303**	**1,947**
Household textiles	132	172	93	95	143
Furniture	467	478	298	487	490
Floor coverings	56	97	16	20	67
Major appliances	223	377	143	171	242
Small appliances and miscellaneous housewares	105	94	46	85	117
Miscellaneous household equipment	782	737	393	445	887
APPAREL AND RELATED SERVICES	**1,886**	**2,035**	**1,981**	**2,195**	**1,830**
Men and boys	**440**	**467**	**420**	**529**	**431**
Men, aged 16 or older	349	366	297	416	347
Boys, aged 2 to 15	91	101	123	112	83
Women and girls	**754**	**877**	**765**	**787**	**747**
Women, aged 16 or older	633	715	635	597	637
Girls, aged 2 to 15	121	162	130	191	111
Children under age 2	**82**	**97**	**77**	**149**	**74**
Footwear	**320**	**303**	**493**	**442**	**278**
Other apparel products and services	**290**	**291**	**226**	**288**	**300**
TRANSPORTATION	**8,344**	**8,899**	**5,850**	**7,900**	**8,791**
Vehicle purchases	**3,544**	**3,516**	**2,350**	**3,280**	**3,765**
Cars and trucks, new	1,931	2,568	988	1,710	2,104
Cars and trucks, used	1,531	898	1,307	1,551	1,566
Other vehicles	82	50	55	20	95
Gasoline and motor oil	**2,013**	**2,011**	**1,546**	**2,171**	**2,063**
Other vehicle expenses	**2,339**	**2,395**	**1,710**	**2,068**	**2,474**
Vehicle finance charges	297	218	229	269	311
Maintenance and repairs	671	619	433	586	721
Vehicle insurance	913	914	747	837	949
Vehicle rentals, leases, licenses, other charges	458	643	301	376	493
Public transportation	**448**	**978**	**245**	**380**	**489**

(continued)

	total households	Asian	black	Hispanic	non-Hispanic white, other
HEALTH CARE	**$2,664**	**$2,262**	**$1,448**	**$1,520**	**$3,005**
Health insurance	1,361	1,357	841	750	1,523
Medical services	677	499	321	444	763
Drugs	521	335	244	273	597
Medical supplies	105	72	43	54	122
ENTERTAINMENT	**2,388**	**1,804**	**1,242**	**1,494**	**2,683**
Fees and admissions	588	647	201	337	682
Audio and visual equipment and services	888	748	797	716	925
Pets, toys, hobbies, playground equipment	420	175	128	244	488
Other entertainment products and services	492	233	117	197	589
PERSONAL CARE PRODUCTS, SERVICES	**541**	**519**	**472**	**501**	**557**
READING	**126**	**117**	**52**	**55**	**148**
EDUCATION	**940**	**1,759**	**500**	**558**	**1,061**
TOBACCO PRODUCTS, SMOKING SUPPLIES	**319**	**124**	**216**	**158**	**357**
MISCELLANEOUS	**808**	**794**	**416**	**665**	**887**
CASH CONTRIBUTIONS	**1,663**	**1,188**	**1,204**	**927**	**1,834**
PERSONAL INSURANCE AND PENSIONS	**5,204**	**6,584**	**3,325**	**3,974**	**5,659**
Life and other personal insurance	381	465	292	140	428
Pensions and Social Security	4,823	6,119	3,033	3,834	5,232
PERSONAL TAXES	**2,408**	**1,966**	**603**	**982**	**2,877**
Federal income taxes	1,696	1,334	287	655	2,054
State and local income taxes	534	440	257	258	614
Other taxes	177	192	59	69	210
GIFTS FOR PEOPLE IN OTHER HOUSEHOLDS	**1,091**	**1,185**	**587**	**636**	**1,229**

Note: Asian and black include Hispanics and non-Hispanics who identify themselves as being of the respective race alone. Hispanic includes people of any race who identify themselves as Hispanic. Other includes people who identify themselves as non-Hispanic and as Alaska Native, American Indian, Asian (who are also included in the Asian column), Native Hawaiian or other Pacific Islander, as well as non-Hispanics reporting more than one race. Spending by category will not add to total spending because gift spending is also included in the preceding product and service categories and personal taxes are not included in the total.
Source: Bureau of Labor Statistics, 2005 Consumer Expenditure Survey, Internet site http://www.bls.gov/cex/

Table 8.2 Indexed Spending by Race and Hispanic Origin of Householder, 2005

(indexed average annual spending of households by product and service category and by race and Hispanic origin of householder, 2005; index definition: an index of 100 is the average for all households; an index of 132 means that spending by households in that group is 32 percent above the average for all households; an index of 68 indicates spending that is 32 percent below the average for all households)

	total households	Asian	black	Hispanic	non-Hispanic white, other
Average household spending, total	$46,409	$52,054	$32,849	$40,123	$49,331
Average household spending, index	100	112	71	86	106
FOOD	100	112	73	94	105
Groceries	100	109	81	101	103
Cereals and bakery products	100	111	82	90	104
Cereals and cereal products	100	151	92	103	101
Bakery products	100	91	76	84	106
Meats, poultry, fish, and eggs	100	117	103	115	98
Beef	100	86	85	125	99
Pork	100	107	111	105	98
Other meats	100	80	87	96	103
Poultry	100	110	132	132	91
Fish and seafood	100	229	107	96	100
Eggs	100	136	106	139	91
Dairy products	100	80	65	96	106
Fresh milk and cream	100	94	67	111	103
Other dairy products	100	72	63	87	107
Fruits and vegetables	100	147	78	116	101
Fresh fruits	100	156	67	120	102
Fresh vegetables	100	178	70	120	102
Processed fruits	100	118	93	112	99
Processed vegetables	100	104	96	103	100
Other food at home	100	93	73	92	105
Sugar and other sweets	100	86	69	76	108
Fats and oils	100	101	93	99	101
Miscellaneous foods	100	93	71	88	106
Nonalcoholic beverages	100	92	76	106	103
Food prepared by consumer unit on trips	100	110	41	80	112
Restaurants and other food away from home	100	116	63	84	108
ALCOHOLIC BEVERAGES	100	75	41	67	113
HOUSING	100	125	77	95	104
Shelter	100	144	74	101	104
Owned dwellings	100	145	54	82	110
Mortgage interest and charges	100	161	60	95	107
Property taxes	100	143	48	69	112
Maintenance, repair, insurance, other expenses	100	97	41	60	114

(continued)

	total households	Asian	black	Hispanic	non-Hispanic white, other
Rented dwellings	100	148	134	165	86
Other lodging	100	111	38	35	118
Utilities, fuels, and public services	**100**	**95**	**102**	**94**	**101**
Natural gas	100	96	116	80	100
Electricity	100	82	104	93	100
Fuel oil and other fuels	100	41	32	30	120
Telephone	100	111	107	108	98
Water and other public services	100	109	90	100	101
Household services	**100**	**118**	**66**	**76**	**108**
Personal services	100	139	90	104	101
Other household services	100	104	50	56	114
Housekeeping supplies	**100**	**72**	**58**	**83**	**109**
Laundry and cleaning supplies	100	68	89	116	99
Other household products	100	73	50	79	110
Postage and stationery	100	73	47	64	113
Household furnishings and equipment	**100**	**111**	**56**	**74**	**110**
Household textiles	100	130	70	72	108
Furniture	100	102	64	104	105
Floor coverings	100	173	29	36	120
Major appliances	100	169	64	77	109
Small appliances and miscellaneous housewares	100	90	44	81	111
Miscellaneous household equipment	100	94	50	57	113
APPAREL AND RELATED SERVICES	**100**	**108**	**105**	**116**	**97**
Men and boys	**100**	**106**	**95**	**120**	**98**
Men, aged 16 or older	100	105	85	119	99
Boys, aged 2 to 15	100	111	135	123	91
Women and girls	**100**	**116**	**101**	**104**	**99**
Women, aged 16 or older	100	113	100	94	101
Girls, aged 2 to 15	100	134	107	158	92
Children under age 2	**100**	**118**	**94**	**182**	**90**
Footwear	**100**	**95**	**154**	**138**	**87**
Other apparel products and services	**100**	**100**	**78**	**99**	**103**
TRANSPORTATION	**100**	**107**	**70**	**95**	**105**
Vehicle purchases	**100**	**99**	**66**	**93**	**106**
Cars and trucks, new	100	133	51	89	109
Cars and trucks, used	100	59	85	101	102
Other vehicles	100	61	67	24	116
Gasoline and motor oil	**100**	**100**	**77**	**108**	**102**
Other vehicle expenses	**100**	**102**	**73**	**88**	**106**
Vehicle finance charges	100	73	77	91	105
Maintenance and repairs	100	92	65	87	107
Vehicle insurance	100	100	82	92	104
Vehicle rentals, leases, licenses, other charges	100	140	66	82	108
Public transportation	**100**	**218**	**55**	**85**	**109**

(continued)

	total households	Asian	black	Hispanic	non-Hispanic white, other
HEALTH CARE	**100**	**85**	**54**	**57**	**113**
Health insurance	100	100	62	55	112
Medical services	100	74	47	66	113
Drugs	100	64	47	52	115
Medical supplies	100	69	41	51	116
ENTERTAINMENT	**100**	**76**	**52**	**63**	**112**
Fees and admissions	100	110	34	57	116
Audio and visual equipment and services	100	84	90	81	104
Pets, toys, hobbies, playground equipment	100	42	30	58	116
Other entertainment products and services	100	47	24	40	120
PERSONAL CARE PRODUCTS, SERVICES	**100**	**96**	**87**	**93**	**103**
READING	**100**	**93**	**41**	**44**	**117**
EDUCATION	**100**	**187**	**53**	**59**	**113**
TOBACCO PRODUCTS, SMOKING SUPPLIES	**100**	**39**	**68**	**50**	**112**
MISCELLANEOUS	**100**	**98**	**51**	**82**	**110**
CASH CONTRIBUTIONS	**100**	**71**	**72**	**56**	**110**
PERSONAL INSURANCE AND PENSIONS	**100**	**127**	**64**	**76**	**109**
Life and other personal insurance	100	122	77	37	112
Pensions and Social Security	100	127	63	79	108
PERSONAL TAXES	**100**	**82**	**25**	**41**	**119**
Federal income taxes	100	79	17	39	121
State and local income taxes	100	82	48	48	115
Other taxes	100	108	33	39	119
GIFTS FOR PEOPLE IN OTHER HOUSEHOLDS	**100**	**109**	**54**	**58**	**113**

Note: Asian and black include Hispanics and non-Hispanics who identify themselves as being of the respective race alone. Hispanic includes people of any race who identify themselves as Hispanic. Other includes people who identify themselves as non-Hispanic and as Alaska Native, American Indian, Asian (who are also included in the Asian column), Native Hawaiian or other Pacific Islander, as well as non-Hispanics reporting more than one race.
Source: Calculations by New Strategist based on the Bureau of Labor Statistics' 2005 Consumer Expenditure Survey

Table 8.3 Total Spending by Race and Hispanic Origin of Householder, 2005

(total annual spending by race and Hispanic origin groups, 2005; households and dollars in thousands)

	total households	Asian	black	Hispanic	non-Hispanic white, other
Number of households	117,356	4,283	14,042	12,462	90,995
Total spending of all households	$5,446,374,604	$222,947,282	$461,265,658	$500,012,826	$4,488,874,345
FOOD	696,038,436	28,404,856	60,647,398	69,176,562	566,261,885
Groceries	386,922,732	15,333,140	37,393,846	41,672,928	307,927,080
Cereals and bakery products	52,223,420	2,107,236	5,097,246	4,984,800	42,130,685
Cereals and cereal products	16,781,908	925,128	1,853,544	1,831,914	13,103,280
Bakery products	35,441,512	1,182,108	3,243,702	3,152,886	29,027,405
Meats, poultry, fish, and eggs	89,659,984	3,820,436	11,051,054	10,916,712	67,882,270
Beef	26,757,168	839,468	2,710,106	3,551,670	20,473,875
Pork	17,955,468	702,412	2,387,140	1,993,920	13,649,250
Other meats	12,087,668	351,206	1,263,780	1,233,738	9,645,470
Poultry	15,725,704	629,601	2,485,434	2,205,774	11,101,390
Fish and seafood	13,261,228	1,109,297	1,699,082	1,358,358	10,282,435
Eggs	3,872,748	192,735	491,470	573,252	2,729,850
Dairy products	44,360,568	1,297,749	3,440,290	4,536,168	36,398,000
Fresh milk and cream	17,133,976	586,771	1,376,116	2,018,844	13,740,245
Other dairy products	27,226,592	710,978	2,064,174	2,517,324	22,657,755
Fruits and vegetables	64,780,512	3,486,362	6,009,976	7,975,680	50,775,210
Fresh fruits	21,358,792	1,216,372	1,713,124	2,729,178	16,834,075
Fresh vegetables	20,537,300	1,336,296	1,713,124	2,617,020	16,197,110
Processed fruits	12,439,736	535,375	1,390,158	1,482,978	9,554,475
Processed vegetables	10,444,684	398,319	1,193,570	1,146,504	8,098,555
Other food at home	135,898,248	4,617,074	11,795,280	13,259,568	110,740,915
Sugar and other sweets	13,965,364	436,866	1,151,444	1,121,580	11,647,360
Fats and oils	9,975,260	368,338	1,109,318	1,046,808	7,825,570
Miscellaneous foods	71,469,804	2,428,461	6,066,144	6,667,170	58,691,775
Nonalcoholic beverages	35,558,868	1,194,957	3,229,660	4,000,302	28,390,440
Food prepared by consumer unit on trips	4,811,596	192,735	238,714	411,246	4,185,770
Restaurants and other food away from home	309,115,704	13,071,716	23,267,594	27,503,634	258,243,810
ALCOHOLIC BEVERAGES	49,993,656	1,366,277	2,429,266	3,564,132	43,950,585
HOUSING	1,779,938,452	81,449,811	163,589,300	178,680,156	1,438,903,935
Shelter	1,033,319,580	54,218,497	91,610,008	111,372,894	831,148,330
Owned dwellings	699,207,048	36,932,309	44,765,896	60,889,332	593,924,365
Mortgage interest and charges	389,269,852	22,931,182	28,055,916	39,454,692	321,940,310
Property taxes	180,845,596	9,435,449	10,306,828	13,184,796	157,421,350
Maintenance, repair, insurance, other expenses	129,208,956	4,565,678	6,403,152	8,249,844	114,562,705

(continued)

	total households	Asian	black	Hispanic	non-Hispanic white, other
Rented dwellings	$275,199,820	$14,900,557	$44,204,216	$48,302,712	$183,172,935
Other lodging	58,912,712	2,381,348	2,653,938	2,180,850	54,051,030
Utilities, fuels, and public services	**373,544,148**	**12,926,094**	**45,678,626**	**37,211,532**	**291,274,995**
Natural gas	55,509,388	1,944,482	7,709,058	4,710,636	43,222,625
Electricity	135,546,180	4,034,586	16,920,610	13,346,802	105,463,205
Fuel oil and other fuels	16,664,552	248,414	631,890	535,866	15,469,150
Telephone	122,989,088	4,993,978	15,783,208	14,082,060	93,269,875
Water and other public services	42,952,296	1,704,634	4,633,860	4,548,630	33,759,145
Household services	**94,002,156**	**4,060,284**	**7,442,260**	**7,539,510**	**78,983,660**
Personal services	37,788,632	1,923,067	4,058,138	4,187,232	29,482,380
Other household services	56,213,524	2,137,217	3,384,122	3,339,816	49,501,280
Housekeeping supplies	**71,704,516**	**1,880,237**	**4,942,784**	**6,330,696**	**60,329,685**
Laundry and cleaning supplies	15,725,704	389,753	1,670,998	1,944,072	12,102,335
Other household products	37,553,920	997,939	2,246,720	3,140,424	32,030,240
Postage and stationery	18,424,892	492,545	1,039,108	1,246,200	16,197,110
Household furnishings and equipment	**207,368,052**	**8,368,982**	**13,915,622**	**16,237,986**	**177,167,265**
Household textiles	15,490,992	736,676	1,305,906	1,183,890	13,012,285
Furniture	54,805,252	2,047,274	4,184,516	6,068,994	44,587,550
Floor coverings	6,571,936	415,451	224,672	249,240	6,096,665
Major appliances	26,170,388	1,614,691	2,008,006	2,131,002	22,020,790
Small appliances and misc. housewares	12,322,380	402,602	645,932	1,059,270	10,646,415
Miscellaneous household equipment	91,772,392	3,156,571	5,518,506	5,545,590	80,712,565
APPAREL AND RELATED SERVICES	**221,333,416**	**8,715,905**	**27,817,202**	**27,354,090**	**166,520,850**
Men and boys	**51,636,640**	**2,000,161**	**5,897,640**	**6,592,398**	**39,218,845**
Men, aged 16 or older	40,957,244	1,567,578	4,170,474	5,184,192	31,575,265
Boys, aged 2 to 15	10,679,396	432,583	1,727,166	1,395,744	7,552,585
Women and girls	**88,486,424**	**3,756,191**	**10,742,130**	**9,807,594**	**67,973,265**
Women, aged 16 or older	74,286,348	3,062,345	8,916,670	7,439,814	57,963,815
Girls, aged 2 to 15	14,200,076	693,846	1,825,460	2,380,242	10,100,445
Children under age 2	**9,623,192**	**415,451**	**1,081,234**	**1,856,838**	**6,733,630**
Footwear	**37,553,920**	**1,297,749**	**6,922,706**	**5,508,204**	**25,296,610**
Other apparel products and services	**34,033,240**	**1,246,353**	**3,173,492**	**3,589,056**	**27,298,500**
TRANSPORTATION	**979,218,464**	**38,114,417**	**82,145,700**	**98,449,800**	**799,937,045**
Vehicle purchases	**415,909,664**	**15,059,028**	**32,998,700**	**40,875,360**	**342,596,175**
Cars and trucks, new	226,614,436	10,998,744	13,873,496	21,310,020	191,453,480
Cars and trucks, used	179,672,036	3,846,134	18,352,894	19,328,562	142,498,170
Other vehicles	9,623,192	214,150	772,310	249,240	8,644,525
Gasoline and motor oil	**236,237,628**	**8,613,113**	**21,708,932**	**27,055,002**	**187,722,685**
Other vehicle expenses	**274,495,684**	**10,257,785**	**24,011,820**	**25,771,416**	**225,121,630**
Vehicle finance charges	34,854,732	933,694	3,215,618	3,352,278	28,299,445
Maintenance and repairs	78,745,876	2,651,177	6,080,186	7,302,732	65,607,395
Vehicle insurance	107,146,028	3,914,662	10,489,374	10,430,694	86,354,255
Vehicle rentals, leases, licenses, other charges	53,749,048	2,753,969	4,226,642	4,685,712	44,860,535
Public transportation	**52,575,488**	**4,188,774**	**3,440,290**	**4,735,560**	**44,496,555**

(continued)

	total households	Asian	black	Hispanic	non-Hispanic white, other
HEALTH CARE	$312,636,384	$9,688,146	$20,332,816	$18,942,240	$273,439,975
Health insurance	159,721,516	5,812,031	11,809,322	9,346,500	138,585,385
Medical services	79,450,012	2,137,217	4,507,482	5,533,128	69,429,185
Drugs	61,142,476	1,434,805	3,426,248	3,402,126	54,324,015
Medical supplies	12,322,380	308,376	603,806	672,948	11,101,390
ENTERTAINMENT	280,246,128	7,726,532	17,440,164	18,618,228	244,139,585
Fees and admissions	69,005,328	2,771,101	2,822,442	4,199,694	62,058,590
Audio and visual equipment and services	104,212,128	3,203,684	11,191,474	8,922,792	84,170,375
Pets, toys, hobbies, playground equipment	49,289,520	749,525	1,797,376	3,040,728	44,405,560
Other entertainment products and services	57,739,152	997,939	1,642,914	2,455,014	53,596,055
PERSONAL CARE PRODUCTS AND SERVICES	63,489,596	2,222,877	6,627,824	6,243,462	50,684,215
READING	14,786,856	501,111	730,184	685,410	13,467,260
EDUCATION	110,314,640	7,533,797	7,021,000	6,953,796	96,545,695
TOBACCO PRODUCTS AND SMOKING SUPPLIES	37,436,564	531,092	3,033,072	1,968,996	32,485,215
MISCELLANEOUS	94,823,648	3,400,702	5,841,472	8,287,230	80,712,565
CASH CONTRIBUTIONS	195,163,028	5,088,204	16,906,568	11,552,274	166,884,830
PERSONAL INSURANCE AND PENSIONS	610,720,624	28,199,272	46,689,650	49,523,988	514,940,705
Life and other personal insurance	44,712,636	1,991,595	4,100,264	1,744,680	38,945,860
Pensions and Social Security	566,007,988	26,207,677	42,589,386	47,779,308	476,085,840
PERSONAL TAXES	282,593,248	8,420,378	8,467,326	12,237,684	261,792,615
Federal income taxes	199,035,776	5,713,522	4,030,054	8,162,610	186,903,730
State and local income taxes	62,668,104	1,884,520	3,608,794	3,215,196	55,870,930
Other taxes	20,772,012	822,336	828,478	859,878	19,108,950
GIFTS FOR PEOPLE IN OTHER HOUSEHOLDS	128,035,396	5,075,355	8,242,654	7,925,832	111,832,855

Note: Asian and black include Hispanics and non-Hispanics who identify themselves as being of the respective race alone. Hispanic includes people of any race who identify themselves as Hispanic. Other includes people who identify themselves as non-Hispanic and as Alaska Native, American Indian, Asian (who are also included in the Asian column), Native Hawaiian or other Pacific Islander, as well as non-Hispanics reporting more than one race.
Source: Calculations by New Strategist based on the Bureau of Labor Statistics' 2005 Consumer Expenditure Survey

Table 8.4 Market Shares by Race and Hispanic Origin of Householder, 2005

(percentage of total annual spending accounted for by race and Hispanic origin groups, 2005)

	total households	Asian	black	Hispanic	non-Hispanic white, other
Share of total households	**100.0%**	**3.6%**	**12.0%**	**10.6%**	**77.5%**
Share of total before-tax income	**100.0**	**4.6**	**8.0**	**8.6**	**83.5**
Share of total spending	**100.0**	**4.1**	**8.5**	**9.2**	**82.4**
FOOD	**100.0**	**4.1**	**8.7**	**9.9**	**81.4**
Groceries	**100.0**	**4.0**	**9.7**	**10.8**	**79.6**
Cereals and bakery products	100.0	4.0	9.8	9.5	80.7
Cereals and cereal products	100.0	5.5	11.0	10.9	78.1
Bakery products	100.0	3.3	9.2	8.9	81.9
Meats, poultry, fish, and eggs	100.0	4.3	12.3	12.2	75.7
Beef	100.0	3.1	10.1	13.3	76.5
Pork	100.0	3.9	13.3	11.1	76.0
Other meats	100.0	2.9	10.5	10.2	79.8
Poultry	100.0	4.0	15.8	14.0	70.6
Fish and seafood	100.0	8.4	12.8	10.2	77.5
Eggs	100.0	5.0	12.7	14.8	70.5
Dairy products	100.0	2.9	7.8	10.2	82.1
Fresh milk and cream	100.0	3.4	8.0	11.8	80.2
Other dairy products	100.0	2.6	7.6	9.2	83.2
Fruits and vegetables	100.0	5.4	9.3	12.3	78.4
Fresh fruits	100.0	5.7	8.0	12.8	78.8
Fresh vegetables	100.0	6.5	8.3	12.7	78.9
Processed fruits	100.0	4.3	11.2	11.9	76.8
Processed vegetables	100.0	3.8	11.4	11.0	77.5
Other food at home	100.0	3.4	8.7	9.8	81.5
Sugar and other sweets	100.0	3.1	8.2	8.0	83.4
Fats and oils	100.0	3.7	11.1	10.5	78.4
Miscellaneous foods	100.0	3.4	8.5	9.3	82.1
Nonalcoholic beverages	100.0	3.4	9.1	11.2	79.8
Food prepared by consumer unit on trips	100.0	4.0	5.0	8.5	87.0
Restaurants and other food away from home	**100.0**	**4.2**	**7.5**	**8.9**	**83.5**
ALCOHOLIC BEVERAGES	**100.0**	**2.7**	**4.9**	**7.1**	**87.9**
HOUSING	**100.0**	**4.6**	**9.2**	**10.0**	**80.8**
Shelter	**100.0**	**5.2**	**8.9**	**10.8**	**80.4**
Owned dwellings	100.0	5.3	6.4	8.7	84.9
Mortgage interest and charges	100.0	5.9	7.2	10.1	82.7
Property taxes	100.0	5.2	5.7	7.3	87.0
Maintenance, repair, insurance, other expenses	100.0	3.5	5.0	6.4	88.7

(continued)

	total households	Asian	black	Hispanic	non-Hispanic white, other
Rented dwellings	100.0%	5.4%	16.1%	17.6%	66.6%
Other lodging	100.0	4.0	4.5	3.7	91.7
Utilities, fuels, and public services	**100.0**	**3.5**	**12.2**	**10.0**	**78.0**
Natural gas	100.0	3.5	13.9	8.5	77.9
Electricity	100.0	3.0	12.5	9.8	77.8
Fuel oil and other fuels	100.0	1.5	3.8	3.2	92.8
Telephone	100.0	4.1	12.8	11.4	75.8
Water and other public services	100.0	4.0	10.8	10.6	78.6
Household services	**100.0**	**4.3**	**7.9**	**8.0**	**84.0**
Personal services	100.0	5.1	10.7	11.1	78.0
Other household services	100.0	3.8	6.0	5.9	88.1
Housekeeping supplies	**100.0**	**2.6**	**6.9**	**8.8**	**84.1**
Laundry and cleaning supplies	100.0	2.5	10.6	12.4	77.0
Other household products	100.0	2.7	6.0	8.4	85.3
Postage and stationery	100.0	2.7	5.6	6.8	87.9
Household furnishings and equipment	**100.0**	**4.0**	**6.7**	**7.8**	**85.4**
Household textiles	100.0	4.8	8.4	7.6	84.0
Furniture	100.0	3.7	7.6	11.1	81.4
Floor coverings	100.0	6.3	3.4	3.8	92.8
Major appliances	100.0	6.2	7.7	8.1	84.1
Small appliances and miscellaneous housewares	100.0	3.3	5.2	8.6	86.4
Miscellaneous household equipment	100.0	3.4	6.0	6.0	87.9
APPAREL AND RELATED SERVICES	**100.0**	**3.9**	**12.6**	**12.4**	**75.2**
Men and boys	**100.0**	**3.9**	**11.4**	**12.8**	**76.0**
Men, aged 16 or older	100.0	3.8	10.2	12.7	77.1
Boys, aged 2 to 15	100.0	4.1	16.2	13.1	70.7
Women and girls	**100.0**	**4.2**	**12.1**	**11.1**	**76.8**
Women, aged 16 or older	100.0	4.1	12.0	10.0	78.0
Girls, aged 2 to 15	100.0	4.9	12.9	16.8	71.1
Children under age 2	**100.0**	**4.3**	**11.2**	**19.3**	**70.0**
Footwear	**100.0**	**3.5**	**18.4**	**14.7**	**67.4**
Other apparel products and services	**100.0**	**3.7**	**9.3**	**10.5**	**80.2**
TRANSPORTATION	**100.0**	**3.9**	**8.4**	**10.1**	**81.7**
Vehicle purchases	**100.0**	**3.6**	**7.9**	**9.8**	**82.4**
Cars and trucks, new	100.0	4.9	6.1	9.4	84.5
Cars and trucks, used	100.0	2.1	10.2	10.8	79.3
Other vehicles	100.0	2.2	8.0	2.6	89.8
Gasoline and motor oil	**100.0**	**3.6**	**9.2**	**11.5**	**79.5**
Other vehicle expenses	**100.0**	**3.7**	**8.7**	**9.4**	**82.0**
Vehicle finance charges	100.0	2.7	9.2	9.6	81.2
Maintenance and repairs	100.0	3.4	7.7	9.3	83.3
Vehicle insurance	100.0	3.7	9.8	9.7	80.6
Vehicle rentals, leases, licenses, other charges	100.0	5.1	7.9	8.7	83.5
Public transportation	**100.0**	**8.0**	**6.5**	**9.0**	**84.6**

(continued)

	total households	Asian	black	Hispanic	non-Hispanic white, other
HEALTH CARE	**100.0%**	**3.1%**	**6.5%**	**6.1%**	**87.5%**
Health insurance	100.0	3.6	7.4	5.9	86.8
Medical services	100.0	2.7	5.7	7.0	87.4
Drugs	100.0	2.3	5.6	5.6	88.8
Medical supplies	100.0	2.5	4.9	5.5	90.1
ENTERTAINMENT	**100.0**	**2.8**	**6.2**	**6.6**	**87.1**
Fees and admissions	100.0	4.0	4.1	6.1	89.9
Audio and visual equipment and services	100.0	3.1	10.7	8.6	80.8
Pets, toys, hobbies, playground equipment	100.0	1.5	3.6	6.2	90.1
Other entertainment products and services	100.0	1.7	2.8	4.3	92.8
PERSONAL CARE PRODUCTS AND SERVICES	**100.0**	**3.5**	**10.4**	**9.8**	**79.8**
READING	**100.0**	**3.4**	**4.9**	**4.6**	**91.1**
EDUCATION	**100.0**	**6.8**	**6.4**	**6.3**	**87.5**
TOBACCO PRODUCTS AND SMOKING SUPPLIES	**100.0**	**1.4**	**8.1**	**5.3**	**86.8**
MISCELLANEOUS	**100.0**	**3.6**	**6.2**	**8.7**	**85.1**
CASH CONTRIBUTIONS	**100.0**	**2.6**	**8.7**	**5.9**	**85.5**
PERSONAL INSURANCE AND PENSIONS	**100.0**	**4.6**	**7.6**	**8.1**	**84.3**
Life and other personal insurance	100.0	4.5	9.2	3.9	87.1
Pensions and Social Security	100.0	4.6	7.5	8.4	84.1
PERSONAL TAXES	**100.0**	**3.0**	**3.0**	**4.3**	**92.6**
Federal income taxes	100.0	2.9	2.0	4.1	93.9
State and local income taxes	100.0	3.0	5.8	5.1	89.2
Other taxes	100.0	4.0	4.0	4.1	92.0
GIFTS FOR PEOPLE IN OTHER HOUSEHOLDS	**100.0**	**4.0**	**6.4**	**6.2**	**87.3**

Note: Asian and black include Hispanics and non-Hispanics who identify themselves as being of the respective race alone. Hispanic includes people of any race who identify themselves as Hispanic. Other includes people who identify themselves as non-Hispanic and as Alaska Native, American Indian, Asian (who are also included in the Asian column), Native Hawaiian or other Pacific Islander, as well as non-Hispanics reporting more than one race.
Source: Calculations by New Strategist based on the Bureau of Labor Statistics' 2005 Consumer Expenditure Survey

Blacks Are Big Spenders on Telephone Service

Black spending is below average on a variety of items because many households are female-headed.

Although black households spend less than the average household on many products and services, they are big spenders on a number of items. Black households spend 5 percent more than the average household on clothes, with spending a substantial 54 percent above average on shoes. On boys' and girls' shoes, blacks spend more than twice the average and control more than 25 percent of the market.

Black households spend 19 percent less than the average household on groceries overall, but they spend 32 percent more than average on poultry. They also spend more than average on fish and pork. Consistently over the years they have spent much more than the average household on noncarbonated fruit-flavored drinks.

Because homeownership is relatively low among blacks, they spend less than average on mortgage interest, but their spending is 33 percent above average on rent. They spend 20 percent more than the average household on residential phone service and 17 percent more on phone cards.

Blacks spend less than the average household on new cars, but 17 percent more than average on used cars. They spend 77 percent more than the average household on mass transit.

■ Because many blacks live in the South, they spend disproportionately on termite and pest control services.

Blacks spend more than average on phone cards

(indexed spending by black households on telephone service and phone cards, 2005)

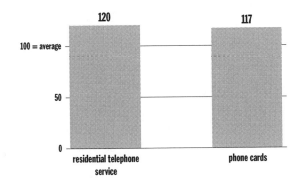

Table 8.5 Spending on Alcoholic Beverages by Black Households, 2005

(average annual, indexed, aggregate, and market share of spending by black households on alcoholic beverages, 2005)

	black average	index	aggregate (in 000s)	market share
ALCOHOLIC BEVERAGES	**$173.48**	**41**	**$2,436,006**	**4.9%**
At home	**100.35**	**46**	**1,409,115**	**5.5**
Beer and ale	66.82	56	938,286	6.7
Whiskey	1.35	21	18,957	2.5
Wine	21.24	28	298,252	3.3
Other alcoholic beverages	10.93	69	153,479	8.2
Away from home	**73.14**	**35**	**1,027,032**	**4.2**
Beer and ale	23.49	30	329,847	3.6
Wine	13.89	38	195,043	4.6
Other alcoholic beverages	26.01	52	365,232	6.2
Alcoholic beverages purchased on trips	9.75	23	136,910	2.8

Note: The index is calculated by dividing black spending on each item by average household spending on the item and multiplying by 100. Subcategories may not add to total because some are not shown.
Source: Bureau of Labor Statistics, unpublished data from the 2005 Consumer Expenditure Survey; calculations by New Strategist

Table 8.6 Spending on Apparel by Black Households, 2005

(average annual, indexed, aggregate, and market share of spending by black households on apparel, accessories, and related services, 2005)

	black average	index	aggregate (in 000s)	market share
APPAREL	**$1,980.82**	**105**	**$27,814,674**	**12.6%**
Men's apparel	**296.85**	**85**	**4,168,368**	**10.2**
Suits	30.41	119	427,017	14.2
Sport coats and tailored jackets	9.82	112	137,892	13.4
Coats and jackets	48.73	130	684,267	15.5
Underwear	10.29	58	144,492	7.0
Hosiery	12.81	81	179,878	9.7
Nightwear	0.92	65	12,919	7.8
Accessories	31.25	82	438,813	9.8
Sweaters and vests	6.25	56	87,763	6.7
Active sportswear	11.06	79	155,305	9.4
Shirts	70.32	72	987,433	8.6
Pants	53.23	84	747,456	10.0
Shorts and shorts sets	7.83	58	109,949	6.9
Uniforms	3.05	130	42,828	15.5
Costumes	0.88	62	12,357	7.4
Boys' (aged 2 to 15) apparel	**123.05**	**135**	**1,727,868**	**16.2**
Coats and jackets	7.63	142	107,140	17.0
Sweaters	3.36	147	47,181	17.6
Shirts	35.11	130	493,015	15.5
Underwear	6.13	104	86,077	12.4
Nightwear	3.92	146	55,045	17.5
Hosiery	5.55	133	77,933	15.9
Accessories	6.40	150	89,869	18.0
Suits, sport coats, and vests	2.22	154	31,173	18.4
Pants	33.66	143	472,654	17.1
Shorts and shorts sets	11.05	156	155,164	18.6
Uniforms	4.74	178	66,559	21.2
Active sportswear	2.96	85	41,564	10.1
Costumes	0.31	28	4,353	3.3
Women's apparel	**634.54**	**100**	**8,910,211**	**12.0**
Coats and jackets	71.23	119	1,000,212	14.3
Dresses	50.45	108	708,419	12.9
Sport coats and tailored jackets	5.41	69	75,967	8.3
Sweaters and vests	36.41	80	511,269	9.5
Shirts, blouses, and tops	116.31	92	1,633,225	11.0
Skirts	22.42	106	314,822	12.7
Pants	111.03	101	1,559,083	12.1
Shorts and shorts sets	6.72	50	94,362	6.0
Active sportswear	18.19	58	255,424	6.9

(continued)

	black average	index	aggregate (in 000s)	market share
Nightwear	$37.15	113	$521,660	13.5%
Undergarments	30.57	91	429,264	10.9
Hosiery	21.62	121	303,588	14.4
Suits	29.47	136	413,818	16.3
Accessories	69.44	123	975,076	14.7
Uniforms	7.21	133	101,243	15.9
Costumes	0.90	42	12,638	5.0
Girls' (aged 2 to 15) apparel	**130.17**	**108**	**1,827,847**	**12.9**
Coats and jackets	6.89	128	96,749	15.3
Dresses and suits	16.24	138	228,042	16.6
Shirts, blouses, and sweaters	34.41	104	483,185	12.4
Skirts and pants	31.11	113	436,847	13.5
Shorts and shorts sets	8.00	118	112,336	14.1
Active sportswear	8.51	77	119,497	9.2
Underwear and nightwear	7.18	119	100,822	14.2
Hosiery	5.45	117	76,529	14.0
Accessories	6.90	70	96,890	8.3
Uniforms	3.66	144	51,394	17.2
Costumes	1.81	94	25,416	11.2
Children's (under age 2) apparel	**77.11**	**94**	**1,082,779**	**11.2**
Coats, jackets, and snowsuits	3.80	141	53,360	16.9
Outerwear including dresses	20.45	89	287,159	10.6
Underwear	38.89	90	546,093	10.8
Nightwear and loungewear	2.95	75	41,424	8.9
Accessories	11.02	116	154,743	13.9
Footwear	**492.63**	**154**	**6,917,510**	**18.4**
Men's	131.35	132	1,844,417	15.8
Boys'	83.13	223	1,167,311	26.7
Women's	204.24	137	2,867,938	16.4
Girls'	73.91	213	1,037,844	25.5
Other apparel products and services	**226.47**	**78**	**3,180,092**	**9.3**
Material for making clothes	5.48	64	76,950	7.6
Sewing patterns and notions	2.20	42	30,892	5.0
Watches	22.54	95	316,507	11.4
Jewelry	64.53	46	906,130	5.5
Shoe repair and other shoe services	0.69	52	9,689	6.2
Coin-operated apparel laundry, dry cleaning	58.40	156	820,053	18.7
Apparel alteration, repair, tailoring services	5.32	97	74,703	11.7
Clothing rental	0.25	12	3,511	1.4
Watch and jewelry repair	2.15	51	30,190	6.1
Professional laundry, dry cleaning	64.17	106	901,075	12.7
Clothing storage	0.73	124	10,251	14.8

Note: The index is calculated by dividing black spending on each item by average household spending on the item and multiplying by 100. Subcategories may not add to total because some are not shown.
Source: Bureau of Labor Statistics, unpublished data from the 2005 Consumer Expenditure Survey; calculations by New Strategist

Table 8.7 Spending on Entertainment by Black Households, 2005

(average annual, indexed, aggregate, and market share of spending by black households on entertainment, 2005)

	black average	index	aggregate (in 000s)	market share
ENTERTAINMENT	**$1,242.07**	**52**	**$17,441,147**	**6.2%**
Fees and admissions	**200.80**	**34**	**2,819,634**	**4.1**
Recreation expenses on trips	8.33	33	116,970	4.0
Social, recreation, civic club membership	25.82	21	362,564	2.5
Fees for participant sports	23.52	30	330,268	3.5
Participant sports on trips	4.85	18	68,104	2.1
Movie, theater, amusement park, and other admissions	60.07	56	843,503	6.7
Movie, other admissions on trips	21.85	45	306,818	5.4
Admission to sports events	10.30	22	144,633	2.7
Admission to sports events on trips	7.28	45	102,226	5.4
Fees for recreational lessons	30.46	34	427,719	4.1
Other entertainment services on trips	8.33	33	116,970	4.0
Audio and visual equipment, services	**797.11**	**90**	**11,193,019**	**10.7**
Television sets	91.08	81	1,278,945	9.7
Cable TV and community antenna	521.77	101	7,326,694	12.0
Tape recorders and players	4.97	121	69,789	14.4
VCRs and video disc players	16.44	80	230,850	9.5
Miscellaneous sound equipment	1.13	59	15,867	7.0
Sound equipment accessories	4.22	49	59,257	5.9
Video cassettes, tapes, and discs	40.58	90	569,824	10.7
Video game hardware and software	29.21	98	410,167	11.7
Streaming and downloading video	0.40	71	5,617	8.5
Repair of TV, radio, and sound equipment	3.49	117	49,007	14.0
Rental of television sets	1.66	307	23,310	36.8
Personal digital audio players	4.17	31	58,555	3.7
Sound components and component systems	5.69	38	79,899	4.5
Satellite dishes	0.62	86	8,706	10.3
Compact discs, records, and audio tapes	34.61	91	485,994	10.9
Streaming and downloading audio	1.10	47	15,446	5.6
Rental of VCR, radio, and sound equipment	0.30	107	4,213	12.8
Musical instruments and accessories	15.49	49	217,511	5.8
Rental and repair of musical instruments	0.63	13	8,846	1.5
Rental of video cassettes, tapes, discs, films	19.43	60	272,836	7.1
Pets, toys, hobbies, playground equipment	**127.60**	**30**	**1,791,759**	**3.6**
Pets	67.54	21	948,397	2.5
Pet food	41.33	31	580,356	3.7
Pet purchase, supplies, and medicines	8.98	13	126,097	1.5
Pet services	5.16	17	72,457	2.0
Veterinarian services	12.06	13	169,347	1.6
Toys, games, hobbies, and tricycles	59.06	67	829,321	8.0
Stamp and coin collecting	0.17	3	2,387	0.3
Playground equipment	0.83	25	11,655	3.0

(continued)

	black average	index	aggregate (in 000s)	market share
Other entertainment supplies, equipment, services	**$116.56**	**24**	**$1,636,736**	**2.8%**
Rental of recreational vehicles	3.38	74	47,462	8.9
Sports, recreation, exercise equipment	74.06	46	1,039,951	5.5
Athletic gear, game tables, exercise equip.	54.45	63	764,587	7.5
Bicycles	7.71	55	108,264	6.6
Camping equipment	4.73	54	66,419	6.5
Hunting and fishing equipment	4.26	15	59,819	1.8
Winter sports equipment	0.13	4	1,825	0.5
Water sports equipment	0.22	4	3,089	0.5
Other sports equipment	2.06	25	28,927	2.9
Rental and repair of misc. sports equipment	0.51	23	7,161	2.7
Photographic equipment and supplies	35.61	40	500,036	4.8
Film	4.37	42	61,364	5.1
Other photographic supplies	0.70	35	9,829	4.1
Film processing	7.80	39	109,528	4.6
Repair and rental of photographic equipment	0.13	28	1,825	3.3
Photographic equipment	12.61	36	177,070	4.3
Photographer fees	9.99	50	140,280	6.0
Pinball, electronic video games	1.41	66	19,799	7.9

Note: The index is calculated by dividing black spending on each item by average household spending on the item and multiplying by 100. Subcategories may not add to total because some are not shown.
Source: Bureau of Labor Statistics, unpublished data from the 2005 Consumer Expenditure Survey; calculations by New Strategist

Table 8.8 Spending on Financial Products and Services by Black Households, 2005

(average annual, indexed, aggregate, and market share of spending by black households on financial products and services, cash contributions, insurance, pensions, and taxes, 2005)

	black average	index	aggregate (in 000s)	market share
FINANCIAL PRODUCTS, SERVICES	**$415.64**	**51**	**$5,836,417**	**6.2%**
Miscellaneous fees	1.56	40	21,906	4.8
Lottery and gambling losses	71.14	93	998,948	11.1
Legal fees	64.75	52	909,220	6.2
Funeral expenses	26.72	42	375,202	5.1
Safe deposit box rental	1.37	33	19,238	4.0
Checking accounts, other bank service charges	18.48	92	259,496	11.0
Cemetery lots, vaults, and maintenance fees	7.10	43	99,698	5.2
Accounting fees	21.14	38	296,848	4.6
Miscellaneous personal services	4.27	11	59,959	1.3
Dating services	0.40	105	5,617	12.6
Finance charges, except mortgage and vehicles	113.93	60	1,599,805	7.2
Occupational expenses	26.85	63	377,028	7.6
Expenses for other properties	52.12	32	731,869	3.9
Credit card memberships	1.31	60	18,395	7.2
Shopping club membership fees	4.50	60	63,189	7.2
CASH CONTRIBUTIONS	**1,204.11**	**72**	**16,908,113**	**8.7**
Support for college students	65.46	71	919,189	8.5
Alimony expenditures	8.78	16	123,289	1.9
Child support expenditures	204.29	104	2,868,640	12.5
Gifts of stocks, bonds, and mutual funds to members of other households	1.82	5	25,556	0.6
Cash contributions to charities and other organizations	56.16	28	788,599	3.4
Cash contributions to church, religious organizations	710.11	100	9,971,365	12.0
Cash contributions to educational institutions	9.10	24	127,782	2.9
Cash contributions to political organizations	3.57	40	50,130	4.8
Other cash gifts	144.83	44	2,033,703	5.2
PERSONAL INSURANCE, PENSIONS	**3,325.18**	**64**	**46,692,178**	**7.6**
Life and other personal insurance	**292.42**	**77**	**4,106,162**	**9.2**
Life, endowment, annuity, other personal insurance	287.32	78	4,034,547	9.4
Other nonhealth insurance	5.10	38	71,614	4.5
Pensions and Social Security	**3,032.76**	**63**	**42,586,016**	**7.5**
Deductions for government retirement	67.77	79	951,626	9.4
Deductions for railroad retirement	2.64	77	37,071	9.2
Deductions for private pensions	227.77	37	3,198,346	4.5
Nonpayroll deposit to retirement plans	173.59	37	2,437,551	4.4
Deductions for Social Security	2,560.99	70	35,961,422	8.4
PERSONAL TAXES	**602.68**	**25**	**8,462,833**	**3.0**
Federal income taxes	287.11	17	4,031,599	2.0
State and local income taxes	256.89	48	3,607,249	5.8
Other taxes	58.67	33	823,844	4.0

Note: The index is calculated by dividing black spending on each item by average household spending on the item and multiplying by 100. Subcategories may not add to total because some are not shown.
Source: Bureau of Labor Statistics, unpublished data from the 2005 Consumer Expenditure Survey; calculations by New Strategist

Table 8.9 Spending on Gifts for People in Other Households by Black Households, 2005

(average annual, indexed, aggregate, and market share of spending by black households on gifts for people in other households, 2005)

	black average	index	aggregate (in 000s)	market share
GIFTS	**$586.87**	**54**	**$8,240,829**	**6.4%**
Food	**50.79**	**46**	**713,193**	**5.5**
Fresh fruit	2.27	60	31,875	7.1
Candy and chewing gum	1.14	12	16,008	1.4
Alcoholic beverages	**9.46**	**69**	**132,837**	**8.3**
Beer and ale	3.06	51	42,969	6.1
Wine	3.70	70	51,955	8.4
Housing	**130.74**	**56**	**1,835,851**	**6.7**
Housekeeping supplies	19.58	62	274,942	7.4
Stationery, stationery supplies, giftwrap	9.98	66	140,139	7.9
Household textiles	10.90	82	153,058	9.8
Bathroom linens	1.14	41	16,008	4.9
Bedroom linens	2.76	47	38,756	5.6
Appliances and miscellaneous housewares	8.45	36	118,655	4.3
Major appliances	2.25	32	31,595	3.9
Small appliances and misc. housewares	6.20	38	87,060	4.5
Miscellaneous household equipment	22.65	34	318,051	4.1
Household decorative items	3.74	23	52,517	2.7
Indoor plants, fresh flowers	3.11	31	43,671	3.7
Apparel and services	**143.87**	**70**	**2,020,223**	**8.4**
Men and boys, aged 2 or older	38.86	81	545,672	9.6
Women and girls, aged 2 or older	49.05	64	688,760	7.6
Children under age 2	22.79	61	320,017	7.3
Jewelry	6.02	32	84,533	3.8
Transportation	**61.56**	**107**	**864,426**	**12.7**
Used cars	24.63	138	345,854	16.5
Airline fares	4.62	47	64,874	5.7
Health care	**5.02**	**11**	**70,491**	**1.4**
Entertainment	**33.02**	**45**	**463,667**	**5.3**
Toys, games, hobbies, and tricycles	10.50	42	147,441	5.0
Personal care products and services	**8.19**	**50**	**115,004**	**6.0**
Reading	**0.14**	**14**	**1,966**	**1.6**
Education	**98.11**	**40**	**1,377,661**	**4.7**
College tuition	68.30	34	959,069	4.1
All other gifts	**45.96**	**52**	**645,370**	**6.2**
Gifts of out-of-town trip expenses	12.80	26	179,738	3.1

Note: The index is calculated by dividing black spending on each item by average household spending on the item and multiplying by 100. Spending on gifts is also included in the product and service categories in other tables. Subcategories may not add to total because some are not shown.
Source: Bureau of Labor Statistics, unpublished data from the 2005 Consumer Expenditure Survey; calculations by New Strategist

Table 8.10 Spending on Groceries by Black Households, 2005

(average annual, indexed, aggregate, and market share of spending by black households on groceries, 2005)

	black average	index	aggregate (in 000s)	market share
GROCERIES	**$2,662.61**	**81**	**$37,388,370**	**9.7%**
Cereals and bakery products	**362.51**	**81**	**5,090,365**	**9.7**
Cereals and cereal products	131.59	92	1,847,787	11.0
Flour	4.02	82	56,449	9.8
Prepared flour mixes	10.34	89	145,194	10.6
Ready-to-eat and cooked cereals	80.69	92	1,133,049	11.0
Rice	20.14	124	282,806	14.8
Pasta, cornmeal, and other cereal products	16.39	75	230,148	8.9
Bakery products	230.92	76	3,242,579	9.1
Bread	73.29	86	1,029,138	10.3
White bread	32.61	102	457,910	12.2
Bread, other than white	40.67	77	571,088	9.2
Cookies and crackers	56.14	70	788,318	8.4
Cookies	34.79	71	488,521	8.5
Crackers	21.36	68	299,937	8.1
Frozen and refrigerated bakery products	20.18	83	283,368	9.9
Other bakery products	81.32	72	1,141,895	8.7
Biscuits and rolls	26.09	63	366,356	7.6
Cakes and cupcakes	30.44	91	427,438	10.9
Bread and cracker products	3.06	74	42,969	8.8
Sweetrolls, coffee cakes, doughnuts	12.41	61	174,261	7.3
Pies, tarts, turnovers	9.32	70	130,871	8.4
Meats, poultry, fish, and eggs	**786.73**	**103**	**11,047,263**	**12.3**
Beef	193.21	85	2,713,055	10.2
Ground beef	88.39	99	1,241,172	11.9
Roast	28.44	85	399,354	10.1
Chuck roast	9.05	94	127,080	11.3
Round roast	5.59	82	78,495	9.8
Other roast	13.79	80	193,639	9.6
Steak	54.00	63	758,268	7.6
Round steak	10.06	74	141,263	8.9
Sirloin steak	11.90	47	167,100	5.6
Other steak	32.05	69	450,046	8.3
Other beef	22.37	112	314,120	13.4
Pork	169.82	111	2,384,612	13.3
Bacon	32.07	113	450,327	13.5
Pork chops	42.91	130	602,542	15.6
Ham	27.10	94	380,538	11.3
Ham, not canned	26.96	97	378,572	11.6
Canned ham	0.14	16	1,966	1.9
Sausage	34.39	126	482,904	15.1
Other pork	33.35	93	468,301	11.1
Other meats	89.67	87	1,259,146	10.4
Frankfurters	23.04	114	323,528	13.6
Lunch meats (cold cuts)	57.44	78	806,572	9.3
Bologna, liverwurst, salami	15.73	84	220,881	10.1
Other lunch meats	41.71	75	585,692	9.0
Lamb, organ meats, and others	9.19	104	129,046	12.5

(continued)

	black average	index	aggregate (in 000s)	market share
Poultry	$177.46	132	$2,491,893	15.8%
Fresh and frozen chicken	144.40	131	2,027,665	15.7
Fresh and frozen whole chicken	31.33	116	439,936	13.8
Fresh and frozen chicken parts	113.07	136	1,587,729	16.3
Other poultry	33.05	137	464,088	16.3
Fish and seafood	121.34	107	1,703,856	12.8
Canned fish and seafood	13.58	87	190,690	10.4
Fresh fish and shellfish	73.68	121	1,034,615	14.5
Frozen fish and shellfish	34.08	92	478,551	11.0
Eggs	35.24	108	494,840	12.9
Dairy products	**245.45**	**65**	**3,446,609**	**7.8**
Fresh milk and cream	98.38	67	1,381,452	8.1
Fresh milk, all types	91.85	70	1,289,758	8.4
Cream	6.53	43	91,694	5.1
Other dairy products	147.07	63	2,065,157	7.6
Butter	14.08	72	197,711	8.7
Cheese	65.72	58	922,840	6.9
Ice cream and related products	42.74	69	600,155	8.2
Miscellaneous dairy products	24.51	67	344,169	8.1
Fruits and vegetables	**427.90**	**78**	**6,008,572**	**9.3**
Fresh fruits	121.56	67	1,706,946	8.0
Apples	19.50	65	273,819	7.8
Bananas	21.48	81	301,622	9.7
Oranges	16.65	85	233,799	10.2
Citrus fruits, excluding oranges	10.10	64	141,824	7.7
Other fresh fruits	53.84	60	756,021	7.2
Fresh vegetables	122.42	70	1,719,022	8.4
Potatoes	26.98	93	378,853	11.2
Lettuce	14.62	64	205,294	7.7
Tomatoes	21.00	66	294,882	7.9
Other fresh vegetables	59.82	66	839,992	7.9
Processed fruits	98.70	93	1,385,945	11.1
Frozen fruits and fruit juices	6.31	64	88,605	7.7
Frozen orange juice	2.14	63	30,050	7.5
Frozen fruits	2.87	68	40,301	8.2
Frozen fruit juices, excluding orange	1.29	58	18,114	7.0
Canned fruits	14.11	76	198,133	9.1
Dried fruits	4.03	55	56,589	6.6
Fresh fruit juice	13.39	80	188,022	9.5
Canned and bottled fruit juice	60.87	114	854,737	13.6
Processed vegetables	85.21	96	1,196,519	11.4
Frozen vegetables	29.18	104	409,746	12.5
Canned and dried vegetables and juices	56.03	92	786,773	11.0
Canned beans	11.26	94	158,113	11.3
Canned corn	6.65	110	93,379	13.2
Canned miscellaneous vegetables	15.59	82	218,915	9.8
Dried peas	0.23	85	3,230	10.2
Dried beans	3.19	106	44,794	12.6
Dried miscellaneous vegetables	6.16	72	86,499	8.6
Fresh and canned vegetable juices	12.60	106	176,929	12.6

(continued)

	black average	index	aggregate (in 000s)	market share
Sugar and other sweets	**$81.55**	**69**	**$1,145,125**	**8.2%**
Candy and chewing gum	38.46	51	540,055	6.1
Sugar	23.53	148	330,408	17.7
Artificial sweeteners	4.33	88	60,802	10.6
Jams, preserves, other sweets	15.22	66	213,719	7.9
Fats and oils	**79.38**	**93**	**1,114,654**	**11.2**
Margarine	6.63	84	93,098	10.1
Fats and oils	36.28	131	509,444	15.6
Salad dressings	20.74	78	291,231	9.3
Nondairy cream and imitation milk	6.98	62	98,013	7.4
Peanut butter	8.75	77	122,868	9.2
Miscellaneous foods	**432.07**	**71**	**6,067,127**	**8.5**
Frozen prepared foods	86.68	67	1,217,161	8.0
Frozen meals	26.94	63	378,291	7.5
Other frozen prepared foods	59.74	69	838,869	8.2
Canned and packaged soups	31.89	78	447,799	9.4
Potato chips, nuts, and other snacks	83.93	69	1,178,545	8.2
Potato chips and other snacks	67.90	74	953,452	8.8
Nuts	16.03	53	225,093	6.4
Condiments and seasonings	77.29	73	1,085,306	8.8
Salt, spices, and other seasonings	23.19	99	325,634	11.9
Olives, pickles, relishes	8.00	62	112,336	7.4
Sauces and gravies	31.40	67	440,919	8.1
Baking needs and miscellaneous products	14.70	65	206,417	7.7
Other canned or packaged prepared foods	152.29	72	2,138,456	8.6
Prepared salads	21.25	66	298,393	7.9
Prepared desserts	7.15	54	100,400	6.5
Baby food	21.60	72	303,307	8.7
Miscellaneous prepared foods	102.29	76	1,436,356	9.1
Nonalcoholic beverages	**230.26**	**76**	**3,233,311**	**9.1**
Cola	62.75	74	881,136	8.8
Other carbonated drinks	35.27	74	495,261	8.8
Coffee	27.17	56	381,521	6.7
Roasted coffee	17.22	54	241,803	6.5
Instant and freeze-dried coffee	9.95	59	139,718	7.1
Noncarbonated fruit-flavored drinks	28.12	155	394,861	18.6
Tea	15.10	66	212,034	7.9
Other nonalcoholic beverages and ice	61.65	76	865,689	9.2
Groceries purchased on trips	**16.76**	**41**	**235,344**	**4.9**

Note: The index is calculated by dividing black spending on each item by average household spending on the item and multiplying by 100. Subcategories may not add to total because some are not shown.
Source: Bureau of Labor Statistics, unpublished data from the 2005 Consumer Expenditure Survey; calculations by New Strategist

Table 8.11 Out-of-Pocket Spending on Health Care by Black Households, 2005

(average annual, indexed, aggregate, and market share of spending by black households on out-of-pocket health care costs, 2005)

	black average	index	aggregate (in 000s)	market share
HEALTH CARE	**$1,448.18**	**54**	**$20,335,344**	**6.5%**
Health insurance	**841.00**	**62**	**11,809,322**	**7.4**
Commercial health insurance	117.58	44	1,651,058	5.3
Traditional fee-for-service health plan (not BCBS)	34.91	48	490,206	5.7
Preferred-provider health plan (not BCBS)	82.67	43	1,160,852	5.2
Blue Cross, Blue Shield	254.44	64	3,572,846	7.6
Traditional fee-for-service health plan	24.65	36	346,135	4.3
Preferred-provider health plan	114.43	70	1,606,826	8.4
Health maintenance organization	99.96	80	1,403,638	9.5
Commercial Medicare supplement	14.51	36	203,749	4.3
Other BCBS health insurance	0.89	24	12,497	2.9
Health maintenance plans (HMOs)	205.49	76	2,885,491	9.1
Medicare payments	197.31	74	2,770,627	8.9
Commercial Medicare supplements and other health insurance	54.86	43	770,344	5.2
Commercial Medicare supplement (not BCBS)	43.67	47	613,214	5.6
Other health insurance (not BCBS)	11.18	33	156,990	3.9
Long term care insurance	11.31	34	158,815	4.1
Medical services	**320.65**	**47**	**4,502,567**	**5.7**
Physician's services	60.70	39	852,349	4.7
Dental services	53.55	21	751,949	2.5
Eye care services	16.15	44	226,778	5.3
Service by professionals other than physician	17.15	33	240,820	4.0
Lab tests, X-rays	10.56	24	148,284	2.9
Hospital room and services	153.24	162	2,151,796	19.4
Care in convalescent or nursing home	4.31	16	60,521	1.9
Other medical services	4.99	35	70,070	4.2
Drugs	**243.99**	**47**	**3,426,108**	**5.6**
Nonprescription drugs	34.70	48	487,257	5.8
Nonprescription vitamins	13.99	32	196,448	3.8
Prescription drugs	195.30	48	2,742,403	5.8
Medical supplies	**42.54**	**40**	**597,347**	**4.8**
Eyeglasses and contact lenses	25.78	48	362,003	5.7
Hearing aids	0.84	7	11,795	0.8
Topicals and dressings	12.22	42	171,593	5.0
Medical equipment for general use	1.31	31	18,395	3.7
Supportive and convalescent medical equipment	1.15	34	16,148	4.0
Rental of medical equipment	0.17	20	2,387	2.4
Rental of supportive, convalescent medical equip.	1.07	147	15,025	17.5

Note: The index is calculated by dividing black spending on each item by average household spending on the item and multiplying by 100. Subcategories may not add to total because some are not shown.
Source: Bureau of Labor Statistics, unpublished data from the 2005 Consumer Expenditure Survey; calculations by New Strategist

Table 8.12 Spending on Household Operations by Black Households, 2005

(average annual, indexed, aggregate, and market share of spending by black households on household services, supplies, furnishings, and equipment, 2005)

	black average	index	aggregate (in 000s)	market share
HOUSEHOLD SERVICES	**$529.72**	**77**	**$7,438,328**	**7.9%**
Personal services	**289.07**	**66**	**4,059,121**	**10.8**
Babysitting, child care in own home	11.12	90	156,147	3.2
Babysitting, child care in someone else's home	39.71	27	557,608	16.5
Care for elderly, invalids, handicapped, etc.	9.18	138	128,906	4.4
Day care centers, nurseries, and preschools	224.32	37	3,149,901	11.9
Other household services	**240.65**	**100**	**3,379,207**	**6.0**
Housekeeping services	11.53	50	161,904	1.5
Gardening, lawn care service	46.71	13	655,902	5.8
Water-softening service	3.53	49	49,568	10.2
Nonclothing laundry, dry cleaning, sent out	0.73	85	10,251	8.4
Nonclothing laundry, dry cleaning, coin-operated	5.69	70	79,899	21.8
Termite and pest control services	6.28	182	88,184	4.8
Home security system service fee	18.96	40	266,236	13.8
Other home services	7.36	115	103,349	5.0
Termite and pest control products	1.03	42	14,463	5.5
Moving, storage, and freight express	26.48	46	371,832	8.7
Appliance repair, including at service center	5.90	73	82,848	4.9
Reupholstering and furniture repair	1.22	41	17,131	1.7
Repairs and rentals of lawn and garden equipment, hand and power tools, etc.	1.56	15	21,906	2.9
Appliance rental	0.99	24	13,902	6.8
Repair of computer systems, nonbusiness use	1.77	57	24,854	4.3
Computer information services	100.84	36	1,415,995	7.8
HOUSEKEEPING SUPPLIES	**352.49**	**58**	**4,949,665**	**6.9**
Laundry and cleaning supplies	**119.18**	**89**	**1,673,526**	**10.6**
Soaps and detergents	67.36	95	945,869	11.3
Other laundry cleaning products	51.83	82	727,797	9.9
Other household products	**159.53**	**50**	**2,240,120**	**6.0**
Cleansing and toilet tissue, paper towels, and napkins	67.83	71	952,469	8.6
Miscellaneous household products	68.32	52	959,349	6.3
Lawn and garden supplies	23.38	25	328,302	3.0
Postage and stationery	73.78	47	1,036,019	5.6
Stationery, stationery supplies, giftwrap	37.25	44	523,065	5.2
Postage	35.48	52	498,210	6.3
Delivery services	1.05	25	14,744	2.9
HOUSEHOLD FURNISHINGS AND EQUIPMENT	**990.76**	**56**	**13,912,252**	**6.7**
Household textiles	**93.41**	**71**	**1,311,663**	**8.4**
Bathroom linens	24.13	110	338,833	13.2
Bedroom linens	48.14	74	675,982	8.9

(continued)

	black average	index	aggregate (in 000s)	market share
Kitchen and dining room linens	$1.21	14	$16,991	1.7%
Curtains and draperies	8.59	46	120,621	5.5
Slipcovers and decorative pillows	8.02	116	112,617	13.8
Sewing materials for household items	2.38	24	33,420	2.8
Other linens	0.95	78	13,340	9.3
Furniture	**298.30**	**64**	**4,188,729**	**7.6**
Mattresses and springs	23.17	40	325,353	4.8
Other bedroom furniture	90.58	97	1,271,924	11.5
Sofas	81.14	76	1,139,368	9.1
Living room chairs	26.86	51	377,168	6.1
Living room tables	11.75	66	164,994	7.9
Kitchen and dining room furniture	21.65	43	304,009	5.2
Infants' furniture	3.39	41	47,602	4.9
Outdoor furniture	5.45	30	76,529	3.6
Wall units, cabinets, and other furniture	34.31	55	481,781	6.6
Floor coverings	**16.23**	**29**	**227,902**	**3.5**
Wall-to-wall carpeting	7.10	27	99,698	3.2
Floor coverings, nonpermanent	9.13	31	128,203	3.7
Major appliances	**143.42**	**64**	**2,013,904**	**7.7**
Dishwashers (built-in), garbage disposals, range hoods	9.57	58	134,382	6.9
Refrigerators and freezers	38.72	64	543,706	7.6
Washing machines	24.67	76	346,416	9.1
Clothes dryers	16.76	73	235,344	8.7
Cooking stoves, ovens	29.32	71	411,711	8.5
Microwave ovens	8.77	81	123,148	9.7
Portable dishwashers	1.02	179	14,323	21.4
Window air conditioners	5.76	102	80,882	12.2
Electric floor-cleaning equipment	7.79	32	109,387	3.8
Sewing machines	1.03	33	14,463	4.0
Small appliances and misc. housewares	**46.27**	**44**	**649,723**	**5.3**
Housewares	32.75	41	459,876	4.9
Plastic dinnerware	1.84	107	25,837	12.8
China and other dinnerware	4.10	31	57,572	3.8
Flatware	1.75	54	24,574	6.5
Glassware	3.52	30	49,428	3.5
Silver serving pieces	3.22	67	45,215	8.0
Other serving pieces	0.36	23	5,055	2.7
Nonelectric cookware	8.60	42	120,761	5.0
Tableware, nonelectric kitchenware	9.36	40	131,433	4.8
Small appliances	13.52	54	189,848	6.4
Small electric kitchen appliances	9.91	53	139,156	6.4
Portable heating and cooling equipment	3.60	56	50,551	6.7
Miscellaneous household equipment	**393.13**	**50**	**5,520,331**	**6.0**
Window coverings	9.24	28	129,748	3.3
Infants' equipment	14.16	101	198,835	12.1

(continued)

	black average	index	aggregate (in 000s)	market share
Laundry and cleaning equipment	$5.95	36	$83,550	4.3%
Outdoor equipment	9.95	35	139,718	4.1
Clocks	1.57	32	22,046	3.8
Lamps and lighting fixtures	5.76	29	80,882	3.5
Other household decorative items	114.88	61	1,613,145	7.2
Telephones and accessories	21.48	69	301,622	8.2
Lawn and garden equipment	24.00	47	337,008	5.6
Power tools	12.52	23	175,806	2.8
Office furniture for home use	2.94	30	41,283	3.5
Hand tools	0.67	11	9,408	1.3
Indoor plants and fresh flowers	14.53	32	204,030	3.8
Closet and storage items	4.07	28	57,151	3.4
Rental of furniture	12.88	428	180,861	51.2
Luggage	2.51	36	35,245	4.4
Computers and computer hardware for nonbusiness use	89.13	60	1,251,563	7.2
Computer software and accessories for nonbusiness use	11.42	58	160,360	6.9
Personal digital assistants	1.66	48	23,310	5.7
Internet services away from home	2.66	74	37,352	8.9
Telephone answering devices	0.57	48	8,004	5.7
Business equipment for home use	1.74	61	24,433	7.3
Other hardware	8.03	32	112,757	3.8
Smoke alarms	0.97	87	13,621	10.5
Other household appliances	4.78	49	67,121	5.9

Note: The index is calculated by dividing black spending on each item by average household spending on the item and multiplying by 100. Subcategories may not add to total because some are not shown.
Source: Bureau of Labor Statistics, unpublished data from the 2005 Consumer Expenditure Survey; calculations by New Strategist

Table 8.13 **Spending on Personal Care, Reading, Education, and Tobacco by Black Households, 2005**

(average annual, indexed, aggregate, and market share of spending by black households on personal care, reading, education, and tobacco products, 2005)

	black average	index	aggregate (in 000s)	market share
PERSONAL CARE PRODUCTS AND SERVICES	**$472.08**	**87**	**$6,628,947**	**10.4%**
Personal care products	**201.10**	**74**	**2,823,846**	**8.8**
Hair care products	34.96	70	490,908	8.4
Hair accessories	6.25	104	87,763	12.4
Wigs and hairpieces	9.15	532	128,484	63.7
Oral hygiene products	20.39	72	286,316	8.6
Shaving products	9.95	67	139,718	8.0
Cosmetics, perfume, and bath products	95.22	72	1,337,079	8.6
Deodorants, feminine hygiene, miscellaneous products	22.85	77	320,860	9.3
Electric personal care appliances	2.32	21	32,577	2.5
Personal care services	**270.98**	**101**	**3,805,101**	**12.1**
READING	**52.44**	**41**	**736,362**	**5.0**
Newspaper and magazine subscriptions	18.44	35	258,934	4.2
Newspapers and magazines, nonsubscription	14.06	89	197,431	10.7
Books	19.85	35	278,734	4.1
EDUCATION	**500.13**	**53**	**7,022,825**	**6.4**
College tuition	269.37	48	3,782,494	5.7
Elementary and high school tuition	99.36	56	1,395,213	6.7
Other school tuition	27.90	84	391,772	10.1
Other school expenses including rentals	22.19	55	311,592	6.6
Books, supplies for college	42.45	66	596,083	7.9
Books, supplies for elementary, high school	11.77	76	165,274	9.1
Books, supplies for day care, nursery school	3.14	75	44,092	8.9
Miscellaneous school expenses and supplies	23.97	57	336,587	6.8
TOBACCO PRODUCTS AND SMOKING SUPPLIES	**216.21**	**68**	**3,036,021**	**8.1**
Cigarettes	206.33	71	2,897,286	8.5
Other tobacco products	9.08	38	127,501	4.5
Smoking accessories	0.80	33	11,234	4.0

Note: The index is calculated by dividing black spending on each item by average household spending on the item and multiplying by 100. Subcategories may not add to total because some are not shown.
Source: Bureau of Labor Statistics, unpublished data from the 2005 Consumer Expenditure Survey; calculations by New Strategist

Table 8.14 Spending on Restaurant Meals by Black Households, 2005

(average annual, indexed, aggregate, and market share of spending by black households on restaurant meals and other food away from home, 2005)

	black average	index	aggregate (in 000s)	market share
Meals at restaurants	**$1,475.65**	**68**	**$20,721,077**	**8.1%**
Lunch	550.17	72	7,725,487	8.7
At fast-food restaurants*	324.35	89	4,554,523	10.7
At full-service restaurants	142.46	50	2,000,423	5.9
At vending machines, mobile vendors	8.98	61	126,097	7.2
At employer and school cafeterias	74.37	78	1,044,304	9.3
Dinner	643.17	62	9,031,393	7.4
At fast-food restaurants*	294.23	87	4,131,578	10.4
At full-service restaurants	343.68	50	4,825,955	5.9
At vending machines, mobile vendors	0.90	25	12,638	3.0
At employer and school cafeterias	4.36	72	61,223	8.7
Snacks and nonalcoholic beverages	122.36	70	1,718,179	8.3
At fast-food restaurants*	60.13	56	844,345	6.7
At full-service restaurants	20.93	74	293,899	8.9
At vending machines, mobile vendors	33.23	98	466,616	11.7
At employer and school cafeterias	8.06	123	113,179	14.7
Breakfast and brunch	159.96	77	2,246,158	9.2
At fast-food restaurants*	94.85	94	1,331,884	11.3
At full-service restaurants	52.90	57	742,822	6.8
At vending machines, mobile vendors	2.69	76	37,773	9.1
At employer and school cafeterias	9.52	91	133,680	10.9
Board (including at school)	**14.79**	**38**	**207,681**	**4.5**
Catered affairs	**17.45**	**23**	**245,033**	**2.7**
Food on trips	**71.05**	**30**	**997,684**	**3.6**
School lunches	**62.86**	**88**	**882,680**	**10.5**
Meals as pay	**14.86**	**55**	**208,664**	**6.6**

* The category fast-food restaurants also includes take-out, delivery, concession stands, buffets, and cafeterias other than employer and school.
Note: The index is calculated by dividing black spending on each item by average household spending on the item and multiplying by 100. Subcategories may not add to total because some are not shown.
Source: Bureau of Labor Statistics, unpublished data from the 2005 Consumer Expenditure Survey; calculations by New Strategist

Table 8.15 Spending on Shelter and Utilities by Black Households, 2005

(average annual, indexed, aggregate, and market share of spending by black households on shelter and utilities, 2005)

	black average	index	aggregate (in 000s)	market share
SHELTER	**$6,524.01**	**74**	**$91,610,148**	**8.9%**
Owned dwellings*	3,187.62	54	44,760,560	6.4
Mortgage interest and charges	1,997.88	60	28,054,231	7.2
Mortgage interest	1,895.11	62	26,611,135	7.4
Interest paid, home equity loan	40.69	50	571,369	6.0
Interest paid, home equity line of credit	61.89	40	869,059	4.8
Property taxes	733.70	48	10,302,615	5.7
Maintenance, repairs, insurance, other expenses	456.04	41	6,403,714	5.0
Homeowner's insurance	202.31	61	2,840,837	7.4
Ground rent	15.31	35	214,983	4.2
Maintenance and repair services	194.87	33	2,736,365	3.9
Painting and papering	26.68	37	374,641	4.5
Plumbing and water heating	17.76	35	249,386	4.2
Heat, air conditioning, electrical work	37.34	44	524,328	5.2
Roofing and gutters	24.35	20	341,923	2.4
Other repair and maintenance services	61.34	31	861,336	3.7
Repair, replacement of hard-surface flooring	24.44	43	343,186	5.2
Repair of built-in appliances	2.96	47	41,564	5.6
Maintenance and repair materials	13.20	16	185,354	1.9
Paints, wallpaper, and supplies	3.92	25	55,045	3.0
Tools, equip. for painting, wallpapering	0.42	25	5,898	3.0
Plumbing supplies and equipment	1.82	30	25,556	3.6
Electrical supplies, heating cooling equip.	0.19	3	2,668	0.4
Hard-surface flooring, repair and replacement	0.39	4	5,476	0.5
Roofing and gutters	0.35	4	4,915	0.5
Plaster, paneling, siding, windows, doors, screens, awnings	0.58	5	8,144	0.6
Patio, walk, fence, driveway, masonry, brick, and stucco materials	0.02	2	281	0.2
Miscellaneous supplies and equipment	5.49	24	77,091	2.9
Property management and security	27.79	60	390,227	7.2
Property management	21.65	66	304,009	8.0
Management and upkeep services for security	6.14	45	86,218	5.3
Parking	2.56	35	35,948	4.2
Rented dwellings	**3,147.57**	**134**	**44,198,178**	**16.1**
Rent	3,018.20	133	42,381,564	15.9
Rent as pay	103.73	268	1,456,577	32.1
Maintenance, insurance, and other expenses	25.63	72	359,896	8.7
Tenant's insurance	11.15	125	156,568	15.0
Maintenance and repair services	10.43	64	146,458	7.6
Maintenance and repair materials	4.05	40	56,870	4.8

(continued)

	black average	index	aggregate (in 000s)	market share
Other lodging	**$188.82**	**38**	**$2,651,410**	**4.5%**
Owned vacation homes	58.41	40	820,193	4.8
Mortgage interest and charges	31.53	61	442,744	7.3
Property taxes	18.15	30	254,862	3.6
Maintenance, insurance, and other expenses	8.73	25	122,587	3.0
Housing while attending school	42.49	69	596,645	8.2
Lodging on trips	87.92	30	1,234,573	3.6
UTILITIES, FUELS, AND PUBLIC SERVICES	**3,252.61**	**102**	**45,673,150**	**12.2**
Natural gas	**549.02**	**116**	**7,709,339**	**13.9**
Electricity	**1,205.40**	**104**	**16,926,227**	**12.5**
Fuel oil and other fuels	**44.82**	**32**	**629,362**	**3.8**
Fuel oil	30.41	38	427,017	4.5
Coal, wood, and other fuels	2.79	34	39,177	4.0
Bottled gas	11.62	22	163,168	2.7
Telephone services	**1,123.60**	**107**	**15,777,591**	**12.8**
Residential telephone and pay phones	681.81	120	9,573,976	14.3
Cellular phone service	415.45	91	5,833,749	10.9
Pager service	1.73	104	24,293	12.5
Phone cards	24.61	117	345,574	14.0
Water and other public services	329.76	90	4,630,490	10.8
Water and sewerage maintenance	**262.66**	**101**	**3,688,272**	**12.1**
Trash and garbage collection	63.56	63	892,510	7.5
Septic tank cleaning	3.54	84	49,709	10.0

* The amount paid in mortgage principal is not shown here because it is considered an asset.
Note: The index is calculated by dividing black spending on each item by average household spending on the item and multiplying by 100. Subcategories may not add to total because some are not shown.
Source: Bureau of Labor Statistics, unpublished data from the 2005 Consumer Expenditure Survey; calculations by New Strategist

Table 8.16 Spending on Transportation by Black Households, 2005

(average annual, indexed, aggregate, and market share of spending by black households on transportation, 2005)

	black average	index	aggregate (in 000s)	market share
TRANSPORTATION	**$5,849.72**	**70**	**$82,141,768**	**8.4%**
Vehicle purchases	2,349.54	66	32,992,241	7.9
Cars and trucks, new	988.19	51	13,876,164	6.1
New cars	476.93	59	6,697,051	7.0
New trucks	511.26	46	7,179,113	5.5
Cars and trucks, used	1,306.61	85	18,347,418	10.2
Used cars	944.78	117	13,266,601	14.0
Used trucks	361.83	50	5,080,817	6.0
Other vehicles	54.73	67	768,519	8.0
New motorcycles	54.60	111	766,693	13.3
Used motorcycles	0.14	0	1,966	0.1
Gasoline and motor oil	**1,545.87**	**77**	**21,707,107**	**9.2**
Gasoline	1,494.84	81	20,990,543	9.7
Diesel fuel	2.17	6	30,471	0.8
Gasoline on trips	43.47	36	610,406	4.3
Motor oil	4.95	54	69,508	6.5
Motor oil on trips	0.44	36	6,178	4.4
Other vehicle expenses	**1,709.81**	**73**	**24,009,152**	**8.7**
Vehicle finance charges	228.74	77	3,211,967	9.2
Automobile finance charges	123.54	109	1,734,749	13.0
Truck finance charges	103.93	63	1,459,385	7.5
Motorcycle and plane finance charges	0.56	14	7,864	1.7
Other vehicle finance charges	0.70	5	9,829	0.6
Maintenance and repairs	432.95	64	6,079,484	7.7
Coolant, additives, brake, transmission fluids	3.08	89	43,249	10.6
Tires—purchased, replaced, installed	60.85	63	854,456	7.6
Parts, equipment, and accessories	17.87	41	250,931	5.0
Vehicle products and cleaning services	4.52	68	63,470	8.2
Vehicle video equipment	9.77	423	137,190	50.6
Miscellaneous auto repair, servicing	24.38	61	342,344	7.3
Body work and painting	16.18	50	227,200	6.0
Clutch and transmission repair	28.13	59	395,001	7.0
Drive shaft and rear-end repair	3.65	57	51,253	6.8
Brake work	40.72	77	571,790	9.2
Repair to steering or front-end	12.04	72	169,066	8.6
Repair to engine cooling system	19.75	95	277,330	11.3
Motor tune-up	27.34	56	383,908	6.6
Lube, oil change, and oil filters	39.12	61	549,323	7.3
Front-end alignment, wheel balance, rotation	10.16	89	142,667	10.7
Shock absorber replacement	3.43	70	48,164	8.3
Tire repair and other repair work	28.07	70	394,159	8.4

(continued)

	black average	index	aggregate (in 000s)	market share
Vehicle air conditioning repair	$11.31	79	$158,815	9.5%
Exhaust system repair	6.25	66	87,763	7.9
Electrical system repair	18.72	79	262,866	9.4
Motor repair, replacement	34.53	55	484,870	6.6
Auto repair service policy	7.73	59	108,545	7.0
Vehicle insurance	747.39	82	10,494,850	9.8
Vehicle rental, leases, licenses, other charges	300.73	66	4,222,851	7.9
Leased and rented vehicles	201.51	73	2,829,603	8.7
Rented vehicles	34.96	89	490,908	10.7
Auto rental	17.51	234	245,875	28.0
Auto rental on trips	12.53	54	175,946	6.5
Truck rental	3.09	113	43,390	13.5
Truck rental on trips	1.83	53	25,697	6.4
Leased vehicles	166.55	70	2,338,695	8.4
Car lease payments	73.96	69	1,038,546	8.3
Truck lease payments	84.32	75	1,184,021	8.9
Vehicle registration, state	39.44	48	553,816	5.7
Vehicle registration, local	4.73	67	66,419	8.1
Driver's license	4.08	55	57,291	6.6
Vehicle inspection	5.32	55	74,703	6.5
Parking fees	16.12	51	226,357	6.1
Parking fees in home city, excl. residence	13.95	54	195,886	6.4
Parking fees on trips	2.17	37	30,471	4.5
Tolls	14.54	102	204,171	12.1
Tolls on trips	2.82	61	39,598	7.3
Towing charges	4.67	93	65,576	11.2
Global positioning services	0.36	25	5,055	3.0
Automobile service clubs	7.14	40	100,260	4.8
Public transportation	**244.50**	**55**	**3,433,269**	**6.5**
Airline fares	97.20	34	1,364,882	4.1
Intercity bus fares	6.77	56	95,064	6.7
Intracity mass transit fares	91.07	177	1,278,805	21.2
Local transportation on trips	3.87	34	54,343	4.1
Taxi fares and limousine service on trips	2.27	34	31,875	4.1
Taxi fares and limousine service	12.81	72	179,878	8.6
Intercity train fares	8.25	43	115,847	5.1
Ship fares	21.05	50	295,584	6.0
School bus	1.21	47	16,991	5.6

Note: The index is calculated by dividing black spending on each item by average household spending on the item and multiplying by 100. Subcategories may not add to total because some are not shown.
Source: Bureau of Labor Statistics, unpublished data from the 2005 Consumer Expenditure Survey; calculations by New Strategist

Time Use

■ After sleep, work is the most time-consuming activity for blacks. Blacks who worked on diary day spent 7.46 hours on the job.

■ Blacks spend more than twice as much time involved in religious activities as the average person. They also spend 11 percent more time in school on an average day.

■ Black men spend 14 percent more time than the average man caring for people in other households and 20 percent more time grooming.

■ Black women are 47 percent more likely to attend class than the average woman and 40 percent more likely to participate in religious activities. They are 16 percent less likely than the average woman to socialize.

Work Ranks Second in Time Use among Blacks

Watching television is third.

We know how blacks use time because of the American Time Use Survey (ATUS), introduced by the Bureau of Labor Statistics in 2003. The ATUS collects data on how Americans spend their time during an average day. ATUS data are now published annually, allowing social scientists to better understand our economy, our lifestyles, and the way policy decisions affect our lives. Through telephone interviews with a nationally representative sample of Americans aged 15 or older, ATUS asks survey respondents what they did minute by minute during the previous 24 hours—or diary day.

The following pages show how blacks aged 15 or older use their time. All of us spend more time sleeping than doing any other activity. Among blacks aged 15 or older, sleep consumes 9.08 hours a day, on average. After sleep, work is the most time-consuming activity for blacks, with the average black working 3.3 hours a day. This figure appears low because it includes weekdays and weekends, people of working age and retirees. Blacks who worked on diary day spent 7.46 hours on the job.

Television is the third most time-consuming activity for blacks. The average black person aged 15 or older spends 3.19 hours a day watching television as a primary activity.

■ Ten percent of blacks aged 15 or older are involved in educational activities on an average day.

One-third of blacks do housework on an average day

(percent of blacks aged 15 or older who participate in selected activities on an average day, 2005)

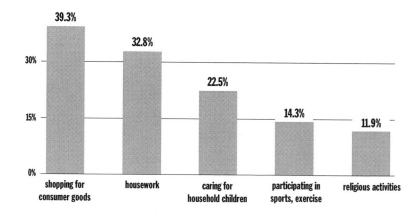

Table 9.1 Time Use of Total Blacks, 2005

(number and percent of total blacks aged 15 or older participating in primary activities on an average day, hours spent doing activity by the average black aged 15 or older and by blacks aged 15 or older who participated in the activity, 2005; numbers of participants in thousands)

	total blacks participating		hours spent doing activity	
	number	percent	average black	black participants
Total, all activities	**26,921**	**100.0%**	**24.00**	**24.00**
Personal care	26,916	100.0	10.09	10.09
Sleeping	26,894	99.9	9.08	9.09
Grooming	21,842	81.1	0.79	0.98
Eating and drinking	25,309	94.0	0.88	0.93
Household activities	18,086	67.2	1.29	1.93
Housework	8,828	32.8	0.47	1.42
Food preparation and cleanup	13,450	50.0	0.49	0.98
Lawn, garden, and houseplants	1,629	6.1	0.13	2.08
Household management	3,948	14.7	0.07	0.49
Consumer purchases (store, telephone, Internet)	11,609	43.1	0.73	1.70
Consumer goods purchases	10,572	39.3	0.37	0.94
Professional and personal care	2,021	7.5	0.08	1.04
Caring for and helping household members	6,958	25.8	0.45	1.74
Caring for and helping household children	6,047	22.5	0.35	1.54
Caring for and helping people in other households	3,810	14.2	0.23	1.64
Caring for and helping adults in other households	1,660	6.2	0.07	0.70
Work and work-related activities	11,271	41.9	3.30	7.89
Working	10,658	39.6	2.96	7.46
Education	2,651	9.8	0.50	5.07
Attending class	2,064	7.7	0.35	4.53
Research, homework	1,464	5.4	0.11	2.08
Organizational, civic, and religious activities	4,567	17.0	0.47	2.74
Religious and spiritual activities	3,192	11.9	0.27	2.26
Volunteer activities	1,829	6.8	0.14	2.04
Leisure and sports	25,812	95.9	5.69	5.94
Socializing and communicating	10,474	38.9	0.78	2.00
Watching television	21,490	79.8	3.19	4.00
Participating in sports, exercise, or recreation	3,839	14.3	0.22	1.54
Telephone calls, mail, and email	6,302	23.4	0.21	0.91

Note: Primary activities are those respondents identified as their main activity. Other activities done simultaneously, such as eating while watching TV, are not included. Time spent doing activities includes related travel time. Numbers may not add to total because not all subcategories are shown.
Source: Bureau of Labor Statistics, unpublished tables from the 2005 American Time Use Survey, Internet site http://www.bls.gov/tus/home.htm; calculations by New Strategist

Table 9.2 Time Use of Black Men, 2005

(number and percent of black men aged 15 or older participating in primary activities on an average day, hours spent doing activity by the average black man aged 15 or older and by black men aged 15 or older who participated in the activity, 2005; numbers of participants in thousands)

	black men participating		hours spent doing activity	
	number	percent	average black man	black men participating
Total, all activities	**12,150**	**100.0%**	**24.00**	**24.00**
Personal care	12,150	100.0	9.87	9.87
Sleeping	12,127	99.8	9.05	9.06
Grooming	9,309	76.6	0.65	0.84
Eating and drinking	11,487	94.5	0.93	0.98
Household activities	7,088	58.3	0.92	1.58
Housework	2,536	20.9	0.23	1.10
Food preparation and cleanup	4,613	38.0	0.26	0.68
Lawn, garden, and houseplants	–	–	–	–
Household management	1,732	14.3	0.07	0.46
Consumer purchases (store, telephone, Internet)	4,959	40.8	0.56	1.36
Consumer goods purchases	4,437	36.5	0.27	0.73
Professional and personal care	–	–	–	–
Caring for and helping household members	2,256	18.6	0.24	1.28
Caring for and helping household children	1,824	15.0	0.18	1.17
Caring for and helping people in other households	1,557	12.8	0.24	1.87
Caring for and helping adults in other households	1,126	9.3	0.06	0.62
Work and work-related activities	5,426	44.7	3.57	7.99
Working	5,062	41.7	3.18	7.63
Education	–	–	–	–
Attending class	–	–	–	–
Research, homework	–	–	–	–
Organizational, civic, and religious activities	2,049	16.9	0.43	2.54
Religious and spiritual activities	1,316	10.8	0.24	2.24
Volunteer activities	–	–	–	–
Leisure and sports	11,864	97.6	6.46	6.62
Socializing and communicating	5,120	42.1	0.87	2.08
Watching television	9,790	80.6	3.66	4.54
Participating in sports, exercise, or recreation	2,302	18.9	0.31	1.65
Telephone calls, mail, and email	2,627	21.6	0.20	0.93

Note: Primary activities are those respondents identified as their main activity. Other activities done simultaneously, such as eating while watching TV, are not included. Time spent doing activities includes related travel time. Numbers may not add to total because not all subcategories are shown. "–" means sample is too small to make a reliable estimate.
Source: Bureau of Labor Statistics, unpublished tables from the 2005 American Time Use Survey, Internet site http://www.bls .gov/tus/home.htm; calculations by New Strategist

Table 9.3 Time Use of Black Women, 2005

(number and percent of black women aged 15 or older participating in primary activities on an average day, hours spent doing activity by the average black man aged 15 or older and by black women aged 15 or older who participated in the activity, 2005; numbers of participants in thousands)

	black women participating		hours spent doing activity	
	number	percent	average black woman	black women participating
Total, all activities	**14,771**	**100.0%**	**24.00**	**24.00**
Personal care	14,767	100.0	10.27	10.27
Sleeping	14,767	100.0	9.11	9.11
Grooming	12,533	84.8	0.91	1.07
Eating and drinking	13,821	93.6	0.84	0.89
Household activities	10,998	74.5	1.60	2.15
Housework	6,292	42.6	0.66	1.56
Food preparation and cleanup	8,838	59.8	0.68	1.14
Lawn, garden, and houseplants	–	–	–	–
Household management	2,216	15.0	0.08	0.51
Consumer purchases (store, telephone, Internet)	6,650	45.0	0.87	1.94
Consumer goods purchases	6,134	41.5	0.45	1.09
Professional and personal care	1,155	7.8	0.10	1.22
Caring for and helping household members	4,702	31.8	0.63	1.97
Caring for and helping household children	4,224	28.6	0.48	1.69
Caring for and helping people in other households	2,254	15.3	0.22	1.47
Caring for and helping adults in other households	1,380	9.3	0.07	0.78
Work and work-related activities	5,845	39.6	3.09	7.80
Working	5,596	37.9	2.77	7.31
Education	1,631	11.0	0.55	4.98
Attending class	1,278	8.7	0.37	4.23
Research, homework			–	–
Organizational, civic, and religious activities	2,519	17.1	0.50	2.91
Religious and spiritual activities	1,876	12.7	0.29	2.27
Volunteer activities	925	6.3	0.14	2.22
Leisure and sports	13,948	94.4	5.06	5.36
Socializing and communicating	5,353	36.2	0.70	1.93
Watching television	11,699	79.2	2.81	3.55
Participating in sports, exercise, or recreation	1,537	10.4	0.14	1.39
Telephone calls, mail, and email	3,675	24.9	0.22	0.90

Note: Primary activities are those respondents identified as their main activity. Other activities done simultaneously, such as eating while watching TV, are not included. Time spent doing activities includes related travel time. Numbers may not add to total because not all subcategories are shown. "–" means sample is too small to make a reliable estimate.
Source: Bureau of Labor Statistics, unpublished tables from the 2005 American Time Use Survey, Internet site http://www.bls .gov/tus/home.htm; calculations by New Strategist

Blacks Spend More Time Participating in Religious Activities

Black women spend 21 percent more time than black men involved in religious activities.

Blacks spend about the same amount of time as the average person doing most activities. They spend more time doing some activities however. The biggest difference is in the amount of time devoted to religious activities. Blacks spend more than twice as much time involved in religious activities as the average person. They spend 11 percent more time in school on an average day and 11 percent less time working.

Black men spend 14 percent more time than the average man caring for people in other households. They spend 20 percent more time grooming than the average man and 31 percent more time watching television. Black women spend more time than the average woman working and going to school. They spend 17 percent more time grooming and 19 percent more time watching television.

■ Black women spend more than twice as much time as black men doing housework, preparing meals, and caring for household children.

Blacks spend more time than the average person in the classroom

(index of black to total people aged 15 or older in time spent doing selected activities on an average day, 2005)

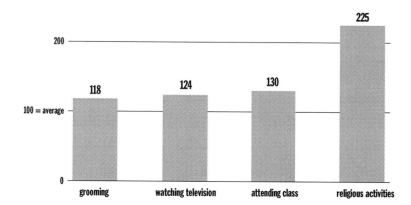

Table 9.4 Indexed Time Use of Total Blacks, 2005

(hours spent doing primary activities on an average day by blacks aged 15 or older and total people aged 15 or older, and index of time spent by blacks to total people, 2005)

	average hours		index, blacks
	blacks	total	to total people
Total, all activities	**24.00**	**24.00**	**100**
Personal care	10.09	9.43	107
Sleeping	9.08	8.63	105
Grooming	0.79	0.67	118
Eating and drinking	0.88	1.24	71
Household activities	1.29	1.82	71
Housework	0.47	0.61	77
Food preparation and cleanup	0.49	0.51	96
Lawn, garden, and houseplants	0.13	0.20	65
Household management	0.07	0.15	47
Consumer purchases (store, telephone, Internet)	0.73	0.80	91
Consumer goods purchases	0.37	0.41	90
Professional and personal care	0.08	0.08	100
Caring for and helping household members	0.45	0.54	83
Caring for and helping household children	0.35	0.42	83
Caring for and helping people in other households	0.23	0.23	100
Caring for and helping adults in other households	0.07	0.08	88
Work and work-related activities	3.30	3.69	89
Working	2.96	3.35	88
Education	0.50	0.45	111
Attending class	0.35	0.27	130
Research, homework	0.11	0.14	79
Organizational, civic, and religious activities	0.47	0.31	152
Religious and spiritual activities	0.27	0.12	225
Volunteer activities	0.14	0.14	100
Leisure and sports	5.69	5.14	111
Socializing and communicating	0.78	0.75	104
Watching television	3.19	2.58	124
Participating in sports, exercise, or recreation	0.22	0.29	76
Telephone calls, mail, and email	0.21	0.18	117

Note: The index is calculated by dividing the average time spent by blacks doing primary activity by average time spent by total people doing primary activity and multiplying by 100. Primary activities are those respondents identified as their main activity. Other activities done simultaneously, such as eating while watching TV, are not included. Time spent doing activities includes related travel time. Numbers may not add to total because not all subcategories are shown.
Source: Bureau of Labor Statistics, unpublished tables from the 2005 American Time Use Survey, Internet site http://www.bls .gov/tus/home.htm; calculations by New Strategist

Table 9.5 Indexed Time Use of Black Men, 2005

(hours spent doing primary activities on an average day by black men aged 15 or older and total men aged 15 or older, and index of time spent by black men to total men, 2005)

	average hours		index, black men
	black men	total men	to total men
Total, all activities	**24.00**	**24.00**	**100**
Personal care	9.87	9.22	107
Sleeping	9.05	8.54	106
Grooming	0.65	0.54	120
Eating and drinking	0.93	1.30	72
Household activities	0.92	1.35	68
Housework	0.23	0.24	96
Food preparation and cleanup	0.26	0.26	100
Lawn, garden, and houseplants	–	0.27	–
Household management	0.07	0.12	58
Consumer purchases (store, telephone, Internet)	0.56	0.63	89
Consumer goods purchases	0.27	0.31	87
Professional and personal care	–	0.06	–
Caring for and helping household members	0.24	0.34	71
Caring for and helping household children	0.18	0.25	72
Caring for and helping people in other households	0.24	0.21	114
Caring for and helping adults in other households	0.06	0.08	75
Work and work-related activities	3.57	4.44	80
Working	3.18	4.02	79
Education	–	0.47	–
Attending class	–	0.28	–
Research, homework	–	0.15	–
Organizational, civic, and religious activities	0.43	0.27	159
Religious and spiritual activities	0.24	0.10	240
Volunteer activities	–	0.14	–
Leisure and sports	6.46	5.50	117
Socializing and communicating	0.87	0.71	123
Watching television	3.66	2.80	131
Participating in sports, exercise, or recreation	0.31	0.39	79
Telephone calls, mail, and email	0.20	0.12	167

Note: The index is calculated by dividing the average time spent by black men doing primary activity by average time spent by total men doing primary activity and multiplying by 100. Primary activities are those respondents identified as their main activity. Other activities done simultaneously, such as eating while watching TV, are not included. Time spent doing activities includes related travel time. Numbers may not add to total because not all subcategories are shown. "–" means sample is too small to make a reliable estimate.
Source: Bureau of Labor Statistics, unpublished tables from the 2005 American Time Use Survey, Internet site http://www.bls .gov/tus/home.htm; calculations by New Strategist

Table 9.6 Indexed Time Use of Black Women, 2005

(hours spent doing primary activities on an average day by black women aged 15 or older and total women aged 15 or older, and index of time spent by black women to total women, 2005)

	average hours		index, black women to total women
	black women	total women	
Total, all activities	**24.00**	**24.00**	**100**
Personal care	10.27	9.62	107
Sleeping	9.11	8.70	105
Grooming	0.91	0.78	117
Eating and drinking	0.84	1.19	71
Household activities	1.60	2.27	70
Housework	0.66	0.96	69
Food preparation and cleanup	0.68	0.75	91
Lawn, garden, and houseplants	–	0.14	–
Household management	0.08	0.17	47
Consumer purchases (store, telephone, Internet)	0.87	0.96	91
Consumer goods purchases	0.45	0.50	90
Professional and personal care	0.10	0.11	91
Caring for and helping household members	0.63	0.72	88
Caring for and helping household children	0.48	0.57	84
Caring for and helping people in other households	0.22	0.25	88
Caring for and helping adults in other households	0.07	0.08	88
Work and work-related activities	3.09	3.00	103
Working	2.77	2.73	101
Education	0.55	0.43	128
Attending class	0.37	0.25	148
Research, homework	–	0.14	–
Organizational, civic, and religious activities	0.50	0.35	143
Religious and spiritual activities	0.29	0.15	193
Volunteer activities	0.14	0.15	93
Leisure and sports	5.06	4.80	105
Socializing and communicating	0.70	0.78	90
Watching television	2.81	2.37	119
Participating in sports, exercise, or recreation	0.14	0.20	70
Telephone calls, mail, and email	0.22	0.23	96

Note: The index is calculated by dividing the average time spent by black women doing primary activity by average time spent by total women doing primary activity and multiplying by 100. Primary activities are those respondents identified as their main activity. Other activities done simultaneously, such as eating while watching TV, are not included. Time spent doing activities includes related travel time. Numbers may not add to total because not all subcategories are shown. "–" means sample is too small to make a reliable estimate.
Source: Bureau of Labor Statistics, unpublished tables from the 2005 American Time Use Survey, Internet site http://www.bls.gov/tus/home.htm; calculations by New Strategist

Table 9.7 Indexed Time Use of Blacks by Sex, 2005

(average hours spent by blacks aged 15 or older doing primary activities on an average day by sex, and index of black women's time to black men's, 2005)

	blacks aged 15 or older, average hours		index of women to men
	black men	black women	
Total, all activities	**24.00**	**24.00**	**100**
Personal care	9.87	10.27	104
Sleeping	9.05	9.11	101
Grooming	0.65	0.91	140
Eating and drinking	0.93	0.84	90
Household activities	0.92	1.60	174
Housework	0.23	0.66	287
Food preparation and cleanup	0.26	0.68	262
Lawn, garden, and houseplants	–	–	–
Household management	0.07	0.08	114
Consumer purchases (store, telephone, Internet)	0.56	0.87	155
Consumer goods purchases	0.27	0.45	167
Professional and personal care	–	0.10	–
Caring for and helping household members	0.24	0.63	263
Caring for and helping household children	0.18	0.48	267
Caring for and helping people in other households	0.24	0.22	92
Caring for and helping adults in other households	0.06	0.07	117
Work and work-related activities	3.57	3.09	87
Working	3.18	2.77	87
Education	–	0.55	–
Attending class	–	0.37	–
Research, homework	–	–	–
Organizational, civic, and religious activities	0.43	0.50	116
Religious and spiritual activities	0.24	0.29	121
Volunteer activities	–	0.14	–
Leisure and sports	6.46	5.06	78
Socializing and communicating	0.87	0.70	80
Watching television	3.66	2.81	77
Participating in sports, exercise, or recreation	0.31	0.14	45
Telephone calls, mail, and email	0.20	0.22	110

Note: The index is calculated by dividing women's time by men's and multiplying by 100. Primary activities are those respondents identified as their main activity. Other activities done simultaneously, such as eating while watching TV, are not included. Time spent doing activities includes related travel time. "–" means sample is too small to make a reliable estimate.
Source: Bureau of Labor Statistics, unpublished tables from the 2005 American Time Use Survey, Internet site http://www.bls .gov/tus/home.htm; calculations by New Strategist

Blacks Are More Likely to Be in School on an Average Day

Black women are more than twice as likely as black men to do housework.

Black participation in some activities is below average. Only 6 percent of blacks spend time taking care of the lawn or garden on an average day compared with 10 percent of all Americans aged 15 or older. Blacks are also 18 percent less likely to participate in sports and exercise. Blacks are more likely to participate in some activities however. The biggest difference is in religious activities. On an average day, 12 percent of blacks participate in religious activities compared with a smaller 7 percent of all Americans. Blacks are 28 percent more likely to attend class on an average day.

Black men's participation in most activities is average, although they are 93 percent more likely than the average man to participate in religious activities on an average day. Black women's participation shows some variation from the average. They are 47 percent more likely to attend class than the average woman (9 percent versus 6 percent), and 40 percent more likely to participate in religious activities. They are 16 percent less likely than the average woman to socialize.

■ Forty-three percent of black women and 21 percent of black men do housework on an average day.

Nearly 8 percent of blacks attend class on an average day

(percent of blacks and total people aged 15 or older who participate in selected activities on an average day, 2005)

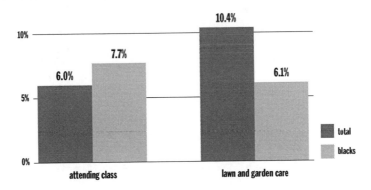

Table 9.8 Indexed Participation in Primary Activities: Total Blacks, 2005

(percent of blacks aged 15 or older and total people aged 15 or older participating in primary activities on an average day, and index of participation by blacks to total people, 2005)

	percent participating		index, blacks
	blacks	total	to total people
Total, all activities	**100.0%**	**100.0%**	**100**
Personal care	100.0	100.0	100
Sleeping	99.9	99.9	100
Grooming	81.1	78.9	103
Eating and drinking	94.0	97.1	97
Household activities	67.2	74.6	90
Housework	32.8	36.9	89
Food preparation and cleanup	50.0	52.0	96
Lawn, garden, and houseplants	6.1	10.4	58
Household management	14.7	18.0	81
Consumer purchases (store, telephone, Internet)	43.1	45.8	94
Consumer goods purchases	39.3	41.4	95
Professional and personal care	7.5	8.9	84
Caring for and helping household members	25.9	26.2	99
Caring for and helping household children	22.5	22.2	101
Caring for and helping people in other households	14.2	13.7	103
Caring for and helping adults in other households	6.2	9.0	69
Work and work-related activities	41.9	46.1	91
Working	39.6	44.5	89
Education	9.8	8.6	115
Attending class	7.7	6.0	128
Research, homework	5.4	5.3	103
Organizational, civic, and religious activities	17.0	13.3	128
Religious and spiritual activities	11.9	7.4	160
Volunteer activities	6.8	7.3	93
Leisure and sports	95.9	96.4	99
Socializing and communicating	38.9	40.4	96
Watching television	79.8	79.8	100
Participating in sports, exercise, or recreation	14.3	17.5	82
Telephone calls, mail, and email	23.4	24.3	96

Note: The index is calculated by dividing percent of blacks doing primary activity by percent of total people doing primary activity and multiplying by 100. Primary activities are those respondents identified as their main activity. Other activities done simultaneously, such as eating while watching TV, are not included.
Source: Bureau of Labor Statistics, unpublished tables from the 2005 American Time Use Survey, Internet site http://www.bls .gov/tus/home.htm; calculations by New Strategist

Table 9.9 Indexed Participation in Primary Activities: Black Men, 2005

(percent of black men and total men aged 15 or older participating in primary activities on an average day, and index of participation by black men to total men, 2005)

	percent participating		index, black men to total men
	black men	total men	
Total, all activities	**100.0%**	**100.0%**	**100**
Personal care	100.0	100.0	100
Sleeping	99.8	99.9	100
Grooming	76.6	75.1	102
Eating and drinking	94.5	97.4	97
Household activities	58.3	64.5	90
Housework	20.9	19.4	108
Food preparation and cleanup	38.0	37.1	102
Lawn, garden, and houseplants	–	11.8	–
Household management	14.3	15.1	94
Consumer purchases (store, telephone, Internet)	40.8	40.0	102
Consumer goods purchases	36.5	36.0	101
Professional and personal care	–	6.7	–
Caring for and helping household members	18.6	20.5	91
Caring for and helping household children	15.0	16.4	92
Caring for and helping people in other households	12.8	12.1	106
Caring for and helping adults in other households	9.3	8.6	108
Work and work-related activities	44.7	52.6	85
Working	41.7	50.9	82
Education	–	8.3	–
Attending class	–	6.1	–
Research, homework	–	5.1	–
Organizational, civic, and religious activities	16.9	11.7	144
Religious and spiritual activities	10.8	5.6	193
Volunteer activities	–	7.0	–
Leisure and sports	97.6	96.7	101
Socializing and communicating	42.1	37.6	112
Watching television	80.6	80.7	100
Participating in sports, exercise, or recreation	18.9	19.4	98
Telephone calls, mail, and email	21.6	18.0	120

Note: The index is calculated by dividing percent of black men doing primary activity by percent of total men doing primary activity and multiplying by 100. Primary activities are those respondents identified as their main activity. Other activities done simultaneously, such as eating while watching TV, are not included. "–" means sample is too small to make a reliable estimate.
Source: Bureau of Labor Statistics, unpublished tables from the 2005 American Time Use Survey, Internet site http://www.bls.gov/tus/home.htm; calculations by New Strategist

Table 9.10 Indexed Participation in Primary Activities: Black Women, 2005

(percent of black women and total women aged 15 or older participating in primary activities on an average day, and index of participation by black women to total women, 2005)

	percent participating		index, black women
	black women	total women	to total women
Total, all activities	**100.0%**	**100.0%**	**100**
Personal care	100.0	100.0	100
Sleeping	100.0	100.0	100
Grooming	84.8	82.6	103
Eating and drinking	93.6	96.8	97
Household activities	74.5	84.0	89
Housework	42.6	53.3	80
Food preparation and cleanup	59.8	66.0	91
Lawn, garden, and houseplants	–	9.0	–
Household management	15.0	20.7	72
Consumer purchases (store, telephone, Internet)	45.0	51.2	88
Consumer goods purchases	41.5	46.5	89
Professional and personal care	7.8	10.9	72
Caring for and helping household members	31.8	31.5	101
Caring for and helping household children	28.6	27.7	103
Caring for and helping people in other households	15.3	15.2	100
Caring for and helping adults in other households	9.3	9.4	99
Work and work-related activities	39.6	40.1	99
Working	37.9	38.6	98
Education	11.0	8.9	124
Attending class	8.7	5.9	147
Research, homework	–	5.5	–
Organizational, civic, and religious activities	17.1	14.9	114
Religious and spiritual activities	12.7	9.1	140
Volunteer activities	6.3	7.7	81
Leisure and sports	94.4	96.1	98
Socializing and communicating	36.2	43.0	84
Watching television	79.2	78.9	100
Participating in sports, exercise, or recreation	10.4	15.7	66
Telephone calls, mail, and email	24.9	30.2	82

Note: The index is calculated by dividing percent of black women doing primary activity by percent of total women doing primary activity and multiplying by 100. Primary activities are those respondents identified as their main activity. Other activities done simultaneously, such as eating while watching TV, are not included. "–" means sample is too small to make a reliable estimate.
Source: Bureau of Labor Statistics, unpublished tables from the 2005 American Time Use Survey, Internet site http://www.bls.gov/tus/home.htm; calculations by New Strategist

Table 9.11 Indexed Participation in Primary Activities: Blacks by Sex, 2005

(percent of blacks aged 15 or older participating in primary activities on an average day by sex, and index of women's participation to men's, 2005)

	blacks aged 15 or older, percent participating		index of women to men
	men	women	
Total, all activities	**100.0%**	**100.0%**	**100**
Personal care	100.0	100.0	100
Sleeping	99.8	100.0	100
Grooming	76.6	84.8	111
Eating and drinking	94.5	93.6	99
Household activities	58.3	74.5	128
Housework	20.9	42.6	204
Food preparation and cleanup	38.0	59.8	158
Lawn, garden, and houseplants	–	–	–
Household management	14.3	15.0	105
Consumer purchases (store, telephone, Internet)	40.8	45.0	110
Consumer goods purchases	36.5	41.5	114
Professional and personal care	–	7.8	–
Caring for and helping household members	18.6	31.8	171
Caring for and helping household children	15.0	28.6	190
Caring for and helping people in other households	12.8	15.3	119
Caring for and helping adults in other households	9.3	9.3	101
Work and work-related activities	44.7	39.6	89
Working	41.7	37.9	91
Education	–	11.0	–
Attending class	–	8.7	–
Research, homework	–	–	–
Organizational, civic, and religious activities	16.9	17.1	101
Religious and spiritual activities	10.8	12.7	117
Volunteer activities	–	6.3	–
Leisure and sports	97.6	94.4	97
Socializing and communicating	42.1	36.2	86
Watching television	80.6	79.2	98
Participating in sports, exercise, or recreation	18.9	10.4	55
Telephone calls, mail, and email	21.6	24.9	115

Note: The index is calculated by dividing percent of women participating in primary activity by percent of men participating in primary activity and multiplying by 100. Primary activities are those respondents identified as their main activity. Other activities done simultaneously, such as eating while watching TV, are not included. "–" means sample is too small to make a reliable estimate. Source: Bureau of Labor Statistics, unpublished tables from the 2005 American Time Use Survey, Internet site http://www.bls .gov/tus/home.htm; calculations by New Strategist

10

Wealth

■ Between 2001 and 2004, the net worth of nonwhite/Hispanic households climbed a substantial 30 percent compared with a small 1.5 percent increase for the average household.

■ In 2004, 85 percent of nonwhite/Hispanic households owned financial assets, which include checking and savings accounts, stocks, and retirement accounts.

■ Between 2001 and 2004, the median value of the nonfinancial assets owned by nonwhite or Hispanic households increased by just 2 percent after adjusting for inflation, much less than the 22 percent gain in the value of nonfinancial assets for all households.

■ The median debt of households headed by nonwhites or Hispanics, at $30,500, is lower thann that for all households, but it grew by a faster 43 percent between 2001 and 2004.

■ Social Security is the major source of income for blacks age 65 or older, 88 percent of whom receive Social Security income.

Blacks Have Little Wealth

But their net worth is growing faster than average.

The median net worth (assets minus debts) of nonwhite or Hispanic households amounted to just $24,800 in 2004. This figure was far below the $93,100 net worth of the average American household. (Note: The Federal Reserve collects wealth data for only two racial and ethnic categories: non-Hispanic whites, and nonwhites or Hispanics. The nonwhite or Hispanic category includes primarily blacks and Hispanics, but also Asians and American Indians.)

On every measure of wealth, nonwhites or Hispanics have less than the average household. Their financial assets are just 22 percent as high as the average, and their nonfinancial assets are only 43 percent of the average. Fortunately for them, their debts are also lower, amounting to 55 percent of the average.

Between 2001 and 2004, the net worth of nonwhite or Hispanic households climbed by a substantial 30 percent, after adjusting for inflation. This gain was much greater than the 1.5 percent increase in net worth experienced by the average household during those years. Behind the gains are rising homeownership rates.

■ The net worth of nonwhite or Hispanic households is below average largely because blacks and Hispanics are less likely than the average household to own a home.

The net worth of blacks is well below average

(median net worth of total and nonwhite or Hispanic households, 2004)

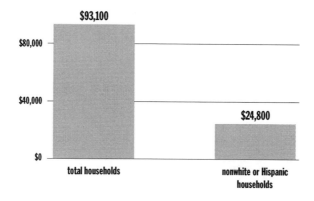

Table 10.1 Net Worth, Assets, and Debt of Total and Nonwhite or Hispanic Households, 2004

(median net worth, median value of assets for owners, and median amount of debt for debtors, for total and non-white or Hispanic households, and index of nonwhite or Hispanic to total, 2004)

		nonwhite or Hispanic households	
	total households	median	index
Median net worth	$93,100	$24,800	27
Median value of financial assets	23,000	5,000	22
Median value of nonfinancial assets	147,800	64,100	43
Median amount of debt	55,300	30,500	55

Note: The index is calculated by dividing the nonwhite or Hispanic figure by the total figure and multiplying by 100.
Source: Federal Reserve Board, Survey of Consumer Finances, SCF Chartbook, Internet site http://www.federalreserve.gov/pubs/oss/oss2/2004/scf2004home.html; calculations by New Strategist

Table 10.2 Net Worth of Households by Race and Hispanic Origin, 2001 and 2004

(median net worth of households by race and Hispanic origin of householder, 2001 and 2004; percent change, 2001–04; in 2004 dollars)

	2004	2001	percent change
Total households	**$93,100**	**$91,700**	**1.5%**
Non-Hispanic white	140,700	129,600	8.6
Nonwhite or Hispanic	24,800	19,100	29.8

Source: Federal Reserve Board, Recent Changes in U.S. Family Finances: Evidence from the 2001 and 2004 Survey of Consumer Finances, Federal Reserve Bulletin, February 23, 2006, Internet site http://www.federalreserve.gov/pubs/oss/oss2/2004/scf2004home.html; calculations by New Strategist

Most Nonwhite Households Have Financial Assets

The median value of financial assets owned by nonwhite or Hispanic households fell between 2001 and 2004.

In 2004, 94 percent of all households owned financial assets, which include checking and savings accounts, stocks, and retirement accounts. Among non-Hispanic white households, the ownership rate was a nearly universal 97 percent. Among nonwhite or Hispanic households, the figure was a smaller 85 percent.

The median value of financial assets plummeted between 2001 and 2004 because of the declining stock market. Non-Hispanic white households experienced a 13 percent loss in the value of their financial assets during those years, while the drop for nonwhite or Hispanic households was a larger 34 percent, after adjusting for inflation. In 2004, the median value of the financial assets owned by nonwhite or Hispanic households was just $5,000.

A checking account is the most widely owned financial asset among nonwhite or Hispanic households, with 81 percent having such an account. The median value of the transaction accounts owned by nonwhites or Hispanics was just $1,500, however. Thirty-three percent of nonwhite or Hispanic households owned a retirement account. The median value of those retirement accounts stood at a modest $16,000 in 2004. Seventeen percent owned a life insurance policy with a median cash value of $5,000.

■ Nonwhite and Hispanic households will need to boost their savings if they want to enjoy a comfortable retirement.

Only three types of financial assets are owned by more than 10 percent of nonwhite or Hispanic households

(percent of nonwhite or Hispanic households that own selected financial assets, 2004)

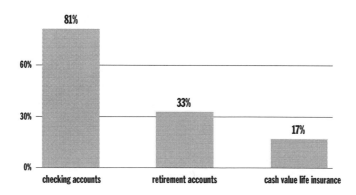

Table 10.3 Ownership and Value of Financial Assets by Race and Hispanic Origin, 2001 and 2004

(percentage of households that own any financial asset and median value of financial assets for owners, by race and Hispanic origin of householder, 2001 and 2004; percentage point change in ownership and percent change in value, 2001–04; in 2004 dollars)

	percent owning any financial asset			median value of financial assets		
	2004	2001	percentage point change	2004	2001	percent change
Total households	**93.8%**	**93.1%**	**0.7**	**$23,000**	**$29,800**	**−22.8%**
Non-Hispanic white	97.2	96.7	0.5	36,000	41,300	−12.8
Nonwhite or Hispanic	85.0	83.2	1.8	5,000	7,600	−34.2

Source: Federal Reserve Board, Recent Changes in U.S. Family Finances: Evidence from the 2001 and 2004 Survey of Consumer Finances, Federal Reserve Bulletin, February 23, 2006, Internet site http://www.federalreserve.gov/pubs/oss/oss2/2004/scf2004home.html; calculations by New Strategist

Table 10.4 Financial Assets of Nonwhite or Hispanic Households, 2004

(percent of nonwhite or Hispanic households that own financial assets, and median value of assets for owners, 2004)

	percent owning asset	median value
Any financial asset	**85.0%**	**$5,000**
Transaction accounts	80.6	1,500
Certificates of deposit	6.0	12,000
Savings bonds	8.5	600
Bonds	–	–
Stocks	8.0	5,300
Pooled investment funds (mutual funds)	5.0	18,000
Retirement accounts	32.9	16,000
Life insurance (cash value)	17.4	5,000
Other managed assets	2.1	40,000
Other financial assets	9.4	2,500

Note: "–" means sample is too small to make a reliable estimate.
Source: Federal Reserve Board, Recent Changes in U.S. Family Finances: Evidence from the 2001 and 2004 Survey of Consumer Finances, Federal Reserve Bulletin, February 23, 2006, Internet site http://www.federalreserve.gov/pubs/oss/oss2/2004/scf2004home.html; calculations by New Strategist

Most Nonwhite Households Own Nonfinancial Assets

Vehicles are the most commonly owned nonfinancial asset.

Most households own nonfinancial assets, with 96 percent of non-Hispanic white households and 85 percent of nonwhite or Hispanic households owning homes, cars, businesses, or other nonfinancial assets. The median value of the nonfinancial assets owned by nonwhite or Hispanic households was just $64,100 in 2004, well below the $147,800 median for all households. Between 2001 and 2004, the median value of the nonfinancial assets owned by nonwhite or Hispanic households increased by 2 percent, after adjusting for inflation, much less than the 22 percent gain in asset value for all households.

Vehicles are the most commonly owned nonfinancial asset. Seventy-six percent of nonwhite or Hispanic households own a vehicle. A home is the second most commonly owned nonfinancial asset among nonwhites and Hispanics. Fifty-one percent own a home. The median value of the homes owned by nonwhites or Hispanics stood at $130,000 in 2004.

■ Because nonwhite and Hispanic households are much less likely than non-Hispanic white households to own a home, their net worth is much lower.

The median value of the nonfinancial assets owned by nonwhite households is below average

(median value of nonfinancial assets for total households and nonwhite or Hispanic households, 2004)

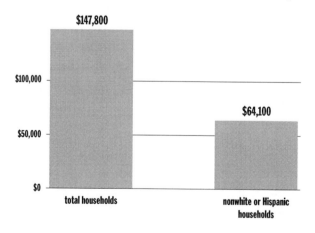

Table 10.5 Ownership and Value of Nonfinancial Assets by Race and Hispanic Origin, 2001 and 2004

(percentage of households that own any nonfinancial asset and median value of nonfinancial assets for owners, by race and Hispanic origin of householder, 2001 and 2004; percentage point change in ownership and percent change in value, 2001–04; in 2004 dollars)

	percent owning any nonfinancial asset			median value of nonfinancial assets		
	2004	2001	percentage point change	2004	2001	percent change
Total households	**92.5%**	**90.7%**	**1.8**	**$147,800**	**$120,900**	**22.2%**
Non-Hispanic white	95.8	94.7	1.1	164,800	141,400	16.5
Nonwhite or Hispanic	84.0	78.4	5.6	64,100	62,800	2.1

Source: Federal Reserve Board, Recent Changes in U.S. Family Finances: Evidence from the 2001 and 2004 Survey of Consumer Finances, Federal Reserve Bulletin, February 23, 2006, Internet site http://www.federalreserve.gov/pubs/oss/oss2/2004/ scf2004home.html; calculations by New Strategist

Table 10.6 Nonfinancial Assets of Nonwhite or Hispanic Households, 2004

(percent of nonwhite or Hispanic households that own nonfinancial assets, and median value of assets for owners, 2004)

	percent owning asset	median value
Any nonfinancial asset	**84.0%**	**$64,100**
Vehicles	76.1	9,800
Primary residence	50.8	130,000
Other residential property	8.9	80,000
Nonresidential property	5.8	30,000
Business equity	5.9	66,700
Other nonfinancial asset	3.8	10,000

Source: Federal Reserve Board, Recent Changes in U.S. Family Finances: Evidence from the 2001 and 2004 Survey of Consumer Finances, Federal Reserve Bulletin, February 23, 2006, Internet site http://www.federalreserve.gov/pubs/oss/oss2/2004/ scf2004home.html; calculations by New Strategist

Debt Is Rising for Nonwhite Households

Nearly half have credit card debt.

Between 2001 and 2004 median debt for all households climbed to $55,300, a 34 percent increase after adjusting for inflation. The median debt of households headed by nonwhites or Hispanics is lower, at $30,500, but grew by a faster 43 percent during those years. Three of four nonwhite or Hispanic households are in debt, slightly below the all-household average.

Credit card debt is the most common type of debt among nonwhite or Hispanic households. Forty-seven percent carried a balance on their credit cards, although the median amount owed was just $1,600. Forty-three percent of nonwhite or Hispanic households had installment loans, typically car loans, owing a median of $9,600. Thirty-seven percent of nonwhite or Hispanic households had debt for a primary residence, owing a median of $83,000.

■ As the homeownership rate of nonwhite and Hispanic households rises, their debt is increasing as well.

Mortgages are the biggest debt for nonwhite households

(median amount owed for selected types of debt by nonwhite or Hispanic households with debt, 2004)

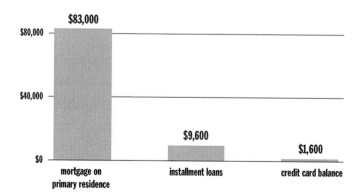

Table 10.7 Debt of Households by Race and Hispanic Origin, 2001 and 2004

(percentage of households with debts and median amount of debt for debtors, by race and Hispanic origin of householder, 2001 and 2004; percentage point change in households with debt and percent change in amount of debt, 2001–04; in 2004 dollars)

	percent with debt			median amount of debt		
	2004	2001	percentage point change	2004	2001	percent change
Total households	**76.4%**	**75.1%**	**1.3**	**$55,300**	**$41,300**	**33.9%**
Non-Hispanic white	78.0	75.8	2.2	69,500	47,700	45.7
Nonwhite or Hispanic	72.5	72.9	–0.4	30,500	21,300	43.2

Source: Federal Reserve Board, Recent Changes in U.S. Family Finances: Evidence from the 2001 and 2004 Survey of Consumer Finances, Federal Reserve Bulletin, February 23, 2006, Internet site http://www.federalreserve.gov/pubs/oss/oss2/2004/ scf2004home.html; calculations by New Strategist

Table 10.8 Debt of Nonwhite or Hispanic Households, 2004

(percent of nonwhite or Hispanic households with debt, and median amount of debt for those with debts, 2004)

	percent with debt	median amount
Any debt	**72.5%**	**$30,500**
Secured by residential property		
Primary residence	37.4	83,000
Other residential property	3.0	66,000
Installment loans	43.2	9,600
Credit card balance	46.7	1,600
Other lines of credit	1.1	400
Other debt	7.3	3,000

Source: Federal Reserve Board, Recent Changes in U.S. Family Finances: Evidence from the 2001 and 2004 Survey of Consumer Finances, Federal Reserve Bulletin, February 23, 2006, Internet site http://www.federalreserve.gov/pubs/oss/oss2/2004/ scf2004home.html; calculations by New Strategist

Older Blacks Depend on Social Security

Some older blacks are still in the labor force.

Social Security is the major source of income for blacks age 65 or older. Eighty-eight percent of older blacks receive Social Security income. Among those who do, the average amount received in 2005 was $9,255.

Only 29 percent of older blacks receive retirement income, and those with retirement income averaged $9,367 from this source. Twenty-four percent receive interest income, but the average amount was just $1,520 in 2005. Fifteen percent of older blacks supplement their Social Security and retirement income by working. Their average earnings were $15,223, a larger amount than from any other source.

■ Without Social Security income, many older Americans would be living in poverty.

Few older blacks receive retirement income

(percent of blacks aged 65 or older with income from selected sources, 2005)

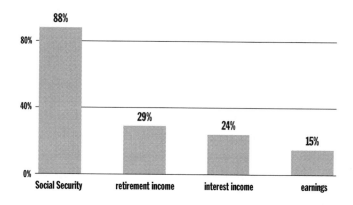

Table 10.9 Sources of Income for Blacks Aged 65 or Older, 2005

(number and percent of blacks aged 65 or older with income from selected sources and average income for those with income, ranked by number receiving income, 2005; people in thousands as of 2006)

	number with income	percent with income	average amount received by those with income
Blacks aged 65 or older with income	**2,862**	**100.0%**	**$11,754**
Social Security	2,519	88.0	9,255
Retirement income	819	28.6	9,367
Interest	678	23.7	1,520
Earnings	428	15.0	15,223
SSI (Supplemental Security Income)	265	9.3	3,385
Dividends	155	5.4	1,786
Rents, royalties, estates, or trusts	130	4.5	2,172
Survivor's benefits	81	2.8	6,324
Veteran's benefits	80	2.8	3,254

Note: Blacks include those who identify themselves as being black alone or as being black in combination with one or more other races.
Source: Bureau of the Census, 2006 Current Population Survey, Internet site http://pubdb3.census.gov/macro/032006/perinc/new08_000.htm; calculations by New Strategist

Glossary

adjusted for inflation Income or a change in income that has been adjusted for the rise in the cost of living, or the consumer price index (CPI-U-RS).

age Classification by age is based on the age of the person at his/her last birthday.

American Community Survey The ACS is an on-going nationwide survey of 250,000 households per month, providing detailed demographic data at the community level. Designed to replace the census long-form questionnaire, the ACS includes more than 60 questions that formerly appeared on the long form, such as language spoken at home, income, and education. ACS data are available for the nation, regions, states, counties, metropolitan areas, and many places.

American Housing Survey The AHS collects national and metropolitan-level data on the nation's housing, including apartments, single-family homes, and mobile homes. The nationally representative survey, with a sample of 55,000 households, is conducted by the Census Bureau for the Department of Housing and Urban Development every other year.

American Time Use Survey Under contract with the Bureau of Labor Statistics, the Census Bureau collects ATUS information, revealing how people spend their time. The ATUS sample is drawn from U.S. households that have completed their final month of interviews for the Current Population Survey. One individual from each selected household is chosen to participate in the ATUS. Respondents are interviewed by telephone only once about their time use on the previous day. In 2005, the sample size was approximately 26,000 households.

Asian Beginning with the 2000 census and in 2003 for government surveys, Asians can identify them-selves as being Asian and no other race (called "Asian alone") or as being Asian in combination with one or more other races (called "Asian in combination"). The combination of the two groups is termed "Asian alone or in combination." In this book, the "Asian alone or in combination" population is shown whenever possible.

average hours per day On the time use tables, the average number of hours spent in a 24-hour day (between 4 a.m. on the diary day and 4 a.m. on the interview day) doing a specified activity. Estimates are adjusted for variability in response rates across days of the week. Average hours per day are shown in decimals. To convert decimal portions of an hour into minutes, multiply 60 by the decimal. For example, if the average is 1.2 hours, multiply 60 by 0.2 to get 12 minutes, so the average is 1 hour and 12 minutes. If the average is 0.05 hours, multiply 60 by .05 to get 3 minutes. If the average is 5.36 hours, multiply 60 by 0.36 to get 21.6, so the average is 5 hours and about 22 minutes.

baby boom Americans born between 1946 and 1964.

baby bust Americans born between 1965 and 1976, also known as Generation X.

black Beginning with the 2000 census and in 2003 for government surveys, blacks can identify themselves as being black and no other race (called "black alone") or as being black in combination with one or more other races (called "black in combination"). The combination of the two groups is termed "black alone or in combination." In this book, the "black alone or in combination" population is shown whenever possible.

Consumer Expenditure Survey The CEX is an ongoing study of the day-to-day spending of American households administered by the Bureau of Labor Statistics. The CEX includes an interview survey and a diary survey. The average spending figures shown in this book are the integrated data from both the diary and interview components of the survey. Two separate, nationally representative samples are used for the interview and diary surveys. For the interview survey, about 7,500 consumer units are interviewed on a rotating panel basis each quarter for five consecutive quarters. For the diary survey, 7,500 consumer units keep weekly diaries of spending for two consecutive weeks.

consumer unit *(on spending tables only)* For convenience, the terms consumer unit and households are used interchangeably in the spending section of this book, although consumer units are somewhat different from the Census Bureau's households. Consumer units are all related members of a household, or financially independent members of a household. A household may include more than one consumer unit.

Current Population Survey The CPS is a nationally representative survey of the civilian noninstitutional population aged 15 or older. It is taken monthly by the Census Bureau for the Bureau of Labor Statistics, collecting information from more than 50,000 households on employment and unemployment. In March of each year, the survey includes the Annual Social and Economic Supplement (formerly called the Annual Demographic Survey), which is the source of most national data on the characteristics of Americans, such as educational attainment, living arrangements, and incomes.

disability The National Health Interview Survey estimates the number of people aged 18 or older who have difficulty in physical functioning, probing whether respondents could perform nine activities by themselves without using special equipment. The categories are walking a quarter mile; standing for two hours; sitting for two hours; walking up 10 steps without resting; stooping, bending, kneeling; reaching over one's head; grasping or handling small objects; carrying a 10-pound object; and pushing/pulling a large object. Adults who reported that any of these activities was very difficult or they could not do it at all were defined as having physical difficulties.

dual-earner couple A married couple in which both the householder and the householder's spouse are in the labor force.

earnings A type of income, earnings is the amount of money a person receives from his or her job. *See also* Income.

employed All civilians who did any work as a paid employee or farmer/self-employed worker, or who worked 15 hours or more as an unpaid farm worker or in a family-owned business, during the reference period. All those who have jobs but who are temporarily absent from their jobs due to illness, bad weather, vacation, labor management dispute, or personal reasons are considered employed.

expenditure The transaction cost including excise and sales taxes of goods and services acquired during the survey period. The full cost of each purchase is recorded even though full payment may not have been made at the date of purchase. Average expenditure figures may be artificially low for infrequently purchased items such as cars because figures are calculated using all consumer units within a demographic segment rather than just purchasers. Expenditure estimates include money spent on gifts for others.

family A group of two or more people (one of whom is the householder) related by birth, marriage, or adoption and living in the same household.

family household A household maintained by a householder who lives with one or more people related to him or her by blood, marriage, or adoption.

female or male householder A woman or man who maintains a household without a spouse present. May head family or nonfamily households.

foreign-born population People who are not U.S. citizens at birth.

full-time employment Full-time is 35 or more hours of work per week during a majority of the weeks worked.

full-time, year-round Indicates 50 or more weeks of full-time employment during the previous calendar year.

Generation X Americans born between 1965 and 1976, also known as the baby-bust generation.

Hispanic Because Hispanic is an ethnic origin rather than a race, Hispanics may be of any race. While most Hispanics are white, there are black, Asian, American Indian, and even Native Hawaiian Hispanics.

household All the persons who occupy a housing unit. A household includes the related family members and all the unrelated persons, if any, such as lodgers, foster children, wards, or employees who share the housing unit. A person living alone is counted as a household. A group of unrelated people who share a housing unit as roommates or unmarried partners is also counted as a household. Households do not include group quarters such as college dormitories, prisons, or nursing homes.

household, race or ethnicity of Households are categorized according to the race or ethnicity of the householder only.

householder The householder is the person (or one of the persons) in whose name the housing unit is owned or rented or, if there is no such person, any adult member. With married couples, the householder may be either the husband or wife. The householder is the reference person for the household.

householder, age of The age of the householder is used to categorize households into age groups such as those used in this book. Married couples, for example, are classified according to the age of either the husband or wife, depending on which one identified him or herself as the householder.

housing unit A housing unit is a house, an apartment, a group of rooms, or a single room occupied or intended for occupancy as separate living quarters. Separate living quarters are those in which the occupants do not live and eat with any other persons in the structure and that have direct access from the outside of the building or through a common hall that is used or intended for use by the occupants of another unit or by the general public. The occupants may be a single family, one person living alone, two or more families living together, or any other group of related or unrelated persons who share living arrangements.

housing value The respondent's estimate of how much his or her house and lot would sell for if it were for sale.

immigrants Aliens admitted for legal permanent residence in the United States.

income Money received in the preceding calendar year by each person aged 15 or older from each of the following sources: 1) earnings from longest job (or self-employment); 2) earnings from jobs other than longest job; 3) unemployment compensation; 4) workers' compensation; 5) Social Security; 6) Supplemental Security income; 7) public assistance; 8) veterans' payments; 9) survivor benefits; 10) disability benefits; 11) retirement pensions; 12) interest; 13) dividends; 14) rents and royalties or estates and trusts; 15) educational assistance; 16) alimony; 17) child support; 18) financial assistance from outside the household, and other periodic income. Income is reported in several ways in this book. Household income is the combined income of all household members. Income of persons is all income accruing to a person from all sources. Earnings are the money a person receives from his or her job.

industry Refers to the industry in which a person worked longest in the preceding calendar year.

job tenure The length of time a person has been employed continuously by the same employer.

labor force The labor force tables in this book show the civilian labor force only. The labor force includes both the employed and the unemployed (people who are looking for work). People are counted as in the labor force if they were working or looking for work during the reference week in which the Census Bureau fields the Current Population Survey.

labor force participation rate The percent of the civilian noninstitutional population that is in the civilian labor force, which includes both the employed and the unemployed.

married-couple family group Married couples who may or may not be householders. Those who are householders are "married-couple households." Those who are not householders are married couples living in a household headed by someone else, such as a parent of the husband or wife. Because married-couple family groups include married-couple households, the

number of married-couple family groups will always outnumber married-couple households.

married couples with or without children under age 18 Refers to married couples with or without own children under age 18 living in the same household. Couples without children under age 18 may be parents of grown children who live elsewhere, or they could be childless couples.

median The median is the amount that divides the population or households into two equal portions: one below and one above the median. Medians can be calculated for income, age, and many other characteristics.

median income The amount that divides the income distribution into two equal groups, half having incomes above the median, half having incomes below the median. The medians for households or families are based on all households or families. The median for persons are based on all persons aged 15 or older with income.

metropolitan statistical area The general concept of a metropolitan area is a large population nucleus with adjacent communities having a high degree of social and economic integration with the core. The Office of Management and Budget defines the nation's metropolitan statistical areas. In general, they must include a city or urbanized area with 50,000 or more inhabitants and a total population of 100,000 or more. The county (or counties) that contains the largest city is the "central county" (counties), along with any adjacent counties that are socially and economically integrated with the central county (or counties). In New England, MSAs are defined in terms of cities and towns rather than counties.

millennial generation Americans born between 1977 and 1994.

mobility status People are classified according to their mobility status on the basis of a comparison between their place of residence at the time of the March Current Population Survey and their place of residence in March of the previous year. Nonmovers are people living in the same house at the end of the period as at the beginning of the period. Movers are people living in a different house at the end of the period than at the beginning of the period. Movers from abroad are either citizens or aliens whose place of residence is outside the United States at the beginning of the period, that is, in an outlying area under the jurisdiction of the United States or in a foreign country. The mobility status for children is fully allocated from the mother if she is in the household; otherwise it is allocated from the householder.

National Ambulatory Medical Care Survey The NAMCS is an annual survey of visits to nonfederally employed office-based physicians who are primarily engaged in direct patient care. Data are collected from physicians rather than patients, with each physician assigned a one-week reporting period. During that week, a systematic random sample of visit characteristics are recorded by the physician or office staff.

National Health and Nutrition Examination Survey The NHANES is a continuous survey of a representative sample of the U.S. civilian noninstitutionalized population. Respondents are interviewed at home about their health and nutrition, and the interview is followed up by a physical examination that measures such things as height and weight in mobile examination centers.

National Health Interview Survey The NHIS is a continuing nationwide sample survey of the civilian noninstitutional population of the U.S. conducted by the Census Bureau for the National Center for Health Statistics. In interviews each year, data are collected from more than 100,000 people about their illnesses, injuries, impairments, chronic and acute conditions, activity limitations, and use of health services.

National Household Education Survey The NHES, sponsored by the National Center for Education Statistics, provides descriptive data on the educational activities of the U.S. population, including after-school care and adult education. The NHES is a system of telephone surveys of a representative sample of 45,000 to 60,000 households in the U.S.

Native Hawaiian and other Pacific Islander The 2000 census identified this group for the first time as a separate racial category from Asians.

nonfamily household A household maintained by a householder who lives alone or who lives with people to whom he or she is not related.

nonfamily householder A householder who lives alone or with nonrelatives.

non-Hispanic People who do not identify themselves as Hispanic are classified as non-Hispanic. Non-Hispanics may be of any race.

non-Hispanic white People who identify their race as white alone and who do not indicate their ethnicity as Hispanic.

nonmetropolitan area Counties that are not classified as metropolitan areas.

occupation Occupational classification is based on the kind of work a person did at his or her job during the previous calendar year. If a person changed jobs during the year, the data refer to the occupation of the job held the longest during that year.

occupied housing units A housing unit is classified as occupied if a person or group of people is living in it or if the occupants are only temporarily absent—on vacation, example. By definition, the count of occupied housing units is the same as the count of households.

outside central city The portion of a metropolitan county or counties that falls outside of the central city or cities; generally regarded as the suburbs.

own children Own children are sons and daughters, including stepchildren and adopted children, of the householder. The totals include never-married children living away from home in college dormitories.

owner occupied A housing unit is "owner occupied" if the owner lives in the unit, even if it is mortgaged or not fully paid for. A cooperative or condominium unit is "owner occupied" only if the owner lives in it. All other occupied units are classified as "renter occupied."

part-time employment Part-time is less than 35 hours of work per week in a majority of the weeks worked during the year.

percent change The change (either positive or negative) in a measure that is expressed as a proportion of the starting measure. When median income changes from $20,000 to $25,000, for example, this is a 25 percent increase.

percentage point change The change (either positive or negative) in a value which is already expressed as a percentage. When a labor force participation rate changes from 70 percent of 75 percent, for example, this is a 5 percentage point increase.

population versus participant measures On the time use tables, average time spent doing an activity is shown for either the population as a whole (such as all 25-to-34-year-olds) or only for those participating in an activity in the previous 24-hours, or diary day. Data referring to the population as a whole include every respondent, even those who did not engage in the activity on diary day. This type of calculation allow researchers to see how Americans prioritize the entire range of daily activities, but it results in artificially short amounts of time devoted to activities done infrequently (such as volunteering). Data referring to participant time show only the time spent on specific activities by respondents who reported doing the activity on diary day. They more accurately reflect the amount of time people spend doing specific activities when they do them.

poverty level The official income threshold below which families and people are classified as living in poverty. The threshold rises each year with inflation and varies depending on family size and age of householder.

principal cities The largest cities in a metropolitan area are called the principal cities. The balance of a metropolitan area outside the principal cities is regarded as the "suburbs."

primary activity On the time use tables, primary activity is the main activity a respondent was doing at a specified time.

proportion or share The value of a part expressed as a percentage of the whole. If there are 4 million people aged 25 and 3 million of them are white, then the white proportion is 75 percent.

race Race is self-reported and can be defined in three ways. The "race alone" population comprises people who identify themselves as only one race. The "race in combination" population comprises people who identify themselves as more than one race, such as white and black. The "race, alone or in combination" population includes both those who identify themselves as one race and those who identify themselves as more than one race.

regions The four major regions and nine census divisions of the United States are the state groupings as shown below:

Northeast:
• New England: Connecticut, Maine, Massachusetts, New Hampshire, Rhode Island, and Vermont
• Middle Atlantic: New Jersey, New York, and Pennsylvania

Midwest:
• East North Central: Illinois, Indiana, Michigan, Ohio, and Wisconsin
• West North Central: Iowa, Kansas, Minnesota, Missouri, Nebraska, North Dakota, and South Dakota

South:
• South Atlantic: Delaware, District of Columbia, Florida, Georgia, Maryland, North Carolina, South Carolina, Virginia, and West Virginia
• East South Central: Alabama, Kentucky, Mississippi, and Tennessee
• West South Central: Arkansas, Louisiana, Oklahoma, and Texas

West:
• Mountain: Arizona, Colorado, Idaho, Montana, Nevada, New Mexico, Utah, and Wyoming
• Pacific: Alaska, California, Hawaii, Oregon, and Washington

renter occupied *See* Owner occupied.

rounding Percentages are rounded to the nearest tenth of a percent; therefore, the percentages in a distribution do not always add exactly to 100.0 percent. The totals, however, are always shown as 100.0. Moreover, individual figures are rounded to the nearest thousand without being adjusted to group totals, which are independently rounded; percentages are based on the unrounded numbers.

self-employment A person is categorized as self-employed if he or she was self-employed in the job held longest during the reference period. Persons who report self-employment from a second job are excluded, but those who report wage-and-salary income from a second job are included. Unpaid workers in family businesses are excluded. Self-employment statistics include only nonagricultural workers and exclude people who work for themselves in incorporated business.

sex ratio The number of men per 100 women.

suburbs *See* Outside principal city.

Survey of Consumer Finances A triennial survey taken by the Federal Reserve Board. It collects data on the assets, debts, and net worth of American households. In the 2004 survey, the Federal Reserve Board interviewed a representative sample of 4,522 households.

unemployed Unemployed people are those who, during the survey period, had no employment but were available and looking for work. Those who were laid off from their jobs and were waiting to be recalled are also classified as unemployed.

white The "white" racial category includes many Hispanics (who may be of any race) unless the term "non-Hispanic white" is used.

Bibliography

Bureau of Labor Statistics
  Internet site http://www.bls.gov
  —2005 Consumer Expenditure Survey, Internet site http://www.bls.gov/cex/home
  .htm
  —2005 American Time Use Survey, Internet site http://www.bls.gov/tus/home
  .htm
  —Labor Force Statistics from the 2006 Current Population Survey, Annual Averages—Household Data, Internet site http://www.bls.gov/cps/home.htm
  —Characteristics of Minimum Wage Workers: 2006, Internet site http://www.bls
  .gov/cps/minwage2006.htm
  —Employee Tenure, Internet site http://www.bls.gov/news.release/tenure.toc.htm
  —Employment Projections, Internet site http://www.bls.gov/emp/home.htm

Bureau of the Census
  Internet site http://www.census.gov/
  —2000 Census, American FactFinder, Internet site http://factfinder.census.gov/
  servlet/BasicFactsServlet
  —2005 American Community Survey, Internet site http://www.census.gov/acs/
  www/
  —2006 Current Population Survey Annual Social and Economic Supplement, Internet site http://www.census.gov/hhes/www/income/dinctabs.html
  —American Housing Survey for the United States in 2005, Internet site http://
  www.census.gov/hhes/www/housing/ahs/nationaldata.html
  —America's Families and Living Arrangements: 2006, Detailed Tables, Internet site
  http://www.census.gov/population/www/socdemo/hh-fam/cps2006.html
  —*The Asian Population*, Census 2000 Briefs, C2KBR/01-5, February 2002, Internet site
  http://www.census.gov/population/www/cen2000/briefs.html
  —*The Black Population*, Census 2000 Briefs, C2KBR/01-16, August 2001, Internet site
  http://www.census.gov/population/www/cen2000/briefs.html
  —Educational Attainment—Historical Tables, Current Population Survey Annual
  Social and Economic Supplement, Internet site http://www.census.gov/
  population/www/socdemo/educ-attn.html
  —Educational Attainment in the United States: 2006, detailed tables, Current Population Survey Annual Social and Economic Supplement, Internet site http://www
  .census.gov/population/www/socdemo/education/cps2006.html
  —Geographic Mobility: 2004 to 2005, Detailed Tables, Current Population Survey
  Annual Social and Economic Supplement, Internet site http://www.census.gov/
  population/www/socdemo/migrate/cps2005.html
  —Health Insurance Tables, 2007 Current Population Survey Annual Social and Economic Supplement, Internet site http://pubdb3.census.gov/macro/032007/health/
  toc.htm
  —*The Hispanic Population*, Census 2000 Briefs, C2KBR/01-3, May 2001, Internet site
  http://www.census.gov/population/www/cen2000/briefs.html

—Historical Income Tables, Current Population Survey Annual Social and Economic Supplements, Internet site http://www.census.gov/hhes/www/income/histinc/h05.html

—Historical Poverty Tables, Current Population Survey Annual Social and Economic Supplements, Internet site http://www.census.gov/hhes/www/poverty/histpov/histpovtb.html

—Housing Vacancies and Homeownership, Annual Statistics: 2006, Internet site http://www.census.gov/hhes/www/housing/hvs/annual06/ann06t20.html

—National Population Estimates, Internet site http://www.census.gov/popest/national/index.html

—*Number, Timing, and Duration of Marriages and Divorces: 2001*, Current Population Report P70-97, 2005; Internet site http://www.census.gov/population/www.socdemo/marr-div.html

—Poverty Tables, 2006 Current Population Survey Annual Social and Economic Supplement, Internet site http://pubdb3.census.gov/macro/032006/pov/toc.htm

—School Enrollment—Social and Economic Characteristics of Students: October 2005, detailed tables, Internet site http://www.census.gov/population/www/socdemo/school/cps2005.html

—State Population Estimates, Internet site http://www.census.gov/popest/states/asrh/SC-EST2006-04.html

Centers for Disease Control and Prevention

Internet site http://www.cdc.gov

—*Cases of HIV Infection and AIDS in the United States and Dependent Areas, 2005*, HIV/AIDS Surveillance Report, Vol. 17, 2006, Internet site http://www.cdc.gov/hiv/topics/surveillance/resources/reports/2005report/default.htm

—Behavioral Risk Factor Surveillance System, Prevalence Data, Internet site http://apps.nccd.cdc.gov/brfss/index.asp

Federal Reserve Board

Internet site http://www.federalreserve.gov/pubs/oss/oss2/scfindex.html

—Survey of Consumer Finances, SCF Chartbook, Internet site http://www.federal-reserve.gov/pubs/oss/oss2/2004/scf2004home.html

National Center for Education Statistics

Internet site http://nces.ed.gov

—*Digest of Education Statistics: 2006*, Internet site http://nces.ed.gov/programs/digest/

—National Household Education Surveys Program, Adult Education Participation in 2004-05, Internet site http://nces.ed.gov/pubs2006/adulted/tables.asp

National Center for Health Statistics

Internet site http://www.cdc.gov/nchs

—*Anthropometric Reference Data for Children and Adults: U.S. Population, 1999–2002*, Advance Data, No. 361, 2005, Internet site http://www.cdc.gov/nchs/about/major/nhanes/advancedatas.htm